CASE

CURRENT PRACTICE

FUTURE PROSPECTS

CASE

CURRENT PRACTICE

FUTURE PROSPECTS

Edited by

Kathy Spurr
Analysis Design Consultants
Chairman, BCS CASE Specialist Group

Paul Layzell
Department of Computation, UMIST, Manchester, UK

JOHN WILEY & SONS
Chichester · New York · Brisbane · Toronto · Singapore

Other Wiley Editorial Offices

John Wiley & Sons, Inc., 605 Third Avenue,
New York, NY 10158-0012, USA

Jacaranda Wiley Ltd, G.P.O. Box 859, Brisbane,
Queensland 4001, Australia

John Wiley & Sons (Canada) Ltd, 22 Worcester Road,
Rexdale, Ontario M9W 1L1, Canada

John Wiley & Sons (SEA) Pte Ltd, 37 Jalan Pemimpin #05-04,
Block B, Union Industrial Building, Singapore 2057

Library of Congress Cataloging-in-Publication Data

Case, current practice, future prospects / edited by Kathy Spurr, Paul
Layzell.
    p.   cm.
Includes bibliographical references.
ISBN 0 471 93304 X
1. Computer-aided software engineering.   I. Spurr, Kathy.
II. Layzell, Paul.
QA76.758.C358   1992
005.1—dc20   91-47691
                                                          CIP

*A catalogue record for this book is
available from the British Library*

ISBN 0 471 93304 X

Typeset from authors' disks by Text Processing Dept, John Wiley & Sons Ltd, Chichester
Printed in Great Britain by Biddles Ltd, Guildford and Kings Lynn

Contents

Authors of Papers

EDITORS

Kathy Spurr

Analysis Design Consultants
Lyndhurst Lodge
41 Lyndhurst Road
Chichester
West Sussex
PO19 2LE

Paul J Layzell

Department of Computation
UMIST
PO Box 88
Manchester
M60 1QD

AUTHORS OF PAPERS

Keith Robinson

Model Systems
No 1 Wendle Court
135 Wandsworth Road
London SW8 2LY

Michael Lloyd-Williams
Paul Beynon-Davies

Department of Computer Studies
Polytechnic of Wales
Pontypridd
CF37 1DL

Jennifer Stapleton
Shirley A Williams

Department of Computer Science
School of Engineering and Information
Sciences
University of Reading
PO Box 225
Whiteknights
Reading
RG6 2AY

Stephen King

Research Fellow
Advanced Technology Centre
University of Warwick
Coventry
CV4 7AL

David M Gee
Barry P Worrall
W D Henderson

Department of Computing
Newcastle Polytechnic
Ellison Building
Newcastle-upon-Tyne
NE1 8ST

John Alexander

AT&T ISTEL
Grosvenor House
Prospect Hill
Redditch

Kenyon Hicks

Bell Labs
Holmdel
New Jersey
USA

Paul Sanders
Keith Short

Texas Instrument Limited
James Martin Associates (UK) Limited
James Martin House
Littleton Road
Ashford
Middlesex
TW15 1TZ

David Law
Tahir Naeem

*The National Computing Centre Limited
Consultancy Group (Software Engineering)
Oxford House
Oxford Road
Manchester
M1 7ED*

Nick Sabanis
Tony Darlison

*Performance Technology Department
Lloyd's Register of Shipping
29 Wellesley Road
Croydon
CR0 2AJ*

T William Olle

*T William Olle Associates Limited
2 Ashley Park Road
Walton-on-Thames
Surrey
KT12 1JU*

Saimond Ip
Louis C-Y Cheung
Tony Holden

*Information Engineering Division
Department of Engineering
University of Cambridge
Trumpington Street
Cambridge
CB2 1PZ*

Peter Haine

*Savant Enterprises Limited
Priory Street
Coventry
CV1 5FB*

William Reynolds
Catherine Kalra

*21 Marks Road
Warlingham
Surrey
CR6 9SH*

Balbir S Barn

James Martin Associates
Information Engineering Limited
James Martin House
Littleton Road
Ashford
Middlesex
TW15 1TZ

Martin Beeby
Vivien Hamilton

Rolls Royce & Associates Limited
PO Box 31
Derby
DE2 8BJ

J. S. Parkinson

NEI Control Systems Limited
Gateshead

Names and Addresses of Reviewers

Babis Theodoulidis
Department of Computation
UMIST
PO Box 88
Manchester
M60 1QD

Christopher G Davies
Department of Computation
UMIST
PO Box 88
Manchester
M60 1QD

Robert E M Champion
Department of Computation
UMIST
PO Box 88
Manchester
M60 1QD

Kathy Gister
43 Loxwood Avenue
Worthing
West Sussex
BN14 7RF

Henry Taylor
56 Mildmay Grove
London
N2 4PJ

Neil Richards
21 Rusland Park Road
Harrow
Middlesex
HA1 1UR

Mr Leslie Jennison
Frogmore House
Market Place
Corsham
Wiltshire
SN14 9NZ

Foreword

'Time present and time Past
Are both perhaps present in time future
And time future contained in time past'.
    T.S. Eliot 1888–1965
    Four Quartets, Burnt Norton.

The British Computer Society CASE specialist group was formed in 1989 to provide a platform for debate on CASE and related issues, with the aim of promoting improvements in the methods and tools available for software development.

Following on from our successful *CASE on Trial* conference in 1990, we were keen to hold a second one (Cambridge, March 1992) based around the general theme of current and future issues in CASE, hence the chosen title, *CASE: Current Practice, Future Prospects.*

In order to fairly represent CASE as it is today, we felt that we needed to look back at past experiences of CASE, look at current 'hot-topics' in the present, and then look to the future of CASE. We have chosen papers that reflect each of these three areas of concern and we are interested as to how effectively CASE tools enhance quality and productivity. Keith Robinson of Model Systems has provided our keynote paper entitled **Putting the SE into CASE**. This ties together the three main areas of investigation, and looks more critically at how CASE tools meet their main objective of providing effective support for software engineering. He proposes that there are benefits in developing an architecture for CASE, possibly similar in concept to the ANSI/SPARC architecture for database systems. By considering such an architecture, Robinson suggests that we may be able to produce CASE tools which have more of a pro-active role in software design and software engineering.

TIME PAST—USER EXPERIENCES OF CASE

The paper by Balbir Barn, formerly of Unitel, reflects on experiences with the HP Interface Architect, used in conjunction with the HP Softbench development environment. The problems of integrating the User Interface Development Environment (UIDE) with the more general software development environment are discussed. Issues relating to productivity and portability are also addressed. The paper concludes with a wish list for the User Interface Development Environment.

Steven King addresses both quality and productivity in his paper entitled "The Quality Gap". Quality is considered in the context of how well CASE tools may be used to support changing customer requirements. The paper looks at an information system developed for the Rover Group, using the ProKit*Workbench and PRO-IV from McDonnell Douglas. Productivity is assessed by comparing actual development effort using CASE technology with an estimate for the equivalent development using third generation language approaches.

Stapleton and Williams consider how the CASE tool, Software through Pictures™, may be used for undergraduate teaching in systems analysis and design. Their paper considers the quality of the analysis and design deliverables produced by the CASE tool with the quality of similar deliverables produced using pencil and paper, or using drawing packages. Also, it examines the delights and frustrations experienced by the students and tutors with the introduction of CASE technology.

Gee, Worral and Henderson look at established methods for the development of real-time systems. Their paper makes comparisons between the Ward/Mellor method, Mascot, JSD, and Harel's statecharts. The need for a real-time CASE tool to provide a variety of viewpoints for a real-time system is discussed, and the role of the repository is considered crucial in this context.

Reynolds and Kalra look at the demarcation between the business enterprise and the computerised information system, discussing conflicts between associated objectives. Their paper suggests that quality should come before productivity, and comments critically as to how existing CASE tools support this.

Beeby, Parkinson and Hamilton discuss their experiences with integrating CASE tools to support real-time control systems. They argue that it is necessary to have a process model to specify the functionality of the integration environment before considering the mechanics of integration.

TIME PRESENT—CURRENT ISSUES IN CASE

Reverse Engineering describes a need expressed by many software development enterprises. It is necessary for transforming existing problematic code into a maintainable state, but there is some doubt currently among software developers as to how effectively this may be achieved. Sabinis and Darlison discuss reverse engineering of data, based on their experience with the REDO maintenance and reverse engineering toolset.

Peter Haine describes second generation CASE (evidenced by Systematica's VSF and the Ipsys tool builder's kit) as consisting of those tools which enable the production of tailor-made bespoke toolsets, rather than the 'off-the-shelf' variety that have commonly been available until recently. He discusses the scope of a proposed bespoke toolset, and considers how it should relate to the corporate repository.

The theme of repositories is continued by Bill Olle, who provides a useful comparison between three standard repository systems: the ISO Information Resource Dictionary System, the ECMA Portable Common Tool Environment and the IBM Repository. Similarities and differences between the three approaches are discussed, and the importance of having an extensible repository for CASE tools is addressed.

Law and Naeem extend the comparison activity with their paper on DESMET, an attempt to determine an evaluation methodology for methods and tools. This reports on a project, funded by the U.K. Department of Trade and Industry, to quantify the effects of methods and tools on developer productivity and quality.

TIME FUTURE—PROSPECTS FOR CASE

Of course, it is a dangerous activity to glance into an imaginary crystal ball to predict the future of such a volatile technology as CASE. However, it is a fairly safe bet that certain developments currently in progress will have an effect on future CASE products. The four papers we have chosen in this category describe work being done to enhance the ability of CASE tools to capture an accurate and complete set of requirements.

The paper by Sanders and Short investigates how declarative techniques may be added to Information Engineering in order to allow the explicit representation of business constraints, rules and policies. In the second paper, Lloyd-Williams and Beynon-Davies consider how artificial intelligence technology in the form of expert systems may be used for database design.

The Knowledge-based Requirement Engineering Assistant (KREA) aims explicitly to represent knowledge relating to the development of an information system. In this third paper, Ip, Cheung and Holden discuss their Lisp based system which can be used by the analyst to build a bridge between the end-user and the designer or programmer.

The paper by Alexander and Hicks on the ISTEL Applications Architecture is included in this category, since it introduces some innovative ideas, although it describes an architecture which has evolved over the last six years. In establishing the architecture, the aim was to eliminate application programming by establishing rigorous, logical definitions of business solutions which could be translated automatically into a form that the computer could understand. In addition, it proposes a Specification Reuse tool that enables systems analysts to take advantage of other analysts' previous experience. The stated goal of this architecture is to improve the quality of the company's software products and to increase the productivity of the development staff.

CASE: CURRENT PRACTICE, FUTURE PROSPECTS

We believe that CASE is here to stay, and is becoming an established part of software development. The original marketing hype that surrounded the introduction of CASE has largely evaporated, and potential CASE users are being encouraged to have more realistic expectations. CASE is not a magic turnkey solution to software development. There are benefits to be gained but these will appear in the long-term rather than in the short-term. CASE makes software development less of a black art and more of a methodical, stimulating and enjoyable activity. Also it does improve quality and productivity.

It is encouraging that CASE is now an established part of the software engineering curriculum in our universities and polytechnics. The cumulative effect of a large number of trained graduate software engineers joining the ranks of productive software developers will, in time, cause a cataclysmic change in our communal approach to development. These software engineers will demand sophisticated CASE products at realistic prices, and we feel confident that the CASE suppliers can meet the challenge.

Some of the fundamental methods supported by CASE have been in existence for 15–20 years, and we are pleased that these are being used to underpin the newer methods and CASE tools. Remembering Yourdon's comment in *Modern Structured Analysis* that 'half of what we learn in this technical field is obsolete within five years', we find it heartening that the software development community is becoming more ready to embrace *knowledge reuse* in the same way that it advocates software reuse. So we see CASE as a maturing technology. The future for CASE is rosy. We can now forget about the hype and get on with some serious software development.

Our thanks to all those who submitted papers for this conference; also to the reviewers who so carefully read the papers and provided valuable feedback. Thanks also to the staff at Wiley's for making the production of this volume so relatively painless for the contributors.

Kathy Spurr
Paul Layzell
March 1992

1

Putting the SE into CASE

Keith Robinson

ABSTRACT

Most current CASE tools are little more than graphical front-ends to data dictionaries. They are too sluggish and unfriendly to be used in real-time assistance in software engineering. This paper examines how qualitative improvements can be made in the way CASE tools are used by:

— enabling the analyst/designer
— better theoretical underpinning
— better support for modularisation
— better support for knowledge acquisition
— better support for transformations.

INTRODUCTION

A comment in a recent issue of the SSADM User Group's newsletter seemed to suggest that CASE tools should not be used by analysts doing a systems development job but should be used only for documenting the system. At the time, I dismissed this as just being a reflection of

CASE: Current Practice, Future Prospects. Edited by Kathy Spurr and Paul Layzell
© 1992 John Wiley & Sons Ltd

the generally poor fitness for purpose of most of the CASE tools on the market. But now I'm not so sure. A client recently expressed almost exactly the same opinion to me. And now I'm worried that the rather primitive tools available have lowered user expectations about what CASE tools should be able to do. This paper is a modest attempt to change those user expectations.

What is CASE?

In this paper CASE is taken to stand for:

C   Computer
A   Aided | Assisted
S   Systems | Software
E   Engineering.

where x|y means either x or y can be chosen. The two key ideas are of:

CA   computer assistance in software development and/or maintenance

SE   an engineering approach to software development and/or maintenance.

The use of a CASE tool as a graphical front-end to a data dictionary seems to deliver neither of these. If an engineering design tool isn't being used by an engineer while he's actually doing the engineering it isn't really helping him.

This paper is about both of these ideas. It could equally well have been entitled "Putting the CA into CASE", or "Putting the CASE into CASE".

What Benefits Are There or Should There Be from CASE?

The two key ideas (of CA and SE) should translate into two benefits:

— Faster development and maintenance
— Low defect solutions

Is there anyone out there getting these benefits from CASE tools? My guess is that there are very few.

What is the Evidence of Benefits?

Of course people are getting advantages from the use of 4GLs. And to the extent that a CASE tool may be a way of programming a 4GL it may appear to give a development advantage. But is it the CASE tool or the 4GL which really delivers the advantage?

What good, controlled, experiments have been done? Who has actually developed the same system twice, once using no tool, and again using a tool? And if they had, wouldn't the second development have profited from end-user and analyst experience to such an extent as to make the comparison meaningless?

The user perceptions discussed above suggest that few people believe in faster development. Maybe some people are using CASE tool documentation in the hope that this will make maintenance easier. But I suggest that this is an act of faith; few people if any have measured maintenance savings. My own (uncontrolled) experience is that automated diagrams which were hard to construct are even harder to maintain.

There is much better experience of translating pictures into code. The advantage of automated transformation is that a more understandable and uncluttered representation can be reviewed for errors; we then have some assurance that the generated system accurately represents the requirements. But where CASE currently helps in this process is more-or-less at the back end. The situation is similar to that in conventional programming at the beginning of the 1980s: then we had good methods for constructing programs from specifications, but no way of guaranteeing that we were producing good specifications.

What can be Done?

Some of things needed to bring CASE tools within the grasp of the systems and software engineers are just to do with usability. Others are to do with theory; unless we really understand what the job is, it's very difficult to help people do it.

Also, a system is a large and complex piece of work; it needs to be split up for development, implementation and maintenance; but it needs to be split in a way that maximises the independence of the components. (Full independence of components cannot be achieved however—the system is a *system*, after all.)

We need better ways of working through the implications of one piece of knowledge gained from the perspective of one component, and ways of deducing its effect elsewhere. And we need better ways of transforming knowledge as we move down the design path.

We might summarise these requirements as:

— Enabling the analyst/designer
— Better theoretical underpinning
— Better modularisation
— Better knowledge acquisition
— Better transformations

In some of these areas we should be able to measure what happens. In others we may still be left with an act of faith, but we should have a better idea of how and why our expectations are reasonable.

ENABLING THE ANALYST/DESIGNER

Almost the first requirement here is that the designer should want to use the tool. The tool should support the way the designer thinks. It should support the way the designer works. It should be faster and easier to use the tool than not use it. (One way of assessing a tool's usability is to let its user choose it. Few organisations do this; if they did they'd get better productivity.)

All of these things can be measured to some degree. It is clearly possible to know whether it is faster to draw a diagram using one particular tool rather than another or whether it is faster to use pencil and paper than a particular tool. And, believe it or not, small-scale experiments have shown advantages of some tools over pencil and paper.

If you watch how a designer works you see lots of things going on which give you some insight into the thought processes going on. Sometimes a designer is just trying out some new idea. Sometimes a designer is evaluating or making some catastrophic change to previous ideas (maybe about 90% of the pictures a designer draws get thrown away). Sometimes a designer is trying to customise something developed for another purpose. Sometimes two designers who have developed separate pieces of a solution are trying to bring them together. Sometimes a designer is checking that all of the ideas hang together. One thing you will see is that very little time is actually spent on the finished product.

What this means is that a truly usable CASE product must be able to support all these modes of working. It must:

— be faster than pencil and paper
— be usable in sketch mode (ie not force consistency between diagrams)

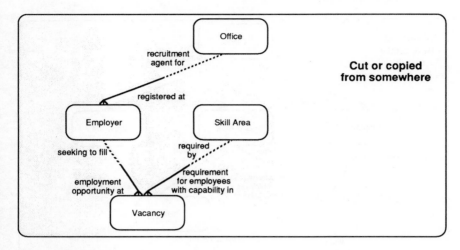

Figure 1

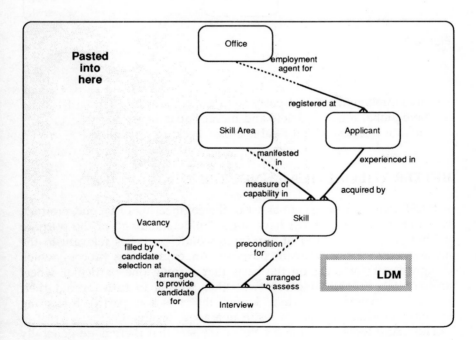

Figure 2

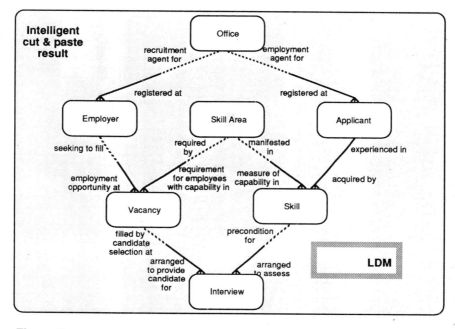

Figure 3

— have intelligent cut and paste facilities
— have global rename, delete and merge capabilities
— provide selectively enforceable cross-checking capabilities.

BETTER THEORETICAL UNDERPINNING

A CASE tool's purpose is to assist in the engineering of an end-product. In order to do this it must have some "understanding" of the purpose of that end-product, and of any intermediate purposes relevant to the achievement of the ultimate purpose. An engineering process which designed part of a car on the basis that turning one particular wheel around its axis should cause two other wheels to turn around their vertical diameters and didn't "know" that this was part of a steering system would be unlikely to result in a good design.

The CASE tools are limited here by the fact that there is no generally accepted theory of what data processing is. Maybe this isn't surprising for a profession which is only about thirty years old. But the fact remains that we are doing to ourselves what we recommend users not to do to themselves, namely automate systems without analysing what they're about.

In these circumstances it's not surprising that people look for CASE tools which are uncommitted to any methodology. But I believe that this approach is even worse than going for a methodology; at least with a methodology-based tool there is some underlying theory that people have tried to make consistent. I exclude from criticism here what we might think of as "platform" tools (eg VSF) which can be used to construct methodology-specific tools.

What agreement about theory is there? Most people seem to agree on something like a "logical"/"physical" or "what"/"how" approach to development; this is developed further in a later section of this paper. Most methodologies seem to agree that some kind of data modelling is desirable. Most methodologies seem to use some form of data flow diagrams, but the purposes they put them to can be surprisingly different. Relational systems are very popular, and they're fine for retrieval; but I believe they're flawed for updating as I'll show shortly. Most CASE tools are based on some or all of these ideas.

Missing—The Event

There's also some growing agreement about gaps in the above ideas. SSADM and MERISE both have some notion of business events. There's growing awareness in IBM that AD/Cycle needs to address business events. There's much less agreement as to how to represent events and their interaction with the rest of the system: an entity-oriented view of events (SSADM v3), an event-oriented view of processing (MERISE), both (SSADM v4), an object-oriented view of events, etc.

But events are necessary to understanding what a system is about. We can see this from a number of perspectives. Firstly, there's a reasonable consensus that what the implemented systems are doing is modelling important real-world concepts:

Data: models the things in the real system
Process: models the activities in the real system

But what do commit units model? Commit units are the ways in which implemented systems maintain consistency. Broadly speaking a commit unit represents a collection of processing that must succeed or fail as a whole, eg a transfer of funds cannot be complete unless the funds have both been moved out of one account and moved into another. This isn't a DP concept; this is an end-user concept. Business events represent the atomic changes in reality the system must model.

Secondly, data flow diagram-based methods which don't take into account how activity is triggered notoriously have difficulty in providing systematic ways of deciding how to move from data flow representations to program-like representations. Remember the famous cartoon where the designer explains how this gap is filled with "... Well. Then a miracle occurs."?

Thirdly all attempts to model reality without them seem to fail. One such attempt is to hang activities directly on data. You can try this non-procedurally using some relational integrity constraints such as CASCADE and RESTRICT, or you can provide data base procedures. Either way there are some problems for which the approach fails.

Consider the following situation. Our system has to maintain customers and a set of contracts which each customer has with us. A customer who has some live contracts comes to us and says he wants to withdraw. We've considered this possibility, and we've decided that we're not going to allow customers to do this; we want them to discharge their obligations under the contracts first. Accordingly we put a RESTRICT constraint on the deletion of a customer with orders. Now no program in the system can delete this customer. Our customer walks out of the door and is knocked down and killed by a passing bus. Now we wish we'd put a CASCADE rule on the deletion of a customer with orders.

If we've decided not to delete defunct customers straightaway we're in even bigger trouble. Now neither of the rules are activated.

Of course, what we want to do is determined by the event which occurred, not by the change we want to make to the customer's stored data.

Where will a better theory come from? There are at least three possibilities:

Euromethod

This project is going to have to find a theoretical framework in which all of the popular European methodologies fit.

AD/Cycle

Some of the AD/Cycle Information Model is likely to become a de-facto standard. There are enough people active in this field who will want to expand its coverage.

User Research

Bob Brown of the Database Design Group, Newport Beach, California, has proposed a historic view of Information Processing theory as ascending up a series of slopes and plateaus. The last major plateau is defined by the emergence of data-centred design. His view is that the next plateau must be an object-centred one which will integrate things like data modelling, object-oriented design, event analysis, window-based operating environments and knowledge-based processing. This can't be developed by theorists alone, but by end-users and theorists co-operating in solving real problems.

My guess is that this latter approach is the one most likely to bring useful new theories.

BETTER MODULARISATION

The best modularisation of a system is one which enables changes to be localised. To understand what changes may be needed we must understand what purpose different system components have. Recent research on the structure of SSADM v4 has suggested what may turn out to be a useful architecture for the future development of most of the modern methodologies. The architecture was suggested in trying to explain why certain products similar in structure were produced by quite different methods in SSADM v4, and was developed in analogy with the ANSI-SPARC 3-Schema Database Architecture.

The ANSI-SPARC 3-Schema Database Architecture

In the mid 1970s a report from the ANSI DBMS standards programme outlined an architecture for database management systems which

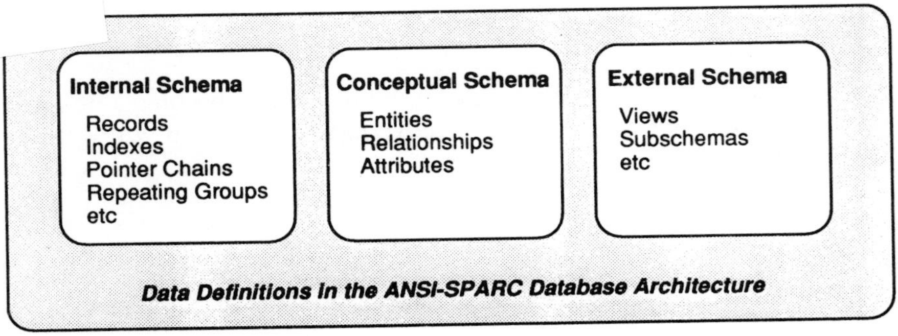

Internal Schema

Records
Indexes
Pointer Chains
Repeating Groups
etc

Conceptual Schema

Entities
Relationships
Attributes

External Schema

Views
Subschemas
etc

Data Definitions in the ANSI-SPARC Database Architecture

Figure 4

supplanted the older, more naive, notion of a division between the "Logical" and "Physical" views of data. The notion of "Physical" data, ie data as actually stored, was retained in the notion of an "Internal Schema" which defines the storage structure of the data. However, data that was previously thought of as "Logical" data was now categorised as either being described in an "External Schema" or in a "Conceptual Schema".

When it was first proposed there was considerable lack of understanding about the role of the Conceptual Schema or "Entity Data". Since then, however, the idea of having a central entity model of the user's business has gained wide acceptance as a way of, among other things:

— understanding the user's business
— gathering data about volumes and driving the physical data design
— mediating between different, co-operating DBMSs
— gaining some portability of design
— providing building blocks for external views to be constructed.

The SSADM v4 3-Schema Processing Architecture

The idea of extending the 3-Schema database architecture into processing was raised (by Jim Lucking of ICL, among others) at the time of publication of the ANSI-SPARC report. The main aim was to extend the

Conceptual Schema to become a "Conceptual Scenario" covering data and processes. At the time, however, no-one knew how to do this.

With hindsight, we can see that SSADM v4 has been developed to conform to such a 3-Schema framework. This is evident in both the structure of SSADM v4, and in its "universal function model".

In SSADM v4 there are three sources of process specifications.

For the **Conceptual** Schema, processing specifications (called Update Process Models and Enquiry Process Models) arise from the Entity/Event Analysis Step and out of Access Path Analysis. These describe that set of processing which is necessarily true, independent of implementation environment.

The Conceptual Schema is both a static and a dynamic model of the user's world and captures all of the semantics, ie all of the necessary business knowledge, about the system to be built.

For the **External** Schema, processing specifications arise out of Function Definition and Dialogue Design. These are about embedding the first set of processing in the user's environment.

For the **Internal** Schema, the processing of "Physical" data (ie processing of data as actually stored rather than of the Logical Data Model) is handled by the Process/Data Interface, as described in SSADM v4.

It is quite clear to which Schema scenario almost all of the SSADM v4 end-products relate.

Internal Scenario	Conceptual Scenario	External Scenario
Records Indexes Pointer Chains Repeating Groups etc	Entities Relationships Attributes	Screen Layouts Printer Layouts etc
Program / Data Interface	Entity Life Histories Events / Commit Units Effect Correspondence Entity Access Paths Update Process Models Enquiry Process Models	Functions Dialogues Batch Runs Scheduling

Data & Process Definitions in the SSADM Architecture

Figure 5

Relevance of the 3-Schema Processing Architecture

The 3-Schema processing architecture suggests:

— how upper and lower CASE tools might modularise systems
— methodology-independent tools
— where prototyping is useful, where animation is useful

Modularity of systems

In theory it ought to be possible actually to construct the implemented system from programs quite clearly belonging to one and only one schema. An internal process *created by the designer* might assemble conceptual data from quite differently structured physical data, and vice versa. (There is a significant difference here from the old ANSI-SPARC architecture in which conceptual data was never supposed to be "materialised".)

However there are some problems about using this architecture directly with some current CASE tools and some implementation products. Some products and tools do not allow such modularisation. A designer might be forced to either structure his conceptual processes in terms of implementation objects, or to restrict his choice of implementation objects.

A further difficulty is with systems like CICS which have no concept of a whole dialogue of several input output messages, and which force commits to take place at the screen in/screen out level. Someone designing for a CICS environment may feel that they are forced to dismember their conceptual processes and distribute them around their screen-handling processes.

A good CASE tool here would take data and processing descriptions from each of the three schemas and automatically perform the dismembering and recombination to form screen-based programs. No such tool exists today.

Methodology-independent tools

Methodologies like IE can now be seen to fail to address adequately the discovery of the Conceptual Scenario. Cultural methodologies such as Mumford's can now be seen as addressing the performance and acceptability of the External Schema. If we can provide tools to support different parts of this architecture they should be portable between methodologies which implement the relevant parts of the architecture.

Prototyping and animation

For the **Conceptual Schema** it is possible to believe that there is in some sense a "right answer". For example, in SSADMv4, through the use of stereotypes, and a disciplined approach to entity-event modelling, the designer can produce a highly objective procedural specification of the database processing. To some extent the Conceptual Schema already exists in the end-users' minds before the analysis starts and only has to be *discovered*.

But the design of the **External Schema** depends on a number of different things:

— organisation structure
— ergonomics
— system efficiency
— end-user input-output device technology
— arbitrary preferences of particular users
— audit principles, security, user politics, etc.

There is certainly no "right answer" to the trading-off of these different requirements. This implies that there will always be a strong subjective element in the definition of "functions" and the development of a user interface.

There is little point in searching for an objectively correct method for building DFDs, or for specifying data input and report programs. Any method for designing the External Schema must be creative, ie it must involve inventing solutions. The External Schema must be *designed* not *discovered*. Heuristic approaches like prototyping clearly have a strong role to play here.

Similarly, the **Internal Schema** depends on tradeoffs between a number of things whose relative importance is subjectively defined: Time Objectives, Space Objectives, Maintainability. Once again, this implies that there is no "right answer" and that a heuristic, prototyping approach is needed. The Internal Schema, too, must be *designed* not *discovered*.

We can create first-cut designs for dialogues and improve them through prototyping. CASE tools clearly have a role to play here, although that role might be best carried out on the implementation product.

CASE tools could also provide performance analysis capability for improvement of Internal Schema prototypes.

But what are we to do about validating the discoveries in the Conceptual Schema? At present all we do is show the end-user's data models and data flow diagrams. Future CASE tools should be able to *animate* the conceptual processes. At first the animations will be crude, eg highlighting the path an event takes through an SSADM v4 effect correspondence diagram, showing what actual values lie behind a particular entity and how they are changed. But maybe in twenty years time we'll be using moving icons to show pictures of lorries arriving at warehouses, unloading and loading, and stock piles depleting!

BETTER KNOWLEDGE ACQUISITION

One of the advantages of the diagrammatic representations that we use is that they contain information not just about what the designer told the tool but also about possible implications of that information. This is information which is also available manually, but the advantage of a CASE tool is that it can bring that information to the designer's attention.

For example, when an SSADM data model is constructed the presence of a "double-V" structure is suggestive of the fact that there may be a relationship between the two entities at the bottom of the "V".

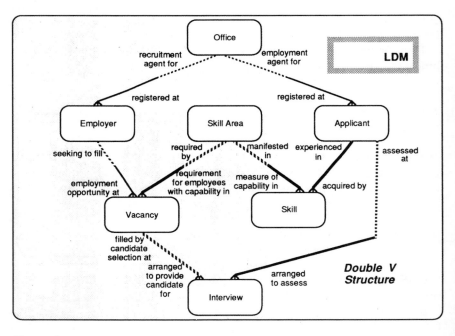

Figure 6

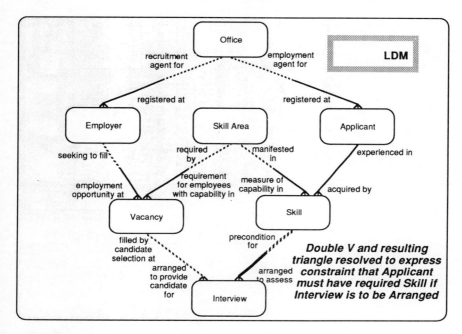

Figure 7

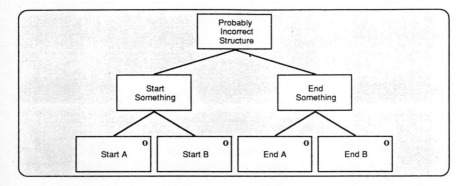

Figure 8

Again, a common mistake in the construction of SSADM entity life histories is to represent what should be a selection of two sequences as a sequence of two selections. The latter structure is rare enough in reality that a tool could make a point of detecting it and querying whether the former was meant, proposing a design which could be chosen by the designer.

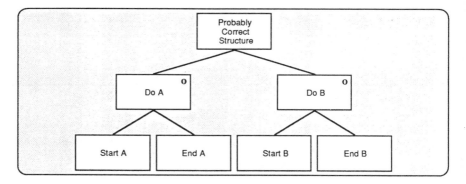

Figure 9

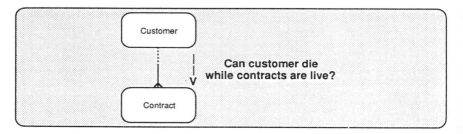

Figure 10

Finally (and there are lots more), a tool could be pro-active in propagating the event-equivalents of RESTRICT and CASCADE around the entities in a data model.

BETTER TRANSFORMATIONS

The architectural framework proposed by John Zachman of IBM can be used to think about the kinds of transformations and other relationships between products of information systems development.

In essence, the Zachman framework is a 3 by 6 matrix tabulating different viewpoints on a system against different development stages. Each cell in the matrix represents a potential product needed by an identifiable audience. In explaining the framework Zachman uses several different analogies, one of which is that of the different models architects use for communicating with different people at different times when designing a building. In another analogy he shows how concentration

The Zachman Framework			
	Data Description	Process Description	Network Description
Scope			
Business Model			
Inform- ation Model			
Techno- logy Model			
Detailed Descript- ion			
Actual System			

Figure 11

on differing combinations of cells to the exclusion of others corresponds to differing modes of running an engineering business with widely differing implications for cost, research and flexibility. Other variants on the framework have been produced; a GUIDE project produced a 6 by 6 matrix.

The 6 layers do **not** represent layers of decomposition. Rather, they represent layers of transformation.

The relevance for CASE tools is twofold. Firstly, the framework defines the kinds of thing that a CASE tool needs to be able to capture information about. Secondly, the framework points to the kinds of product transformations (downwards, in the implementation direction, and across, to reconcile products in different views or to produce a product in one view from a product in another) needed in information processing. Zachman doesn't discuss the lines between cells much in his papers or presentations, but in conversation says that they're as important as the cells. From the perspective of this paper, much of the engineering takes place on the lines.

I've already discussed earlier how engineering transformations down the framework could be used to take products representing the separation of concerns in a 3-Schema framework and repackage them for a hostile environment such as CICS.

Transformations across the model could for example be used to take data models, extract subsets hit on particular access paths and transform those access paths into skeleton enquiry processes, as in SSADM v4:

SSADM in the Zachman Framework

	Data Description	Process Description	Network Description
Scope	*Requirements Catalogue*	*Soft Systems Guide?* *Requirements Catalogue*	↑?
Business Model	*Overview LDM?*	*Resource & Service Flows*	?
Information Model	*LDM:* *LDS* *Entity & R'ship Descritp'ns* *TNF Contents* *Data Catalogue*	*Data Flow Diagrams* *Functions* *ELHs I-O Structures* *ECDs Dialogues* *EAPs* *Update Process Models* *Enquiry Process Models* *Process Data Interface*	*Guide on distributed systems in preparation*
Technology Model	*Database Block Planning & R'ship Implementation Plans*	*Function Component Implementation Map* *3 GL Interface Guide*	↓ ?
Detailed Description			
Actual System			

Figure 12

For example, from the following data model:

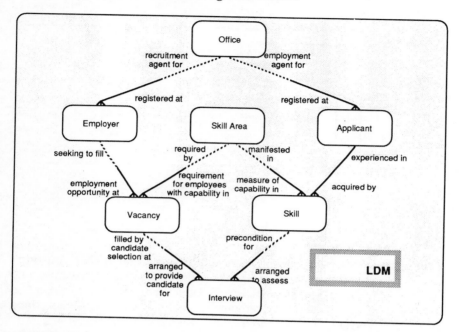

Figure 13

cut an access path:

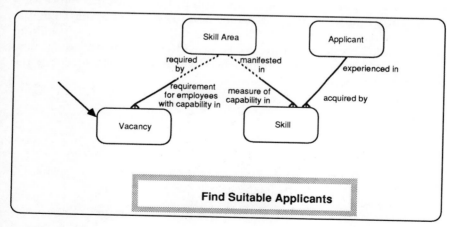

Figure 14

and transform it automatically into a processing skeleton:

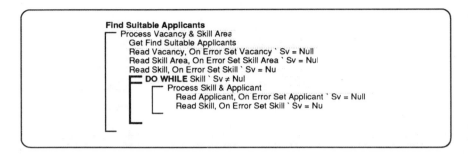

Figure 15

CONCLUSION

One of the great pleasures of a keynote presentation is that you don't really have to deliver. You can strike attitudes, savage colleagues and make wild claims. But the criticisms I make here are real ones, and so are the suggestions for improvement I'm making. Just about everything I've talked about is being done to some degree somewhere.

There are tools which satisfy the usability criteria I'm talking about. We're a substantial way up Brown's slope to the last plateau where we have put together a much better theory which combines data modelling, object orientation etc. People are using the 3-schema processing architecture and there are tools which address the Conceptual/External schema separation to some degree or other. People are working on animation systems. Some tools provide ways of encoding new knowledge. And a demonstrator exists which animates aspects of the Zachman framework.

2

User Interface Development: Our Experience with HP Interface Architect

Balbir S. Barn

ABSTRACT

The increasing use of graphical user interfaces to applications has led to the development of User Interface Development Environments (UIDE). These tools considerably ease the task of development of user interfaces. Indeed it is this ease which has led to somewhat inflated claims about increased productivity. This paper describes some of the problems we have experienced in using a User Interface Development Environment. An overview of the X Window System architecture and its relationship to the UIDE is presented. The specific problems that we had with integrating the UIDE to our development environment (programming languages etc) are described. Our approach for providing a practical solution for interfacing user interface C code and tool C++ code is described. Finally a requirements wish list for future UIDEs is presented.

CASE: Current Practice, Future Prospects. Edited by Kathy Spurr and Paul Layzell
© 1992 John Wiley & Sons Ltd

INTRODUCTION

This paper describes our initial experience with a User Interface Development Environment (UIDE) based on the X Window System™ (Scheiffler, Getty 1986) and supporting the Motif Toolkit™. This section provides an overview of the X Window System architecture and its relationship to UIDEs. Subsequent sections discuss some of the problems we were forced to overcome when we attempted to combine the use of different programming languages. Some specific problems to the CASE tool we selected are also highlighted. We indicate how the usage of the tool has directed future technical and project management considerations for the selection of such tools. In the final section a wish list of some basic requirements for future generations of UIDEs is presented.

The X Window System and Toolkit layers

The X Window System is composed of a number of layers. These are shown in the diagram below (see Figure 1). There are a number of primitive layers. The X Protocol layer implements the network transparent aspects of the X Window System. This is the layer that implements the functionality that allows the user to display an application (in its own window) on another X terminal. All X terminals run a copy of the X server. The Xlib C Language Interface contains all the necessary low level primitives to construct X Window applications. This would be the lowest level that an application developer would work at.

The next two layers present a greater level of abstraction. The Xt Intrinsics layer collects together the Xlib primitives and provides a basic framework to construct and use widgets (graphical objects—scroll bars, pushbuttons, lists etc.). The Toolkit layer has been subject to bruising confrontation between two rival camps attempting to define standards for the look and feel of user interfaces. The groups have done this by developing Toolkits (utilizing the Intrinsics layer) comprised of widgets based on their standards. The first group—Unix International—have produced a toolkit called OPEN LOOK™, the second group—Open Software Foundation (OSF)—have produced a toolkit called Motif. Organisations involved in the development of Graphical User Interfaces (GUI) have aligned themselves with one or other of the two groups. At the time of writing it would appear that the OSF camp is becoming the standard choice.

Although both toolkits go a considerable way towards easing the burden for production of a GUI, the process is still resource expensive. The final layer, the UIDE layer, attempts to solve this problem.

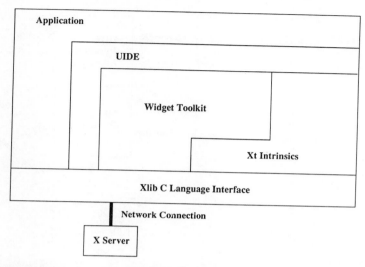

Figure 1   The X Window System Architecture

Architecture of a UIDE

GUI builders or UIDEs as they are now commonly called have a long history of research. The early tools captured the object oriented nature of user interfaces and the notion of reusability but failed to provide any standardisation of the graphical objects. The tools were also largely built using custom graphics libraries. The development of window systems saw the introduction of the notion of a toolkit based on "standards". The following diagram describes the basic structure of a UIDE (see Figure 2).

Currently the range of UIDEs is large and continually expanding. The tools have been marketed in a similar manner. They all emphasise a rapid prototyping ability and all claim to reduce development costs. The tools are also directed towards Interface Designers rather than Software Engineers; however experience has shown that X expertise is essential when building the final product.

Corporate Environment

Unitel is a new company, whose main activity is the development of mobile telecommunication network. The Software Engineering Group

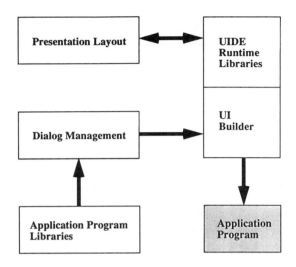

Figure 2   UIDE Structure

(SEG) provides a internal software development service to users within the company in order to perform the main activity. Project requirements supplied to the SEG are defined by the users within the company.

OUR EXPERIENCE

The HP Interface Architect™ was chosen because of its availability for the SEG development environment (based on HP workstations) and other corporate decisions. The Architect allows wysiwyg manipulation of the presentational layer of the user interface being constructed. Widgets that are used to build the interface can be further manipulated by altering their property values via a property editor. Widgets that are manipulated by users and which alter the state of the UI or the underlying application have points where additional source code can be called. These points (Callback positions) are accessible to the engineer via the property editor. The Architect supports the testing of the interface within the tool. It also generates the C code associated with the interface created. The code generated can either be Motif standard code and thus allow portability across to other platforms supporting Motif, or it can be specifically for HP environments which have Interface Architect installed. The latter option allows the use of a number of powerful library functions. This section describes some of the difficulties that arose from using Interface Architect to design and construct user interfaces for tools used within the company. Some of the major problems stemmed from software engineering issues, others arose from more pragmatic development needs.

Software Engineering Issues

The basic target application produced output which was of a graphical nature (terrain plots based on Ordnance Survey data). The design of the GUI of the application was left to the SEGs understanding of the user requirements. The SEG identified the GUI as a major work package of the tools. Thus in terms of project plans, it was a separate activity and required its own resourcing and scheduling. Further, it was regarded as a separate project and was subject to normal project management rules. Thus there should be the usual project deliverables of requirements specification, functional specification and design specification which cover the specification phase of a development project.

The requirements were not a problem for the SEG. They were supplied externally and stated that the GUI should be of a graphical, dynamic manipulation nature. The functional specification standard (Unitel has adapted the IEEE Standard (IEEE 1984)) was too inflexible for the needs of the GUI. Other techniques such as formal specification were inappropriate considering the time constraints.

Thus a more pragmatic approach was accepted—that of prototyping. Prototyping provided a powerful evaluation tool and the prototype could become the basis for subsequent development. But the prototype was not appropriate as a deliverable for our fledgeling standards. It raised some important configuration management issues. Should prototypes be baselined? How does one sign off a prototype? What criteria should apply for the acceptance of a prototype? Our standards are now being modified to support the development of user interfaces with respect to prototypes.

Development Issues

The Architect was the main software tool used during the GUI development. The presentational aspect of the GUI was prototyped relatively quickly and mock results displayed. The GUI was subject to approval from the users. However their lack of experience in using graphical tools of this nature meant that many of the graphical aspects requirements came from the SEG. There has been limited feedback as to the usability of the final interface. Certainly, there have been no overriding major criticisms.

Once the presentational aspects were complete, the dialog management (that layer which linked the UI with the application) had to be written. This would not normally have been a problem as the Architect provides ample support for this process. Our problems arose out of the use of mixed programming languages.

The application functionality of the tool was designed and built in an object oriented manner using C++. The Architect provided only C support. Thus the callback functions (in the dialog management layer) that implement the functionality of the tool had to be written in C. They could not call the C++ class methods. Using Ansi C, it is possible to call C++ methods directly; however, Architect is based on X11 Release 3.0 and is based on standard C (Kernighan, Ritchie 1978). So it was necessary to create a new interface and protocol for communication between the UI and the tool functionality (see Figure 3).

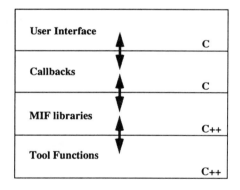

Figure 3   The MIF Communication Layer

The protocol is based on a client-server model, in that the UI (client) makes requests to the server (the main functional body of the tool) via a set of services defined as the MIF (Microwave Interface Functions). The MIF layer made it possible to share data that was relevant to the UI and the C++ objects created within the main functional body of the tool. Their basic operation was as follows. A number of global data structures were declared within the Architect so that declarations appeared in the generated source code. Pointers to these data structures were passed to the MIF functions. The MIF functions called C++ methods which then populated the global data structures. The data could then be used as required by those C functions necessary to modify the state of the UI. The MIF functions were written in Ansi C. Although the protocols were very simple, this approach had a number of overheads. Firstly there was the necessary development of an additional library. Secondly there was a need for a highly stylised approach in both the development practice and code. Both these overheads had some effect on the final delivery date.

User interface code generation

It is possible to develop prototype user interfaces within the Architect by the use of a built-in interpreter. The Architect handles the presentational aspects via the graphical editor. The behaviour is coded by writing C code (within the Architect) which is interpreted during testing.

A second approach is to use the code generation facilities provided. For each interface object, the Motif code is generated thus allowing the user interface to be built independently of the Architect. The code written by the user is also part of the generated code. This approach makes it possible to port the user interface to platforms which support X11/Motif but not Architect. However care must be taken to avoid using Architect library functions. The generated code can easily be modified but there is the real danger that the code can very quickly become out of step with the user interface definition file (used by the Architect). The test mode facility and the interpreter are used to make rapid changes to the interface in response to user feedback; thus the code has to be repeatedly generated in order to build the interface outside of the Architect.

The main advantage of building the interface as a standalone process was that the full power of a software development environment was available (editors, compilers, debuggers etc). But this approach was feasible if and only if the user interface had been baselined and subsequent changes were unlikely. For incremental development (the natural GUI development paradigm) the danger of inconsistencies and overheads of this approach were too great to make this approach a practical reality.

Development within the Architect

The dialog component includes those elements (callbacks) which modify both the behaviour and the appearance of the user interface and also the procedures that implement the functionality of the underlying application. This section is concerned with the development of this component. Again there were two possible approaches.

Approach A

The Architect toolset provides a capability to rebuild the Architect executable by augmenting it with external library functions. Thus the callback functions are developed separately as modules. The object files for these modules are linked with the Architect object files to provide an augmented Architect executable. The functions in the external modules are thus available within the Architect built-in Interpreter facility to allow rapid testing. This approach is eminently feasible but when we consider the actual steps that are required to perform a simple compile and test we can see that this approach is not that practical.

Table 1. Sample timings for an Augmented Architect executable

Step	Time (sec)
Compile separate module uif.o	180
Build Architect with uif.o	240
Load User Interface (ui.i)	350

Our callbacks were confined to one object module—uif.o. The user interface specification for the Architect was stored in the ui.i file. As the table shows, for a complex interface the loading process provides a unacceptable delay to the development cycle. It is worth bearing in mind, that we were using workstations with 16Mbytes of RAM.

Approach B

Alternatively we can use the built-in interpreter for all our development by simply declaring the code by judicious use of #include statements within the declaration sections of the user interface. Thus the code could be written outside of the Architect using the more powerful editing tools available with HP Softbench™. The simple text editor available within Architect was not suitable for editing large files.

This approach proved the most satisfactory but there were some interpreter characteristics which were irritating. Namely, once a variable had been declared of a type, it could not be re-declared as a different type even after the original declaration had been removed. It was necessary to restart the Architect to overcome this problem. In addition, as the included source code grew in size, the time taken to interpret the code was a significant overhead and again led to unacceptable delays in the development cycle.

The final approach was as follows. The code was written so that it could be used both by the interpreter and it could be separately compiled outside of the interpreter. Thus stepwise development was done within the interpreter allowing ad hoc changes to the GUI. At certain key points the Motif code was generated and the GUI built with the uif module as a separate process. Some modules, for example the MIF layer, were developed separately and once complete were not subject to many changes. These module functions were linked to the Architect executable to reduce the included code. Figure 4 shows the usage of the Architect in this manner.

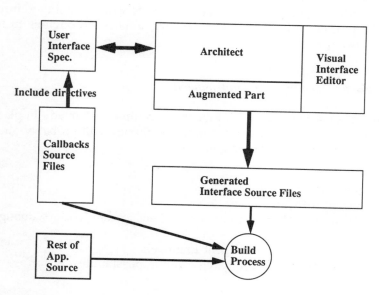

Figure 4   Architect Usage

Debug evils

Our general software development environment is based within HP SoftBench™. A good overview of SoftBench is described in (Cagan 1991). This tool provides a platform for integrating software tools. A number of tools including editors, compilers and debuggers are provided. Our particular version of Softbench and its integrated toolset was targeted for C++ development. This only became a problem when we were attempting to debug the GUI and the Callbacks code which were written in C. We found that the symbolic debugger provided could not be used for debugging the C code.

GENERAL CONSIDERATIONS FOR SELECTING A UIDE

Firstly, it is important to not lose sight of the fact that tool selection is essentially a marriage between meeting requirements and short term pragmatics. In most professional development environments (outside of academic institutions) it is not possible to make considered decisions after lengthy research. The project for which the tool has to be used is almost certainly about to begin. The process for purchasing the tool is almost certainly going to have an elapsed time which is going to intrude into the project time schedules. A scenario almost too obvious to most project managers ...

The Current Development Environment

It is most likely that the development environment is already in place. If it is not the key decisions concerning technology will probably already have been made. Thus major issues are:

- The hardware platform;
- The system software;
- The development tools—compilers, linkers, loaders, editors, debuggers etc.
- The skills base of Development Engineers;
- General resource availability, eg training possibilities.

Immediately, we can conclude that the required UIDE must run on our hardware supporting our version of the operating system and must generate GUI for our hardware or it must generate source code in development language(s) which must be suitable for our version of the compiler.This was in fact the major factor in the choice of our UIDE. However the importance of this factor can be reduced if we consider that certain operating systems provide at least some support for portability.

Product Maturity

In many ways this is related to the earlier point. A mature product is usually available across a variety of platforms and can be ported to new environments easily. The product company is also stable and there is a considerable client base. It also makes sense to consider the support availability for the product. Generally, support should be available from sources within the same country originating the support request. Transatlantic support causes considerable time delay.

Often, the support is provided by a distributor, in which case the distributor should be subject to same sort of screening as the product company. In our case, the product was not mature, in fact it was at Beta release, documentation was late in arriving but excellent support was available although it was overly bureaucratic.

A WISH LIST

The Architect proved to be a powerful tool for generating prototypes of user interfaces and on that basis alone it justified its presence. However, like all other tools of its type it does not provide any support or automation for developing the interactive elements which are perhaps application specific. Typically, these elements have now become relatively well defined such that support should be possible. For example, why not provide a framework for interactive zooming and panning?

Training was not necessary as the users were experienced in the use of the underlying technology. To other users some aspects of the tool may not be immediately transparent. Subsequent product development was problematic but could be made simpler by adopting function prototyping c.f. ANSI C. This will not be possible unless the Architect is ported to X11 Release 4.

The following list is a set of ideal requirements we would wish from a next generation UIDE. The list is not exhaustive but it could be used as a yardstick to measure a current generation vendor's intentions for their product's future releases.

(i) The UIDE must support C++. This is a key requirement, but we suspect that it will not be met until there are C++ Motif Class Libraries. As a short term pragmatic solution, the generated code should conform to ANSI C. This would at least allow the GUI functions to be callable from the C++ portion of the application. The use of C++ is constantly growing and GUI technology is a particularly good example of its use.

(ii) The UIDE should provide a build environment in which it is possible to build an application from either compiled code or interpreted code. This would allow interpreted development for unstable code and a simple switch mechanism to cause that code to be compiled once it had stabilised.

(iii) The UIDE must provide graphical browsers for the widget hierarchies which are created within the interface.

(iv) The UIDE should provide version management facilities (based on the proprietary operating system if necessary). The version management should extend to dependency management between interface source files and generated code. A finer grain of version control would ideally extend to graphical objects and their associated operational source code.

(v) The UIDE should allow the creation of templates (to be defined at the widget and/or interface layer). These templates would then be used to support house styles.

(vi) The UIDE should optionally generate UIL code and load UIL code. UIL (User Interface Language) is a facility provided by the Motif Toolkit. The facility allows user interfaces to be expressed in terms of UIL. The UIL compiler reads a UIL specification and generates the Motif code. This facility would provide a useful generic means of importing and exporting User Interfaces between UIDE tools and platforms.

(vii) The UIDE should provide a symbolic debugger specifically for X11/Motif applications.

(viii) The UIDE should provide a direct manipulation interface for assigning property values to widgets for as many property types as possible. Thus widget attachments, colours, fonts should be supported in this manner.

(ix) The UIDE must allow widgets developed separately to become part of the widget set used in the construction of interfaces.

REFERENCES

Scheiffler R.W; J. Getty. 1986. The X Window System. *ACM Transactions on. Graphics*. 5: 79–89.
IEEE. 1984. *IEEE Guide to Software Requirements Specifications*. ANSI.
Kernighan B.W; Ritchie D.M.1978. *The C Programming Language*. Prentice-Hall.

Cagan M.R. 1990. The HP SoftBench Environment: An Architecture for a New Generation of Software Tools. *Hewlett Packard-Journal.* 3. 36–47.

TRADEMARKS

UNIX is a registered trademark of AT&T. The X Window System is a trademark of Massachusetts Institute of Technology. Motif is a trademark of the Open Software Foundation. Open Look is a trademark of UNIX International. HP Interface Architect is a trademark of Hewlett-Packard Corporation. HP SoftBench is a trademark of Hewlett-Packard Corporation.

3

The Quality Gap: A Case Study in Information System Development Quality and Productivity using CASE Tools

Stephen King

ABSTRACT

The ISO definition of quality states that a product must satisfy the customer's stated or implied needs. These needs change over time. A simple graphical indicator is introduced to illustrate the danger of failing to match system deliverables to changing requirements. This indicator is called *"The Quality Gap"*. The quality of an information system developed for the Rover Group using CASE technology is assessed. The CASE tools used were *ProKit*WORKBENCH*™ and *PRO-IV*™ from McDonnell Douglas Information Systems Ltd. Three quality techniques are applied to the project: Gilb's Attribute Specification, Function Point Analysis and a User Satisfaction Survey. The results show that a *functionally-correct* system was developed but was not updated in line with changing user requirements. In other words, a *Quality Gap* appeared. Development productivity is also assessed by comparing actual development effort

CASE: Current Practice, Future Prospects. Edited by Kathy Spurr and Paul Layzell
© 1992 John Wiley & Sons Ltd

with an estimate for an equivalent development in COBOL. The results show a six-fold productivity improvement over the estimated COBOL figure. The reasons for the difference are discussed.

INTRODUCTION

"Quality" may well be the buzzword of the 1990s. The Prime Minister of the United Kingdom extols quality in public services in the form of The Citizens Charter (HMSO, 1991). The letters page of the Times Higher Education Supplement[1] carries heartfelt articles on the applicability of BS5750 to the processes of higher education. And, most importantly for the theme of this Conference, CASE tool vendors claim that by using their products the system developer will produce high quality information systems.

Central to this debate is the definition of *"quality"*. Definitions of quality abound. Wesselius and Ververs (1990) list a number of them with particular reference to software quality. One of the most concise, and appropriate from an information systems point of view is the definition given by ISO (1986):

"Quality: The totality of features and characteristics of a product or service that bear on its ability to satisfy stated or implied needs".

The point here is that a quality information system must clearly satisfy the *customer.*

System development does not take place in a vacuum. While the system is being developed the business moves on. Some businesses move faster than others and the information needs of the customer change over time. When assessing the quality of system development it is therefore essential to include the time taken to develop the system. Figure 1 shows the relationship between customer requirements, system deliverables, time and quality. Failure to match the system deliverables to the customer requirements results in the *"Quality Gap"*. The greater the gap, potentially the more problems in store. The impact of CASE technology on system development quality, productivity and elapsed time is considered in this paper with reference to a system development project within the Rover Group.

The Rover Project

The project in question was undertaken as a collaboration between the Advanced Technology Centre (ATC) of the University of Warwick, the

---

[1]   2 August 1991 and 19 July 1991.

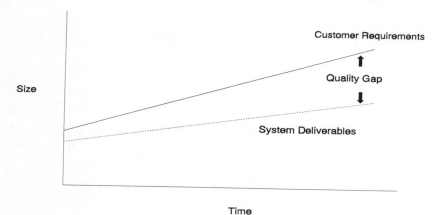

Figure 1   The Quality Gap

Rover Car Group and McDonnell Douglas Information Systems Limited. The tools evaluated are McDonnell Douglas Prokit*WORKBENCH and PRO-IV. ProKit*WORKBENCH is a CASE tool, PRO-IV is a fourth-generation language.

The project entailed the development of a Design Problem Tracking System for the pre-production build phases of Rover new model development, based at the Longbridge and Cowley manufacturing plants. The aim of the system was to enable tracking of problems from identification to resolution and to provide various problem status reports. A system-level data flow diagram for the PSR system[2] drawn using ProKit*WORKBENCH is shown in Figure 2. Data from part of a Problem Status Report (PSR) Form, which is the primary input to the system, are shown in Figure 3.

CASE Tool Support for Quality Measurement

Like many CASE tools, Prokit*WORKBENCH does not explicitly provide support for quality measurement. Instead, emphasis is placed on process and data modelling. However, the user may *extend* the repository to enable quality data to be recorded and presented. This paper indicates, where appropriate, how this facility might be used to support quality assessment.

---

[2] PSR System will be used as a more concise alternative to Design Problem Tracking System in the remainder of the paper.

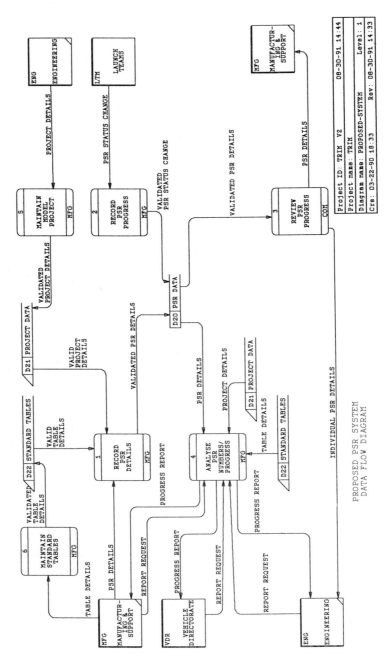

Figure 2 PSR System Data Flow Diagram

ORIGINATOR S. G. CROMPTON		CELL 2	DATE 21/02/90	CELL/ZONE REF.	
EVENT R8 QP	MODEL R8 3.0R		LAUNCH TEAM T	P.S.R Nº 3QP1-137	

PROBLEM	PART Nº EFP S111 EFP S110	Nº OFF	ISSUE	SIGNAL
	PART DESCRIPTION FINISHER - SixTHLight L/H - /RH			V.P.G 1105 DG

PROBLEM DESCRIPTION / ILLUSTRATION / SUGGESTED SOLUTION

Operator is Having great difficulty of clipping the clip's marked with (*). It's sort of a Blind spot to work on.

(*) Clip fixing (EYC 10008)

(+)

The two clips marked with an (+) is like a 5-door. Easy to Reach and operate.

PARTS OK TO DRG ISSUE	YES / NO
SIGNED	

JOB 1 CHANGE	
R.G	H.M

NEXT CHANGE POINT	
R.G	H.M

PROBLEM ANALYSIS

22.2.90   Suggest more operator Training is Required. I.e. monitor QP2 end of "A" Shift in Particular. No Apparent Problems with 'B' Shift Operators.

CYCLE TIME EFFECT	YES / NO	
OWNER N. Hubbard		
DATE 22.2.90		
RESOLUTION PRIORITY	S (A) B	
RESOLUTION OWNER		
MANUFACTURING		
HONDA R&D		
ROVER R&D		
PCA NO.		
HONDA R&D		DATE
ROVER R&D		DATE
SUPPLIER		DATE
PURCHASE		DATE
S.Q.D		DATE
PROCESS		DATE

TEMPORARY ACTION

Figure 3   PSR Form

QUALITY IN INFORMATION SYSTEM DEVELOPMENT

How do we know if we have produced a *"quality"* information system? A useful approach is to split quality into three distinct components (Wesselius and Ververs, 1990):

(i) An objectively assessable component: does the product have all the characteristics stated in the requirements specification?

(ii) A subjectively assessable component: do the characteristics of the product comply with the preferences and expectations of the customer?

(iii) A non-assessable component: does the system behave according to our expectations in situations that have not been foreseen?

In the following sections the quality of the PSR system is assessed using three different techniques. The ability of each technique to measure the objective and subjective components of the system is evaluated. The presence of any non-assessable components is also considered.

Gilb's Attribute Specification

The first technique is Gilb's Attribute Specification (Gilb, 1988). An attribute, in Gilb's definition, is a "quality concept or resource which describes a system quantitatively". Examples of system attributes include maintainability, usability and performance. Attributes should be specified as part of the requirements specification since they influence the design of the system. By stating attributes *quantitatively*, the successful achievement of the target attribute values can be measured.

Whilst the attributes should be specified early in the development cycle, they relate to the end product, the information system, and so cannot be measured until the system has been produced. Therefore Gilb's metrics must be supplemented with additional metrics in order to monitor quality prior to implementation. The following examples illustrate how attribute specification could be applied to the objectives of the PSR system[3].

---

[3] The objectives were not quantified at the start of the project. The following examples are therefore *suggested* quantifications.

PSR system objectives

The system objectives were identified at the start of the project as:
Engineering:

(i) To save time spent by the engineering team leader in compiling statistics.

(ii) To improve management focus on outstanding problems.

Manufacturing:

(iii) To ensure that the problem tracking system recognises all problem-related activities which need to be controlled during the pre-production build phase of product development.

(iv) To ensure that the system is adequate to support future product development projects.

Quantified objectives

The above objectives are clearly *qualitative*. Achievement of qualitative objectives is difficult to measure. Attribute templates[4] can be used to quantify objectives. For example, objectives (i) and (iv) could be quantified as follows.

Objective (i):

SCALE = hours spent by engineering team leader in compiling statistics.

DATE (training in use of system) = January next year.

TEST = at least ten consecutive statistics compilation sessions to be completed within the planned time specified below for each session.

WORST (by initial release DATE) = 3 hours.

PLAN (by initial release DATE) = 1 hour.

RECORD (Rover 200 statistics session, 17.2.90) = 20 minutes.

NOW (old system, last year average) = 5 hours.

---

[4] Gilb defines an *attribute template* containing a number of slots such as SCALE, DATE, TEST etc. The template can be customized as required.

SEE (PSR System Business Specification, Issue 1, March 1990) = specification of this requirement.

SOURCE = GW April 14th 1990.

Objective (iv):

SCALE = work-hours to implement change in requirements.

DATE (training in support of system) = January next year.

TEST = at least 10 representative requirement changes to be generated and implemented in the system within the planned time specified below.

WORST (by initial release DATE) = 20 work-hours per change on average.

PLAN (by initial release DATE) = 5 work-hours per change on average.

RECORD = not defined.

NOW (old system, last year average) = 30 work-hours per change on average.

SEE (PSR System Business Specification, Issue 1, March 1990) = specification of this requirement.

SOURCE = SK April 19th 1990.

CASE tool support for attribute specification

ProKit*WORKBENCH does not directly support attribute specification. The repository does not provide pre-defined objects to represent business objectives or attribute templates. A link therefore has to be defined between these new objects and the pre-defined objects supplied by Prokit*WORKBENCH.

Since the business objectives are stated at the start of a project, they should be linked to early life-cycle objects in the repository. One solution is to link each business objective to the process or processes that will deliver the objective. A simple solution would be to add a *Business Objective Supported* text field to the *Process* object via the *Extend Repository*[5] facility provided by ProKit*WORKBENCH. For example, objective (i)

---

[5] The Extend Repository facility enables the *user* to add new fields to the pre-defined repository objects.

"To save time spent by the engineering team leader in compiling statistics"

could be recorded in the *Business Objective Supported* field of *Process 4.2.4 Analyse Problem Status for Single Launch Team*[6].

The second new object, *Attribute Template*, could be recorded in the *Business Objective Supported* field following the qualitative description of the objective. Alternatively an existing ProKit*WORKBENCH field, such as the *Test Plan* field in the *Design Unit* object, could be used. This field is an appropriate location for the attribute template since the template is, in effect, a test plan. The pre-defined *Test Plan Report* can subsequently be used to automatically generate test scripts from the attribute templates. The *number of test failures recorded* is therefore an appropriate metric to associate with Gilb's technique.

Attribute specification is clearly an attempt to make all quality components *objectively assessable*.

Function Point Analysis

Function Point Analysis (FPA) (Symons, 1988) is a technique for measuring the size of an information system based on the number of inputs, outputs and files in the system. FPA is becoming increasingly widely-used and is recommended for use in UK government departments by the CCTA. After adjustment for complexity factors, a figure of 320 function points was calculated for the PSR system using the transaction-based Mark 2 counting conventions.

Function Points can be used to assess quality by calculating the ratio:

user-reported defects per year/system size in function points.

Capers Jones (1989) suggests a benchmark for system quality. This benchmark states that "a high quality" system should result in the receipt of fewer than 10 user-reported defects per 100 function points per year. Using this benchmark we can claim that the PSR system is a high quality system if we receive fewer than 32 user-reported defects per year. The first 10 weeks of system operation were monitored and user communications categorised as either defect reports or change requests. The details are described in the following sections.

---

[6] Process 4.2.4 is the process that generates the statistical report for the engineering team leader.

Defects reported

A total of *six* user-reported defects were received during this period. Two defect related to errors in changing the PSR status. Two defects related to violations in operator security levels. One defect related to the problem incidence reports, whereby PSRs were printed that did not match some of the selection criteria specified. The final defect related to the omission of help messages from the functional specification.

Change requests

A total of *eleven* change requests were received during this period. Five of the requests related to changes in the data model to reflect the different requirements of the Longbridge and Cowley assembly plants. The sixth request was to direct report output to screen as well as printer. The seventh was to support a new type of printer. The eighth to add a new report: Problem Incidence by Part Number. The ninth to select PSRs by partial key. The tenth request was to allow a PSR to be assigned to a launch team for information purposes only. Finally, the eleventh request was to automatically carry-over some field values from one PSR to the next to save unnecessary re-keying of data.

Assessment of quality

Six defects were reported in the first 10 weeks of operation. Since it is likely that the majority of defects will be reported in the early stages of operation, it is fair to assume that the figure of 32 defects will not be exceeded in a full year. Therefore, according to the Capers Jones benchmark we can claim to have produced a *"high quality"* information system.

CASE Tool Support for Function Point Analysis

In order to count the number of function points, the system needs to be defined down to transaction level[7]. A transaction is defined as something that

"gives rise to separately distinguishable processing as seen in the system requirements of the user." (Nolan Norton, 1989)

---

[7] Assuming the transaction-based Mark 2 counting conventions are used.

In practice, this definition is open to interpretation. The interpretation adopted for this project is that a data flow diagram needs to be exploded down to the level where there are separate processes for adding, changing, deleting and viewing data *for each primary file maintained by the process*. For example, with reference to *Process 1 Record PSR Details* (figure 2), the data store *D20 PSR DATA* is a composite data store containing several simple data stores which result from normalising the data shown on the PSR form (figure 3). Each of these simple data stores is maintained by *Process 1*. Therefore *Process 1* needs to be exploded into 28 transactions[8].

A separate function point figure is calculated for each transaction using the formula defined in (Nolan Norton, 1989):

*FP count = number of input fields * 0.54 + number of files referenced * 1.66 + number of output fields * 0.29.*

The individual transaction counts are then added together to get a total (unadjusted) count for the whole system. The count for *Process 1* was 141 unadjusted function points.

ProKit*WORKBENCH does not support function point analysis. However, the information required to calculate the unadjusted figure does reside in the repository. The following steps should be followed to calculate the unadjusted figure:

(i) Explode the DFDs down to transaction level.
(ii) Identify the primary data stores and the system (master) data stores.
(iii) Extract the figures for the number of input and output fields from the data flow contents held in the repository.
(iv) Do the calculations.

The unadjusted function point count is multiplied by the Processing Complexity Adjustment (PCA) factors giving the final function point count. There are 19 such factors in the Mark 2 guide including performance of target system, design for end-user efficiency and security/privacy/auditability requirements.

Unfortunately, calculation of the Processing Complexity Adjustment is not easy to automate. Of the 19 PCA factors, only one could be derived automatically. The remaining 18 factors require subjective, human judgement.

---

[8] 7 (simple data stores) * 4 (add, change, delete and view transactions).

The system size in function points is not, in itself, of interest. What is of interest are the quality and productivity metrics that can be derived using the size figure. In order to support the Capers Jones quality metric we need to know both the system size and the number of user-reported defects received. Again, ProKit*WORKBENCH does not directly support the collection of quality metrics such as user-reported defects. However, it is possible to extend the repository to include a *defect list* text field associated with the defective process, data store, data flow etc.

The other quality metric based on function points is a measure of the volatility of user requirements. This is the ratio

change requests per year/system size in function points.

ProKit*WORKBENCH does provide a pre-defined change history mechanism, associated with one object type, the *Module*. This facility needs to be extended to other object types.

Criticism of defect-related metrics

The Capers Jones quality benchmark is expressed in terms of the number of user-reported defects per 100 function points per year. There are two problems with this metric. Firstly, no attempt is made to differentiate between severe defects, which could lead to system failure, and more cosmetic defects.

Secondly, defects relate to faults in the *operational system*. A similar metric such as:

number of inspection errors per 100 function points

could be used to assess the quality of early life-cycle deliverables such as the *requirements specification* and *design specification*. This metric relies on the application of a document inspection technique such as Fagan's Inspection Method (Fagan, 1976).

The defect-based metric, like attribute specification, is an attempt to make system quality *objectively assessable*.

User Satisfaction Survey

A review of the PSR system was carried out some six months after the system was implemented. The aim of the review was both to assess user satisfaction with the delivered system (ie. the *subjectively assessable* component of quality) and to review the system development process.

The questionnaire

The following questions were asked of a number of key users.

1. What was expected of the project?
2. What was achieved?
3. What were the perceived problems with the project?
4. Were the techniques useful?
5. Were the right people involved? If not, why not?
6. Was the scope established correctly?
7. Were the right issues/objectives established?
8. Would locally-based system support have helped?

Extracts from two of the interviews follow.

The senior user's response

The first interview was with the senior user (initials KL) who had originally commissioned the system.

KL viewed this project as an opportunity to extend the existing spreadsheet-based Longbridge PSR system to embrace all pre-production problem management activities at both Longbridge and Cowley.

The extended PSR system was delivered in time to provide useful support to the new model development at Cowley. KL viewed the system as "suffering from its own success" in that as more areas began to use the system, there was demand for a greater range of reports than had originally been envisaged. It was intended that a member of the Longbridge PSR team provide end-user support for the system. However, due to the company re-organisation, the Longbridge operation separated from the Cowley operation and the support became no longer available. The lack of local system support meant that new reports could not be created without some delay and the users at Cowley became frustrated with the apparent inflexibility of the system.

In the meantime the new model project had progressed to the stage where forward considerations of problem control post-production were being explored with the Cowley Product Support Group (PSG). PSG had developed their own post-production problem tracking system in conjunction with a major systems house. The system had been refined by a member of the PSG team and was being used successfully at Cowley. A decision was made to combine the two systems. The issue of flexibility was seen as crucial here. Since the PSG system was supported locally by both a member of PSG staff and the systems house, whilst the PSR system had no established local support, the choice was made to use the PSG system as the basis for the combined system.

KL saw the major problem with the project as being the lack of local support for the PSR system once it was installed at Cowley. The time pressure imposed by the tight schedule for the new model project meant that Cowley staff could not be made available for training in system support. The requirement to combine the PSR and PSG systems could not have been envisaged by KL at the start of the project since at that time his attention was completely focused on pre-launch activities. KL was aware of the Cowley PSG system but did not think it appropriate for PSR management at that time.

The PSR control manager's response

The second interview was with the engineer (initials SO) who had day to day responsibility for running the PSR system at Cowley.

SO described the need for an improved PSR system. The spreadsheet-based system developed at Longbridge was seen as very difficult to use, slow and storing minimal data. SO was looking for a more flexible system that would provide a wide variety of management reports for all stages of pre-production build.

The PSR system delivered by this project did provide a greater variety of reports and was easier to use. However, the variety of reports required by different users was far greater than SO had envisaged. The lack of local support for the new system meant that new reports could not be developed sufficiently quickly to meet this demand. SO became frustrated at the lack of flexibility of the system. The ideal reporting system was seen as one where the user could specify a report containing any number of attributes from the database selected on any combination of attributes.

SO was not involved in the initial specification of the PSR system and was surprised that the Longbridge staff who were involved had not emphasised the need to interface to the PSG system since the need for an interface must have become evident in the previous new model project at Longbridge. The scope of the project should therefore have been extended to include the PSG interface.

Comments on the interviews

These comments show that a technically correct system[9] can fail to satisfy user requirements. In this instance, a combination of lack of on-

---

[9] Judged by the user-reported defects received.

site support and the need for specialised training in PRO-IV meant that changes were not made to the PSR system in time to satisfy the changing user requirements.

The users' expectation of a highly-flexible system is an example of a *subjectively assessable* component of quality, whilst the unforeseen need to interface to the PSG system is a good example of a *non-assessable* component.

CASE tool support for user satisfaction surveys

The user satisfaction survey consisted of two components: the list of questions and the interview transcripts. Since the interviews were not confined to any particular part of the system, it seems appropriate to link the questionnaire to the highest-level object in the ProKit*WORKBENCH repository: the *Project*. The transcripts reflect the views of a number of users. The users are modelled by *External Entities* in the DFDs; therefore it would be appropriate to add a *User Satisfaction Survey Response* text field to the *External Entity* object type.

Other quality issues

ProKit*WORKBENCH provides a number of facilities that are likely to enhance the quality of the system by automating error-prone manual processes. In particular, horizontal and vertical balancing reports can be produced that check the data flow diagrams to ensure that data flowing into a process or data store flows out again and vice versa. An orphans report lists any object in the repository that is not used in the diagrams. This enables redundant objects to be identified and deleted if required.

The interface between ProKit*WORKBENCH and PRO-IV is particularly useful in that screen and report images, file specifications and field validation checks are automatically transferred from the CASE tool to the 4GL thereby saving time-consuming and error-prone rekeying of data. However, the developer still needs to undertake additional work in the 4GL in order to produce a working system. Full integration of the tools has not yet been achieved but some useful progress has been made.

Maintainability has yet to be measured. However, the lack of a fully-integrated repository meant that the system documentation (stored in Prokit*WORKBENCH) had to be updated separately from the application (stored in PRO-IV). The overhead incurred by this task meant that the working system gradually moved away from the system described by the CASE tool. It is therefore important that the CASE tool and 4GL be integrated, at least to the extent whereby alterations made to the system description in the CASE tool can be propagated through to the working system without destroying any additional work required to produce the working system.

PRODUCTIVITY IN INFORMATION SYSTEM DEVELOPMENT

Time is a vital contributor to system quality. Systems must be delivered in time to make a useful contribution to the business, otherwise the *Quality Gap* may grow too large.

Comparison with a 3GL Development

An estimate for the development of an equivalent system for an IBM mainframe environment, using the hierarchical database IMS DB/DC and COBOL, was provided by the in-house IS development department of another large manufacturing company. The department consists of about 15 analysts and 15 programmers. Systems are developed using functional decomposition and data modelling. A program specification is then written for each function showing the files accessed, screen/report layouts and processing logic (in structured english). Only the effort required to write the program specifications and then code and test the programs was estimated by the IS department; the project determination and requirements specification activities were assumed to be the same. The figures are as follows:

PRO-IV actual effort: 135 work-hours
COBOL estimated effort: 141 work-days
                        (= 141*6 = 846 work-hours)

The difficulty in comparing languages is clearly illustrated by this example. A six-fold productivity increase is shown but this could be due to any combination of development factors. Boehm (1981) quantifies the impact of a number factors on IS development productivity including:

— personnel/team capability (4.18)[10]
— product complexity (2.36)

---

[10] The figures in parentheses indicate the productivity difference between the best and worst examples of the factor.

— use of modern programming practices (1.51)
— use of software tools (1.49).

These four factors differ between the PRO-IV team and the IS department team. Certainly it is difficult to isolate the contribution made by the 4GL, although both the capability of the small, highly-motivated ATC team and use of the 4GL are likely to have been significant.

CASE Tool Support for Productivity

We have not attempted to measure productivity during the feasibility study and requirements specification stages because a worthwhile analysis would require the evaluation of many subjective organisational factors. It is likely that the use of rigorous structured techniques will slow down analysis in comparison to a more informal approach since the techniques encourage more comprehensive analysis. Given that structured techniques are being used, a CASE tool should improve analyst productivity over a non-CASE approach because many of the time-consuming tasks such as drawing diagrams, checking the consistency of diagrams and transferring specification details into a form that can be used by programmers to develop code have been fully or partly automated.

More measurable productivity improvements appear downstream; at the coding stage. Here, the screen, report and file-processing algorithms pre-coded into PRO-IV enable the majority of routine data processing functions to be implemented with a minimum of hand-written code. Hand-coding is both time-consuming and error-prone; therefore the use of the 4GL should improve both development productivity and the quality of the resulting system. The six-fold increase in productivity over a comparable COBOL development substantiates the former claim, whilst the receipt of only three user-reported defects that were caused by coding errors[11] substantiates the latter.

The *portability* of PRO-IV is emphasised by the fact that the application was developed on a PC at the University and ported to a Rover VAX™ for operation with the minimum of alteration.

---

[11] The other three defects related to the inadequate specification of operator security and help messages.

CONCLUSIONS

The experience of this project shows that a combination of CASE tool and 4GL can be used to develop a *technically-correct* information system, that conforms to the original requirements specification, with considerably less effort than the estimate for an equivalent 3GL development. The benefits for the developer are significant, especially the automation of time-consuming and error-prone tasks such as diagram verification and coding of the application.

However, quality is in the eye of the *customer*. Whilst the CASE tool and 4GL used on this project assist the developer, they do not directly support the customer-oriented quality techniques described in this paper. The danger here is that developers will concentrate on producing a *functionally-correct* system since the techniques supported by the CASE tool are *function-oriented*, whilst failing to address the *quality* issues.

The PSR system development fell into this trap. Changes in customer requirements were not effectively addressed after the initial implementation of the system. By using the quality-oriented techniques described here, a more accurate picture of the true quality of the system can be gained. Indeed, by making some simple extensions to the ProKit*WORKBENCH repository, the three techniques can be accommodated in the CASE tool. However, this alone will not be enough to change the *focus* of the structured techniques supported by ProKit*WORKBENCH away from function and towards quality. The methodology needs to be changed to give due emphasis to quality-oriented techniques. At present these techniques are overshadowed by process and data-oriented methods.

Many factors contribute to information system quality and productivity. The claim that the 4GL can deliver a six-fold improvement in productivity over a 3GL fails to highlight at least one other major factor: that the PSR system was developed by an experienced two-person team keen to explore the impact of new tools and techniques. Given the restrictions of a large systems development group it is unlikely that the same enthusiasm would result. It is therefore essential that further research be undertaken into the influence of the various *environmental factors* on system development quality and productivity.

Finally, three lessons should be learnt from this project:

(i) *Organizational support for the delivered information system is vital.* The lack of on-site support from trained personnel meant that changes could not be implemented when required.

(ii) *The information system implementation must be easy to change in line with changing requirements*. PRO-IV is a tool for the IS professional and cannot be easily mastered by end users. An easy to use query language would have helped considerably here by enabling end users to make changes, thereby satisfying the demands for additional reports. This would also have reduced the need for trained on-site support described in (i).

(iii) *The scope of the project must be correctly defined*. This is a very difficult issue. *Scope* is one type of customer requirement, and is therefore subject to change during the lifetime of the system. The unforeseen requirement to merge the PSR system with the PSG system is a good example of changing scope. Techniques such a *portfolio analysis* may help to contain this problem by revealing closely-related systems that are operated by different functions within the business. Top-down *strategic planning* may also help by giving a broader, more long term view of the IS requirements.

The message from all this is clear. *Change* is inherent in IS development, therefore a *Quality Gap* is never far away. The next generation of CASE tools must support techniques that reduce the impact of change whilst making the implementation of change as painless as possible.

ACKNOWLEDGEMENT

The author would like to thank Graham Warren of McDonnell Douglas Information Systems Limited for many hours of fruitful discussion during this project.

REFERENCES

Boehm B.W. 1981. *Software Engineering Economics*, Prentice-Hall, Englewood Cliffs.
Capers Jones. 1989. Metric with Muscle, *System Development*, 9(8):1–3.
Fagan M.E. 1976. Design and code inspections to reduce errors in program development, *IBM Systems Journal*, 3:182–211.
Gilb T. 1988. *Principles of Software Engineering Management*, Addison-Wesley, Wokingham.
HMSO 1991. *The Citizen's Charter: A Guide*, HMSO.
ISO 1986. *ISO-8402: Quality Vocabulary*. International Standardisation Institute.
Nolan Norton 1989. *Application Productivity Measurement Workbook*.

Symons C.R. 1988. Function Point Analysis: Difficulties and Improvements, *IEEE Transactions on Software Engineering*, 14(1).
Wesselius J. and Ververs F. 1990. Some elementary questions on software quality control, *Software Engineering Journal*, November 319–330.

TRADEMARKS

ProKit*WORKBENCH and PRO-IV are trademarks of McDonnell Douglas Corporation. VAX is a trademark of Digital Equipment Corporation.

4

Experiences of Introducing a CASE Tool into Undergraduate Teaching of Systems Analysis and Design

Jennifer Stapleton, Shirley Williams

ABSTRACT

In January of 1991, the Department of Computer Science at Reading University took delivery of Interactive Development Environment's CASE tool for analysis and design, Software through Pictures. This was used to enhance the teaching of systems analysis and design to second year undergraduates for honours degrees in Computer Science and joint subjects.

After the first year the students were competent programmers but had no experience of more than program design. Hence they were learning the basic methods of structured systems analysis and design concurrently with learning the use of the CASE tool. This paper describes the delights and frustrations introduced through Software through Pictures into the course from both the teacher and the student point of view.

CASE: Current Practice, Future Prospects. Edited by Kathy Spurr and Paul Layzell
© 1992 John Wiley & Sons Ltd

Although the learning curve lengthened, the general opinion amongst the students is that it is far easier to use a CCASE tool than pencil and paper but they found some aspects of tool usage limiting. The quality of work produced using the CASE tool was considerably higher than had previously been achieved using manual methods.

INTRODUCTION

One of the aims of the Department of Computer Science at Reading University is to expose students to current practical methods and environments in addition to teaching fundamental and leading edge theory. One result of this aim was the decision, after the delivery of several SUN workstations, to incorporate upper CASE tool usage into the teaching of systems analysis and design. The platform made the number of CASE tools available for consideration smaller than if a PC environment had been chosen. However the CASE tools that are available are of a high standard and it was after a considerable evaluation process that Interactive Development Environment's Software through Pictures was selected.

HISTORY

Delivery of Software through Pictures was taken in January 1991. Its target users were second year undergraduates studying for honours degrees in Computer Science and joint subjects. After the first year, computing students at Reading are competent programmers, but they have no experience of design at a higher level than that of program design. They have no experience of basic systems analysis, but they have been introduced to data analysis. Hence with the introduction of Software through Pictures, the students would be learning the methods and techniques of structured analysis and design alongside mastering the usage of the CASE tool.

Many members of the teaching staff were new to the idea of using CASE tools (indeed some were new to the idea of using structured analysis). So it was determined that if CASE tools were to be successfully introduced into the undergraduate teaching it was important that staff teaching on related courses should also be familiar with the concepts, abilities and limitations.

At the start of the Lent term (i.e. in January) the second-year students who were to use the tool had spent a sixth of their time in the previous term on the first part of an extensive commercially-based analysis and design case study. They had completed the interviewing process and had produced a feasibility study which contained data flow diagrams of the current system. Since the students were learning structured systems analysis techniques and had not been exposed to higher level design problems than that of program design before the beginning of the second year, these were the first and only DFDs that they had ever produced. The DFDs had necessarily been produced using pencil and paper, though some students made use of personally-owned drawing packages.

The students had found the production of DFDs time-consuming and tedious. They knew what they wanted their diagrams to express and disliked the constant draughting and re-draughting with the concommitent consistency checking, that manual techniques necessitate. The DFDs that were produced for the feasibility study were generally both syntactically and semantically incorrect.

INITIAL INTRODUCTION TO UNDERGRADUATES

To introduce the students to Software through Pictures, they were allocated a series of practical sessions. They were each given worksheets providing tutorial instruction on the data flow, data structure and data dictionary parts of the CASE tool. This included consistency and completeness checks on the data dictionary produced from the data flow and data structure diagrams. Later on, as they graduated from structured analysis to structured design, further practical sessions were arranged to instruct them in the use of the CASE tool for the creation of module structure charts and consistency checks with earlier stages.

Like many Computer Science students, they were already familiar with working in the UNIX™ environment under Windows and were quickly able to gain understanding of the Software through Pictures environment.

To ensure the students concentrated on the use of the tool, rather than practising their analytic skills, it was decided to use a trivial domestic example of preparing a meal (most of our second year students are in self catering accommodation), with much of the specification given in a textual form, with some initial diagrams to ease the transition from verbal description of the problem to diagrammatic.

During this time we found about six occasions when the documentation supplied with the tool was insufficient to answer student problems. For instance there is no comprehensive error message listing. Consequently we had to resort to phoning the help line at IDE with

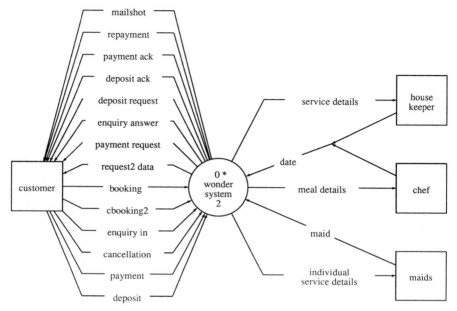

Figure 1   A student case study context diagram from Software through Pictures

varying degrees of success, but usually they were able to untangle the webs the students had woven.

The most nagging problem was that of stray anchor points. (Software through Pictures uses anchor points in DFDs to position the loose ends of data flows: they are represented by miniscule dots.) Unfortunately the tool allows the creation of anchor points one on top of the other and even singleton anchor points are not readily visible on the screen or paper copy. The result was a number of students with "unconnected nodes" and the staff with the equivalent of magnifying glasses hunting these down. Experienced users create single anchor points and connect them immediately, thus avoiding this problem.

There was an intense dislike of the editing facilities available, particularly when it came to correcting mistakes. Names of flows etc. are typed in and mistakes can only be corrected by deleting and retyping from the corrected error—very annoying when the mistake is in the first few characters of a name. Mistakes in annotations needed the use of backspace which was inconsistent with the use of the delete key for labelling diagrams.

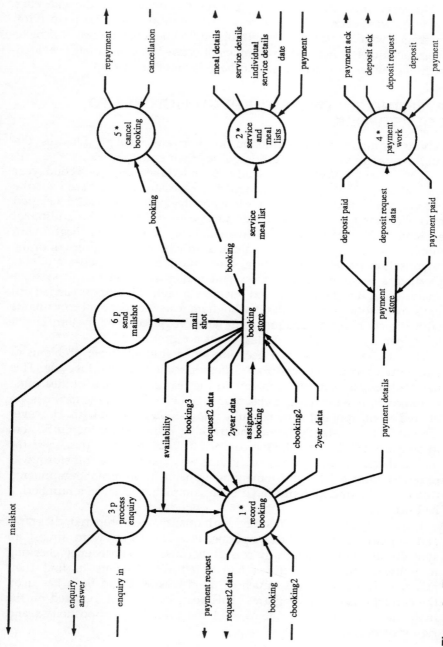

Figure 2 Figure 1 exploded

However the production of the data dictionary and the checking facilities were seen as a great boon, although at times the terse error messages were considered unhelpful: only experience helped to isolate their meanings. A list of the meanings of errors in the manuals provided or fuller online explanation would have been of great help.

APPLYING SOFTWARE THROUGH PICTURES TO COURSEWORK

Having completed the induction to Software through Pictures the students progressed to using the tool for their course work.

Each year a different case study is undertaken by the second year students. For the year in question, the case study was based on the automation of clerical procedures in a country pub which had developed into a conference centre and was unable to cope with the additional administrative load that this entailed. The case studies begin with interviews with members of academic staff who role-play the staff of the organisation under investigation. From the initial interviews, students produce a feasibility study, after which they progress to full systems analysis and design of a selected business option. All work is carried out in teams of four to five students who operate as independent consultants with direction from teaching staff when required. The system is not implemented but quality and test plans are produced.

The case study is the first occasion when students meet problems of integrating work products from different sections of the lifecycle. This has traditionally caused problems to the teams. Their difficulties often stemmed from an inability to keep track of everything: these facilities are offered by the tool but were not fully understood to begin with. However the students eventually found the tracking provided by the CASE tool to be extremely beneficial. One complaint which arose as they used the tool to incrementally produce diagrams was that when a transform was removed from a DFD the remaining transforms were not renumbered (there would undoubtedly have been complaints if such renumbering had occurred).

The completed reports included high quality, well prepared, diagrams and supporting process descriptions, etc. The DFDs were almost all syntactically and semantically correct, because the consistency checking in Software through Pictures had aided the students to find their mistakes. In earlier years, much of the assessment had been based on the correctness of the diagrams. This year, assessment focussed on the understanding of the problems, and the originality, appositeness and rigour of the solutions.

RESULTS

At the end of the course the students were given a questionnaire on Software through Pictures.

The results of the first three questions on the quesionnaire are summarised below:

1. How easy was Software through Pictures to understand at first?
   easy 20% ok 70% hard 10%

2. How easy was it to use?
   easy 20% ok 80% hard 0%

3. How did it compare with using paper and pencil for DFDs?
   worse 10% not much different 10% better 80%

This shows that the majority of the students believed that the tool was superior to hand drawn diagrams, although few had found it easy to use.

We suspect that some of the problems with the students learning Software through Pictures were because it was new to the department and problems such as the "unconnected nodes" took longer to solve than they should have done (this was not seen as a problem at all in the later course for staff).

The questionnaire also asked what they particularly liked and disliked about the tool. Almost all students liked the neat pictures from Software through Pictures and gave this answer to the question.

What they disliked varied much more. Most of the problems related to local network problems: e.g. printing, memory usage, delays when the server was busy. Several students mentioned unfriendly error messages.

Finally they were asked what they would like to see changed given a totally free hand. Many of the answers to this question reflected the points in the previous paragraph, e.g. get a bigger disc. One student requested an online manual. Several other students mentioned that the editors needed enhancing, even citing VI as a possibility!

CONTINUED USE OF CASE

The students who learned about CASE tools in their second year were encouraged to use these skills in later courses, which include vision, graphics, advanced systems analysis (with a real project), real-time processing, the design of compilers and parallel programs.

At the time of writing, the first batch of students to be introduced to CASE are beginning their final year projects. They are required to undertake a software engineering approach to their work and will be encouraged to use the facilities of Software through Pictures to capture and document their design processes.

COURSE ENHANCEMENTS

The introduction of Software through Pictures half way through a course running through the two winter terms was not ideal. This year we will introduce the tool along with the concepts thus eliminating the need to draw diagrams by hand. This approach will take the emphasis away from the teaching of Software through Pictures and enable the students to see it as a tool which will make their life easier in the same way as a word processing package makes the production of their reports easier. Our emphasis will remain on structured analysis and design, using CASE tools as an enabling technology.

Beyond that we would wish to move the use of data flow diagrams, data structure charts and module structure charts into a first year course on Program Design, that would form a very sound basis for the teaching of Software Engineering. Within our modular system this course could then be made available to other departments, hopefully facilitating the use of CASE across the University.

EDUCATING THE STAFF

Prior to the delivery of the CASE tool a number of lunch time seminars for staff were organised on structured analysis and design. The objectives of these seminars were to ensure an integrated approach across course modules. These seminars introduced the concepts of data flow diagrams, data structure charts, module structure charts and supporting data dictionaries and documentation.

In addition to the target audience, of staff concerned with teaching and postgraduate students, these seminars attracted a number of staff working on research and development projects who continue to take a keen interest in the use of structured methods and tools.

At the point when Software through Pictures was delivered it was decided it was impractical to organise a course for staff. Hence the course for staff on the CASE tool was scheduled for the Easter vacation (after the students were familiar with it!). The staff course took the

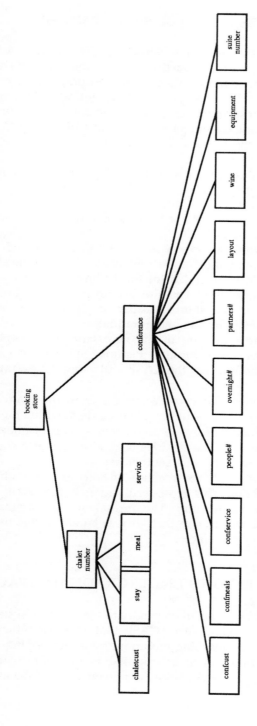

Figure 3 A high-level Jackson data structure. Repetitions and selections are shown on lower level diagrams

form of an intensive two day workshop. The format followed the lines of the undergraduate practicals of starting with DFDs and Data Structure Charts, generating data dictionaries, progressing onto Module Structure Charts, and then additionally generating code templates. The discrepancies in background resulted in different levels of progress. The most advanced members emulating Yourdon's lifts using Control Flow information, while most were happy to produce the simple example from the worksheet.

The staff worksheets were based on the computation of a simple mathematical function:

$$f(x) = 1.2 \ x * x + 2.0 \ x - 10.6$$

where the user would supply a series of values of x and require the display of x, f(x) and the square root of x. The worksheet instructed that a check should be included for f(x) having a negative value before calculating the square root. The aim was to provide an exercise which could be completed in a short timespan, as opposed to the ambitious case study undertaken by the undergraduates.

The first session took care of the necessary housekeeping such as how to get into Software through Pictures. Subsequent sessions gave detailed steps of how to use the CASE tool using the example from the worksheets.

The staff sessions were voted a success from the point of bringing everyone up to date on this subject. Holding them within the department was a problem since there were a constant stream of interruptions for some members of staff. The sessions were also seen as a success from a social point of view, but that's another matter.

Many staff saw a role for the use of Software through Pictures in their course modules. This cross-fertilisation is important in giving a consistent approach to learning. The time taken to ensure that colleagues understood CASE will ensure that what is taught in one module of the course is reinforced elsewhere.

USE OF CASE BEYOND UNDERGRADUATE TEACHING

As well as enhancing the undergraduate teaching of systems analysis and design the introduction of CASE tools has had other impacts in the department. The teaching environment is developing the research activities of the department as opposed to the more usual model of teaching following research! Below are given some of the aspects which have felt the impact of the introduction of Software through Pictures into the department.

- Software through Pictures was used on an internal project for automating the registration of students on different modules within the choices offered by the school.

- A postgraduate project to compile an annotated functional language to run on a parallel computer is described in terms of data flow diagrams produced by the CASE tool.

- A development team associated with the department are considering tendering for a project that will use CASE in the development of a constraint satisfaction problem.

- A research team is developing tools to reverse engineer existing real time programs up into the CASE tool (up to the data flow diagrams).

- The use of CASE is incorporated into methodologies for the design and development of parallel programs.

RECOMMENDATIONS TO OTHERS ABOUT TO INTRODUCE CASE TOOLS INTO UNDERGRADUATE TEACHING

Like us you will want to consider many different tools: price and capability will be important as will be the target machine to run it on. We had a number of evaluation copies which helped us choose. However, short of getting undergraduates to actually use the software, it is sometimes difficult to see things from the novice's perspective, but we do not regret the choice of Software through Pictures. Indeed its open interface has made it very easy to adapt on a research project and we will consider modifications after evaluation of the use of the tool on the next run of the second year module.

There are many CASE tools on the market of varying suitability to a learning environment: some are offered at substantial discounts to higher education via the CHEST scheme. The choice of Unix platforms in higher education limits the choice available. Currently many more CASE tools are available for PCs than for workstations. Although the power of the hardware platform can limit facilities, this does offer a cheap entry point. We are aware of at least one CASE tool that is now on offer, as shareware, to the home computer market (it only draws DFDs). It could be worth considering if budgets were tight. However the full functionality of a true CASE tool, whether upper or lower CASE, is unlikely to be offered by a cheap tool.

We considered many of the tools covering different stages of software development, e.g. formal methods, support tools and code generators. The decision was made to purchase an upper CASE tool to support structured analysis and design based on the wide usage in industry of such tools. This means that our current students are at the forefront of modern software engineering practice. For the future, we are considering CASE tools to support other areas of software development.

We believe that it is preferable to teach the use of any CASE tool in parallel with the concepts that it supports, such as our proposed teaching of the upper CASE tool Software through Pictures in parallel with structured analysis and design techniques. The only time it is acceptable to teach them separately is when the tool is initially unavailable.

It can be very tempting to postpone the introduction of CASE tools into the undergraduate curriculum, since the price of software and the necessary platforms falls year by year and the facilities increase. However the use of CASE tools does make the engineering of software an easier process, freeing the students to concentrate on the principles rather than the tedious production of correct documentation and software.

If you are committed to encouraging good and current practice amongst your students, CASE tools will help you and them. The support of the rest of the department will help to guarantee the successful use of CASE tools throughout a course. So we recommend you gather your arguments and ensure that CASE tools are high on the budget for your department next year, and high on the list of skills required by your colleagues.

5

Real-time CASE Tools: A Review of Current Tools and Future Prospects

David M. Gee, Barry P. Worrall, W. D. Henderson

ABSTRACT

Modern CASE tools should not merely automate existing (manual) methods; they should provide *advances* in method based on their use. We propose that one way of achieving this, as far as real-time systems are concerned, is to use a *repository* as the means of drawing together information derived via different means. A suitable design for such a repository is proposed, based on fundamental components of real-time systems. Suitable components are proposed, and their possible internal representation is discussed. The representation is related to existing development methods; goals for a new development method to meet are proposed, and a possible method outlined.

INTRODUCTION

There has been increasing development of CASE tools over the last several years. However, such tools principally automate *manual* development methods and do not provide advances in methods based on their use, as suggested by Jackson at the 1990 BCS *CASE on Trial* Conference (Jackson, 1990). If we are to use many different descriptive notations, as Jackson suggested, we need to be able to draw together the information provided by each of the different notations.

The vast majority of CASE tools rely on visual notations. These are more readily understood by users than (say) mathematically-based notations such as Z or VDM; they are also familiar to many software engineers.

This paper considers the problems and opportunities of developing a CASE tool which permits the user to employ different visual notations to express the different aspects of real-time systems, and which also permits the generation of executable 3GL code.

Current CASE tools catering for real-time systems suffer insofar as the methods on which they are based are often not defined with sufficient rigour. As rigour is essential if code is to be generated, it comes as no surprise that the number of CASE tools which generate full, executable code is very small. (The vast majority of CASE tools which claim to generate code in fact produce only procedure headers based on structure charts, or—in a different application area—SQL schemas based on entity-relationship diagrams and data-dictionary information.)

Wassermann's concept of a three-layer architecture for CASE tools is now widely accepted (Wassermann, 1988). The bottom layer of this model comprises a repository for design information. The authors believe that if we are to employ many languages in the design of systems, as suggested by Jackson (1990) a repository should be used as the means of bringing the information thus derived together. The design of the repository is the key to the success or otherwise of such a venture. Since there is inevitably overlap between the information provided by different notations, the authors feel that it is necessary to identify a set of fundamental components of real-time systems, around which the design of the repository may be based. The 'languages' or visual notations used may be regarded as projections of the information in the repository—which we regard as the canonical form.

We consider below the overall architecture of the proposed CASE tool. We then look at how the design of such a repository may be derived, and the components on which it should be based. We also consider the relationships between the proposed design and existing development methods and notations, and present an outline of a proposed development method drawing on features of JSD, statecharts and other methods. Finally, we present a summary of work currently being carried out within the Department of Computing at Newcastle Polytechnic aimed at the development of a prototype CASE tool to test the ideas proposed in this paper.

ARCHITECTURE OF PROPOSED CASE TOOL

The authors propose that the architecture should be based on the three-layer model proposed by Wassermann. In particular, the bottom layer should be a *repository* for design-related information.

There are numerous ways in which the repository could be implemented. Hitchcock and Brown have, in a recent paper, considered some of the possible methods (Hitchcock *et al.*, 1990), namely a commercial implementation of SQL, the PCTE Object Management System, and two object-oriented databases (both advanced prototypes). SQL was shown to compare very well with the other alternatives; in particular it was found to offer several advantages over PCTE.

The authors feel that the use of a relational database management system to implement the repository is advantageous, particularly given the availability of a powerful standardised query language in the form of SQL. The version of SQL available to the authors—VAX™/VMS™ SQL—in fact offers a number of facilities over and above the version assessed by Hitchcock and Brown:

- it *is* possible to maintain the uniqueness of keys using, for example, the *primary key* constraint. Combinations of attributes may also be declared as unique (compound keys);

- in addition to the ability to declare attributes as *not null*, it is also possible to associate *default* values with certain attributes.

In addition, VAX/VMS SQL possesses facilities for declaring referential constraints, albeit using a slightly different syntax to the version given in (Hitchcok *et al.*, 1990). Further features include *triggers* which enable actions to be taken when certain events occur. All of these features—together with the generic strengths of relational databases—assist in ensuring the integrity of data. Both embedded SQL and the module language are supported. Accordingly, we have decided to use VAX/VMS SQL to implement the repository.

The top layer of the architecture—which does not form part of the current project—would comprise a human-computer interface through which the tools in the middle layer could be accessed. The following tools could potentially be included in the middle layer:

- graphical editors which provide information to the repository
- verification tools to ensure the accuracy of the contents of the repository
- code generation, animation and interpretation tools
- performance, effort and schedule estimation tools
- deadlock detection tools.

The underlying concept behind the present research is that the information stored in the repository should be regarded as the canonical form of any design; the various diagrams used may be treated as projections of some of the information contained in the repository—in database terminology, they are *views*. These views form, in effect, an additional layer of the repository above the bottom layer, thus yielding a four-layer architecture (see figure 1).

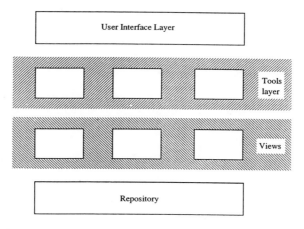

Figure 1   A Four-layer Architecture

EXISTING METHODS

The repository design of existing CASE tools is usually based on the components of the diagrams which form the basis of the supported methods. The diagrams are used to express different aspects (conceptual models) of real-time systems. The most common conceptual models are as follows:

- the *data model* which deals with the stored data within the system, normally in the form of an *entity-relationship diagram*, depicting the relationships of the entities in the system to one another;

- the *behavioural model*, depicting the response of the system to events, as influenced by the passage of time and the history of previous events;

- the *functional model*, showing the relationship between the functions carried out by a system and the stored data.

The functional model is usually depicted by means of a set of data-flow diagrams. State-transition diagrams and their variants, together with Jackson's structure diagrams, have been used to represent the behavioural aspects of systems. However, the authors believe that—in most present methods—the different forms of diagram are not integrated as well as they might be. To investigate this matter further, let us consider some of the current methods used in the specification, design and implementation of real-time systems. We shall consider the following:

- the Ward and Mellor version of structured development for real-time systems (Ward *et al.*, 1986);

- Mascot (RSRE, 1986), a popular method used in the design of real-time systems in the U.K.;

- Jackson System Development (Jackson, 1983), a method which has been used with some success in the real-time area.

We shall also look at David Harel's statechart/activity-chart notations, which, while less familiar than the above methods, offer a number of novel concepts.

Ward and Mellor

The Ward and Mellor method (Ward *et al.*, 1986) is based on the earlier Yourdon/DeMarco standards (DeMarco, 1978), with considerable extensions in order to cater for the additional complexity inherent in real-time systems. Data-flow diagrams, enhanced to show control processes, event flows and event stores, together with both continuous and discrete data flows, form the centrepoint of the method.

Control processes are state-machines, defined by means of state-transition diagrams. They may trigger, enable or disable other (non-control) processes. Entity-relationship diagrams also form part of the method, but they are not clearly linked in any way to the other diagrams—a data store on a DFD need not necessarily represent an entity or relationship on an ERD. In fact, data stores on DFDs may also be used, if required, to represent buffering of data flows.

The Ward and Mellor method is event-based. Development usually commences with identification of the events to which the system must respond, and construction of an *event list* to store this information. The top-level DFD includes one process for each event; this is responsible for providing the appropriate response. These processes may be combined (levelled upwards) or further subdivided (levelled downwards) as necessary.

Some of the DFD constructs used have been found to be imprecise. Consequently, rules have been suggested to restrict the constructs which may be used (Ward, 1986), (Bennett, 1988). These also facilitate symbolic execution of the diagrams.

Any control processes are described by means of state-transition diagrams. The resulting network of processes must then be transformed *manually* into a hierarchical structure chart, although there are a few tools which attempt to assist in this process. With the increasing acceptance and availability of efficient multi-processor systems—such as the INMOS transputer—the authors believe that an "ideal" approach would be to generate code directly from the DFD.

Hatley/Pirbhai

This is basically similar to Ward and Mellor, in that it is derived from the Yourdon approach. However, separate diagrams for control flow and data flow are used; thew treatment of state-machines is also different, since control flows in the Hatley/Pirbhai methodology represent the truth or falsity of a condition rather than a "triggering" signal (Hatley *et al*, 1987).

Both the Ward and Mellor and Hatley/Pirbhai methods have been used to develop large real-time systems; the latter principally on aerospace systems (it was developed in-house at Boeing, Inc.).

Mascot

The Mascot method is intended specifically for the *design* and *implementation* of real-time software. Unlike Ward and Mellor, the method does not attempt to address the specification stage. Only one form of diagram is used: the ACP (Activity, Channel, Pool) diagram. This is similar to the data flow diagrams of Ward and Mellor.

The ACP diagram contains two main forms of component; *activities* (processes), and *intercommunication data areas (IDAs)* (data stores). Activities possess *ports* through which data is communicated; IDAs have *windows* which provide access methods to stored data. *All* communication between activities must be by means of IDAs.

The present version of Mascot is Mascot 3. This, unlike earlier versions (RSRE, 1986) provides, via subsystems, a means of hierarchical decomposition. The general concept of an IDA includes two special cases (which were the *only* forms of IDA allowed in earlier versions:

- the *channel* (buffer), characterised by a destructive read;

- the *pool*, characterised by a destructive write. (This component is equivalent to a collection of variables which may not be deleted but whose values may be changed.)

Synchronisation in Mascot uses the concept of a *control queue*. This is not easy to implement satisfactorily in modern concurrent languages (Jackson, 1986). The majority of Mascot systems employ a specific run-time kernel.

Jackson System Development

This method (Jackson, 1983) places primary importance on the observable events or actions which occur within the environment of a system. These must be identified, and their ordering with respect to the "entities" in the system determined. (An entity, in JSD, is something which responds to events, and which may be uniquely identified.) This ordering is depicted using a tree-like structure diagram called a *process structure diagram* (PSD).

The identified entities in both level-0 (external) and level-1 (internal) form yield the basis of the *system specification diagram* (SSD). The entities (and other processes, which may be added later) communicate using two principal methods:

- data-stream; an infinitely-buffered connection which is written to by one process and read by another;

- state-vector inspection. The *state-vector* of a process is a collection of its local variables, including the *text-pointer* (an indication of the stage reached in its execution). It may be inspected without the knowledge of the "owning" process.

In addition to processes representing entities, additional processes—function processes—may be added if required. Also it may be necessary to create *level-2* processes where the response to an action is not an elementary operation.

One process is assumed to exist for every *instance* of each entity type. Thus, whilst JSD specifications are in principle directly executable, the number of concurrent processes will potentially be very large (and variable). It is therefore frequently necessary to *transform* the specifications for efficient execution. There are a number of methods available, but none that can be automated in all cases. The transformed form is represented by a *system implementation diagram* (SID).

In the latest version of JSD, the concept of *entity roles* has been introduced to deal with potential concurrency within a single entity. Also, the concept of *static entities* (which have a state vector but no PSD) has been introduced. These entities are similar to conventional, "database-type" entities.

Harel's Notations—Statecharts and Activity Charts

Conventional state-transition diagrams possess a number of disadvantages. In particular, they do not readily permit hierarchical decomposition, and, in a complex system, the number of states may be very large. Statecharts (Harel, 1988) overcome many of these problems.

In statecharts, states are allowed to contain other states; the decomposition of a state may be by either AND or OR decomposition. Where two states (say) are grouped together in AND-form, we understand that to be in the enclosing "superstate" is to be in both of the substates simultaneously. The substates are orthogonal to one another. In an OR-decomposition, the states are mutually exclusive, and a transition from the enclosing superstate is equivalent to transitions from *each* of the substates. A transition *to* the enclosing state goes to the *default* substate (there must be one in this case, to avoid ambiguity).

Transitions may be dependent on events, the truth or falsity of a condition, or both. Several orthogonal sections of a statechart may be affected by the same event; also, a transition can generate an event which may cause other transitions to occur—a form of "chain reaction".

Harel has applied similar techniques to data-flow diagrams; the result is "activity charts". The interaction between these diagrams is in a similar manner to Ward and Mellor—there are control processes on the activity chart which are described by means of statecharts.

These diagrams have been incorporated into the tool STATEMATE™ (Harel *et al.*, 1990) which is capable of generating the controlling code for the statecharts (in Ada) but not procedural code—which must be written in the normal way.

Conclusions

The authors believe that, in order to obtain a full picture of a real-time system, several different descriptive notations are required. The methods surveyed—with the exception of Mascot—do provide more than one notation, but these are not closely integrated. None of the methods, for example, provides an *overall* behavioural view of systems; the integration between the behavioural and functional models is by means of control processes. The methods do not, in general, address the relationship between data stores and ERD entities adequately.

JSD stands out from the other methods to an extent. It *does* provide a means of clearly relating the behavioural model to the functional (although the data model is implicit). On the other hand, the need for complex manual transformations is a disadvantage. There is also no *overall* behavioural model. The *framework* of JSD, on the other hand, is adequate for real-time system development, and provides clear guidelines as to how that development should be carried out.

THE DESIGN OF THE REPOSITORY

In existing CASE tools, the repository design is based upon the diagram components. This makes it very difficult to relate the different conceptual models. Consequently, the authors believe that it is essential to identify the *fundamental components* of real-time systems, and to use these as the basis for the repository design.

If fundamental components are to be derived, this can only be by considering the components of *existing* notations. By following a process of generalisation, we ought to be able to derive more fundamental components.

Some of the concepts of existing notations are:

- processes and activities
- states
- transitions
- entities and relationships
- data stores, channels, pools and IDAs
- data flows, event flows, data streams, events and actions.

The concept of a process is one of the most important in real-time and concurrent systems. It is to be found in all of the notations discussed. We can class activities and transforms as processes.

Hoare has defined a process as something which "responds to events". Data stores may be regarded as equivalent to Mascot IDAs. These may be handled as a set of data attributes together with defined access methods. Using Hoare's definition, IDAs may be regarded as a form of process, since they respond to "get" and "put" events.

Let us now consider the question of entities and relationships. We may deal with the latter by insisting that all relationships on ERDs are one:many. These relationships are, therefore, only of use in determining the presence or absence of foreign keys. Entities themselves may be treated as in JSD (i.e. be regarded as processes, with state-vectors and zero, one or more roles); those with no state-changes (and therefore no roles) may be regarded as static entities (Cameron, 1988).

There have been many different definitions of states; however, we regard these in a similar light to CCS (Milner, 1989)—that is, as processes (in effect, sub-processes of state-machines). Transitions may be regarded as processes which encapsulate the response to an event under certain conditions.

We turn now to the treatment of events. If a process responds to events, then it would seem that events must be distinct from processes, and are therefore fundamental. Data-flows are regarded as either representing interactions between processes and events, in which the process acts as transmitter or receiver, or as interactions between a processes, one of which acts as a data store. The two cases are equivalent to datastreams and state-vector inspections in JSD.

Data is itself clearly important, and appears in a system design as attributes of processes or events. We conclude therefore that the fundamental components of real-time systems are *processes, events* and *data*. Other components may be seen as interactions between processes or as groups of either processes or data.

INTERNAL REPRESENTATION OF FUNDAMENTAL COMPONENTS

Since we are dealing with components which we have generalised to be either processes, events or data, or groups of processes and/or data, we see that there is an hierarchical structure inherent in some of the components being stored.

We regard the system itself as a process; it is the ancestor of all other components. As its children we have entities and other processes. Entities themselves are the parents of zero, one or more entity-role processes and up to one state-vector process. These processes themselves have children.

All processes—other than the system itself—may possess data attributes, i.e. be linked to components which are either variables or groups of variables. As far as interactions between processes are concerned, these are addressed by events or by process interaction. Events may also have associated data attributes. States are also regarded as processes, and can if desired be related to sub-states in the same manner as statecharts.

The database tables to store this information have been based around the ideas already outlined. There are three "base" tables to handle processes, events and data respectively. Additionally, several further tables are required to deal with the relationships involved— specifically, the ownership of data, transitions, datastreams and state-vector inspections. The entity-relationship diagram for the system (see figure 2) depicts these relationships.

RELATIONSHIP OF PROPOSED REPRESENTATION TO OTHER DEVELOPMENT METHODS

One of the advantages of the proposed repository design is that it may be related to a number of development methods. Let us consider those methods which we have referred to above.

Ward and Mellor

This may be regarded as a system wherein all the entities are static (and are thus represented by data stores on the DFDs) and where there are both control and ordinary processes as children of the system. Data and event flows are represented by events; the latter have no

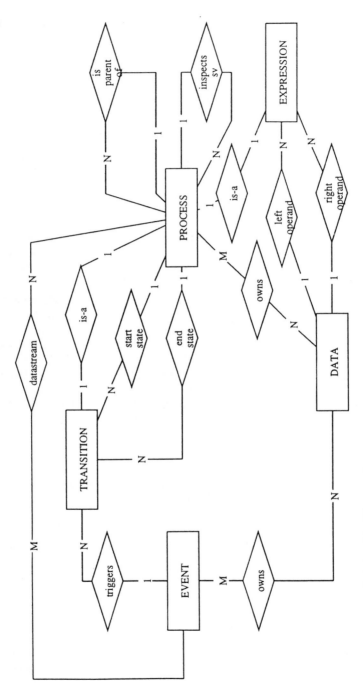

Figure 2 Entity-Relationship Diagram for system

attributes. Continuous flows may be dealt with—if restricted, as we propose, to interaction with the outside world—as interaction with an external process.

Mascot

The representation of Mascot designs would be in a similar manner to that in the previous section; subsystems could be children of the system itself and could have both IDAs and activities—or other subsystems—as their children. Here we have a situation where interactions are restricted in that one of the partners must be an IDA and the other an activity. Ports and windows could be treated as children of the activities and IDAs respectively.

JSD

Here, the "entities" and other processes would be children of the system node, and their interactions would be by means of data streams or by state-vector inspection. (As with other forms of data flows, the directionality values can be used to show which process is the source, and which the destination.) The descendants of the processes would indicate their structure. Note that processes may be "constructors" if required (e.g. for WHILE statements) and that individual statements and conditions can be described in terms of their parent, operands and operator.

Harel's Notations

These are essentially hierarchical in nature, so are ideally suited for storage in the repository. The representation would be broadly similar to those above, with the addition of hierarchical arrangements of states, and a more complex treatment of transitions.

A PROPOSED DEVELOPMENT METHOD

Whilst we believe that the proposed representation may be related to existing development methods, we nevertheless feel that it is possible to devise a new method, consistent with the proposed representation, which offers advantages over existing methods. The proposed method is based on concepts derived from JSD (Jackson, 1983), CSP (Hoare, 1985) statecharts (Harel, 1988) and Mascot.

The method has been derived with the following goals in mind:

- to provide *overall* behavioural, data and functional models
- to integrate the different conceptual models
- to provide a framework for real-time system development
- to permit (and encourage) hierarchical decomposition and a structured approach to development
- to permit a designer to approach his task starting with any one of the conceptual models
- to support code generation without requiring manual transformation of systems.

In order that the data model should be integrated into the whole, we begin from a similar standpoint to Jackson, holding that systems comprise entities which respond to events. The *behaviour* of these entities over time is described using statecharts. The statechart for each entity may contain AND-decomposition at the top level only (this indicates the existence of entity roles) but may contain OR-decomposition at any level.

The concept of events is treated in two ways: firstly, by associating a number of data-flows with each event, and secondly by associating with each event a process which is responsible for recognising it and distributing it to those entities (or entity roles) which can respond to it. Such a process would:

- wait for an occurrence of the event from *any* possible source;
- once the event has occurred, communicate knowledge of that event as appropriate.

This allows events to be explicitly represented on DFDs, as the proposed notation shows (see figure 3).

Entities exist concurrently with one another, and possess zero, one or more roles. Their state-vectors are regarded (along with the roles) as sub-processes. The state-vectors may be used in the same manner as Mascot pools (by creating a static entity if need be) whilst the event recognition processes can buffer input and serve the function of Mascot channels. Note that *all* communication between processes is by means of events.

The response to an individual event, when the entity or role is in a given state, would need to be defined by some form of procedural logic diagram, such as Jackson diagrams, or perhaps using an extended state-transition notation such as SDL (Davis, 1988).

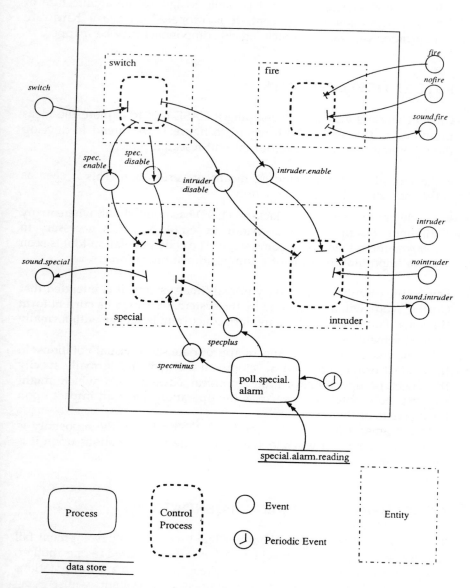

Figure 3 A Proposed Notation for DFDs

In real-time systems, it is not possible to ignore the architecture of the implementation environment. It is proposed to use a hardware configuration diagram to which logical components may be mapped.

FUTURE DEVELOPMENTS

Current work is aimed at developing a CASE tool to explore the ideas presented in this paper. With regard to figure 1, we intend to develop the following tools as part of our current research project:

- the repository itself, including means of verification. This is seen as the most crucial part of the work;

- a code-generation tool. As Jackson (1990) has pointed out, where many different descriptions of a system are employed, it is necessary to *compose* these together at some stage. The code-generation tool is seen as an important example of a compositional operation.

Due to the essential concurrency of real-time systems, it is intended that *Occam*™ code will be generated by the system. Occam in its current form (May and Pountain, 1990) is a modern concurrent language with formally defined semantics.

Furthermore, we shall define an appropriate set of visual notations, in the context of the proposed development method, and formally specify the effect of operations within graphical editing tools which might support these notations insofar as the operations have an impact upon the contents of the repository.

At the present time (September 1991), the design of the repository is largely complete and work to specify the effect of operations upon it is progressing.

CONCLUSIONS AND RECOMMENDATIONS

The majority of existing methods for real-time system development fail to provide a set of notations which may clearly be related to one another. This paper has shown that it is practicable to develop a set of notations which provide distinct conceptual models of a system, whilst being closely related. Using the ideas of higraphs—a generalisation of statechart concepts—permits the notations to have a similar means of supporting hierarchical decomposition.

Overall, the authors feel that by proceeding along the lines given, we will be able to meet the stated goals. The most closely related current work is:

- Harel's work on statecharts and related notations, and the tool STATEMATE
- certain modern CASE tools, such as 'Software through Pictures'.

As far as the latter area is concerned, our work differs in a number of important respects:

- rather than using existing (and often imprecise) notations unchanged, we are devising more precise visual forms which may be clearly related both to one another and to the contents of the repository
- the link between the different representations of fundamental components does not rely on added annotations, but is inherent in the design.

Statecharts and activity charts (DFDs) in Harel's notations are not related other than through control processes. One result of this is that it is not easy to see the sources and possible destinations of events; to do so requires one to resolve an arbitrary number of text-based references (Ward, 1990). This does not make the best possible use of visual forms, and we consider that our proposals overcome this problem. Furthermore, by allowing the use of global variables, statecharts are geared more towards shared-memory systems. We anticipate that falling costs in the future will generate increased use of distributed systems, exemplified by the INMOS transputer.

REFERENCES

Bennett, Stuart. *Real-Time Computer Control - An Introduction*. Prentice-Hall: 1988
Cameron, J.R. The Modelling Phase of J.S.D. *Information and Software Technology*, pp.373-383, July/Aug.: 1988
Davis, A. M. A comparison of techniques for the specification of external system behaviour. *Communications ACM*, 31 (9) 1988.
Harel, David. On visual formalisms. *Communications ACM*, 31 (5), 1988.
Harel, D., H Lachover, A Namaad, A Pneuli, M Politi. *STATEMATE: A Working Environment for the Development of Complex Reactive Systems* In Proc. 10th Int Conf Soft Eng, IEEE, April: 1988.
Hatley, D.J. and I.A. Pirbhai. *Strategies for Real-Time System Specification*. New York: Dorset House, 1987.

Hitchcock, P. and A. W. Brown. A Comparison of Databases for Software Engineering. *Proceedings Software Engineering 90*, Cambridge University Press, pp. 27–64, 1990.
Hoare, C.A.R. *Communicating Sequential Processes*. Prentice-Hall, 1985.
Jackson, K. Using Mascot with Ada. *Software Engineering Journal*, Special Issue on MASCOT, May 1986, pp. 121–135.
Jackson, M.A. Case tools and development methods. In *Proceedings BCS CASE On Trial*, 1990.
Jackson, M.A. *System Development*. Prentice-Hall, 1983.
RSRE. *The Official Handbook of MASCOT*. RSRE, 1986.
Ward, Paul T. The Transformation Schema: An extension of the DFD to represent control and timing. *IEEE Trans Software Engineering*, SE-12 (2) February: 1986.
Ward, P.T. and S. J. Mellor. *Structured Development for Real-Time Systems*. Yourdon Press, 1986.
Wassermann, A. The Architecture of CASE tools. Internal Paper, IDE Ltd.

ACKNOWLEDGEMENTS

The use of the following trademarks is acknowledged:
Occam is a registered trademark of INMOS Ltd., Bristol.
STATEMATE is a registered trademark of i-Logix, Inc., Burlington, Mass., USA.
VAX and VMS are trademarks of Digital Equipment Co., Inc.

6

The Business v. IS: A Case Of Breach Of Promise

William Reynolds, Catherine Kalra

ABSTRACT

Despite great technological progress, the benefits of IT (Information Technology) have often been disappointing. Many enterprises have built an increasingly complex and unmanageable portfolio of stand-alone "applications" which are often overlapping, mutually inconsistent, unable to respond to inevitable business changes and, in extreme cases, major inhibitors to business plans. These failings are normally traceable to aspects of system development that seem to be largely ignored. Until these basic problems are faced and our focus shifts from doing things fast to doing the right thing, the promised benefits of CASE technology seem bound to remain a seductive dream.

Against this background, the paper describes a framework for managing business systems in an integrated manner. Within that framework it outlines an approach to business systems which starts by creating a stable "core model" of the essential, permanent aspects of the business. This then serves as a basis for expressing and prioritising real business needs, for deciding the boundaries and contents of future

CASE: Current Practice, Future Prospects. Edited by Kathy Spurr and Paul Layzell
© 1992 John Wiley & Sons Ltd

system components, and for controlling migration to a stable and unified business system. Both business people and IS staff seem able to accept this approach, which has been successfully used in a number of enterprises. The paper then draws some conclusions on what it is realistic to expect from CASE technology—and what not.

INTRODUCTION

Over the past 35 years the emphasis of commercial computing has shifted from the automation of specific clerical tasks to the provision of pervasive information support for entire business functions. Many enterprises have become totally reliant on their information systems and some areas of ordinary life have been revolutionised as a result.

In the same period there have been spectacular technological innovations and major improvements in price-performance. Despite this, it is not uncommon for senior management to express concern that IT keeps falling short of its promise. The problem is often perceived as one of maintenance and application backlog.

IS (Information Systems) departments have normally responded to this criticism by seeking to improve productivity. Vendors have in turn responded by developing new products: initially assemblers, control systems, high-level languages, documentation aids, project control tools, dictionaries, screen-painters—and so on. Each of these advances in computer assistance to developers made it possible to produce systems faster—but with inadequate attention to producing the *right* thing this often meant that businesses simply moved faster to a point where the web of wrong, overlapping and inconsistent components became virtually unmanageable.

Enterprises are now being invited to deal with the backlog problem by investing heavily in CASE—Computer Assisted Software (or Systems) Engineering—supported by some kind of "repository" or "encyclopedia".

We believe that without some fundamental re-thinking, this will only exacerbate the situation. Rapid development is only of value if the things that are developed are valid in their own right, avoid conflict and unnecessary overlap with each other, and are able to meet changing needs.

We argue that this calls for reducing the number and complexity of overlapping information systems (not adding more) and that this can be done only by adopting a common framework of understanding. We shall describe initial work on such a framework.

THE PRODUCTIVITY PARADOX

It is arguable that eliminating misconceived or wasteful effort is the single most useful thing an IS department can do. One IS department, for example, built eleven different versions, giving different answers, of the enterprise's primary measure of sales performance. The building of each ranked as productive work! Another decided "something must be done" when it found it was using 28 different coding structures for its products; ten years later it had 42. A survey of applications in yet another revealed an *average* duplication factor of over 5 systems per business function (e.g. there were five order processing systems).

The industry seems to be so numbed by examples of "computers getting it wrong" that people are no longer outraged by the damage and waste that result. In a 1954 "Goon Show" the ineffable Eccles was acting as lookout and shouted that there was a mine ahead—adding, after a moment: "There's no need to worry: it's one of ours".[1] The audience accepted that this was too absurd to be anything but invention; yet 30 years later major loss was suffered because an onboard computer in a British ship followed exactly this absurd logic in treating an incoming missile as friendly; it had been made in France, was emitting a "friendly" signal, and was therefore "one of ours".

Examples abound of the damage done by similar misconceptions in commercial computer systems. One enterprise discovered it had spent £12M on developing systems that no one had ever used. The finance director in another was told it would take IS staff six months to answer the simple question: "how much money is tied up in stocks?"—and the answer would then be six months out of date.

The above examples are chosen because they were incontrovertibly wasteful—but some of them only came to light because of a specific disaster or investigation. Legions of lesser errors are quietly accepted, covered up, or never detected at all.

Most such errors can be traced to aspects of system development that seem to be largely ignored: unawareness of the intrinsic difficulties exposed by Kent[2], basic misunderstanding of the enterprise itself, unwitting adoption of inconsistent definitions, wrong business assumptions, and a tradition of defining pieces of the business system without due consideration of the whole.

The cost of tearing down and rebuilding systems which are defective is often very heavy—typically far heavier than that of incorporating the necessary accuracy and flexibility in the first place. Ironically, the pressure to rebuild quickly when a system is found to be inadequate makes it only too likely that similar problems will recur.

CASE EXPECTATIONS

There is a lack of clarity as to the proper purpose, scope and structure of "CASE". To understand what people might expect of CASE it is instructive to examine the abbreviation, which is variously expanded to "Computer Assisted Systems/Software Engineering".

Engineering?

The word suggests precision, sound practice, and processes that can be automated. We would also argue that the first requirement of engineers is to build things that do their job properly, stand up under pressure, and do not need constant repair or replacement. Given that the IT industry has yet to demonstrate that it has mastered the trick of specifying what is required, let alone that of hand-crafting a design. it could be argued that the term is an aspiration rather than a reality and that it would be premature to rush into large-scale automation using CASE.

By comparison with many branches of engineering, information systems engineering is relatively young and has had little time to establish high professional standards, with proper certification of those who achieve competence. The understanding of available materials that characterises most engineering disciplines is missing and there are few experts, and even fewer masters, to guide beginners.

Systems or Software?

If engineering systems, then which and how many? We would argue that any single organism such as an enterprise has one and only one system, no matter how informal and ill-fitting the mechanisms for combining its components. We would further argue that until the CASE community accepts the need to build single integrated systems, conflict, overlap and waste will be inherent.

If software, then purpose, scope, content and interfaces must be defined particularly rigorously and clearly as the informal mechanisms available in business systems are excluded.

Computer Assisted?

Computer assistance can reasonably be expected to include:

- Automating transformations (e.g. generators)
- Guiding the user through standards and procedures

- Recording and retrieving results
- Reporting on tasks and products
- Predicting the effects of change
- Making necessary inputs available at the right time
- Extending human skills (e.g. diagramming aids)

The more one tries to replace rather than support human endeavour, and then to share and combine the results of that endeavour, the greater the need for clear definition and agreement on constructs, transformation rules, and areas of judgment such as in the well-known and varied problems of generalisation.

Any assumptions made will have formal consequences for subsequent decisions and these must be explicit, sound and mutually consistent if CASE tools and repositories are to work together. Disparate tools can hardly share a repository if they do not correctly understand each other's constructs, definitions and assumptions.

Domain?

In terms of activities, there seems general agreement that the engineering of systems (or software) legitimately covers all phases of the development of systems. Some, however, seek to extend it to the areas of planning and strategy-setting for the IS department—and even for the business itself. Clearly these lie outside "Engineering" as generally understood. Unless boundaries are properly drawn, the systems/software engineer risks inventing specialised approaches, the output of which may not be usable by others working in related areas.

When it comes to mechanisms, everyone would include *tools*; nowadays most would include *repositories*; the last few years have seen a major shift in understanding the importance of including *methods* (or "methodologies" as they are sometimes, regrettably, called); a similar shift is beginning towards the importance of *models*.

Disciplines?

Some effort has been made to introduce disciplines to CASE, but this has been hampered by the fact that there is no agreed body of principles, rules and guidelines such as one would expect from engineers. Growing from notations and techniques, methods are widely accepted as necessary in order for CASE to be effective. However, yet again, confusion exists as to what is the proper scope of method and many existing methods, while seen as in competition, are actually quite different in what they are addressing. Within the context of automated CASE we would distinguish four different types of method (workstyles and facilities methods are external to this context):

- *"Product method"*—a set of rules which take account of the properties of components and the effect on the developer, the user, the business sponsor and those impacted by the final business system.

- *"Process management method"*—a set of standard procedures used in development.

- *"Resource management method"*—the rules for obtaining and using shared resources e.g. repository data.

- *"Project management method"*—a set of controls for applying the right resources and processes to a specific project.

Each of these types of methods is separate and discrete. The implications of one should not dictate the structure of any other. Much pain is caused by trying to mix and match methods and their supporting CASE tools because these boundaries are not observed.

By analogy consider the different types of rules that apply to cooking food, running a kitchen, managing kitchen resources, and putting on a banquet.

To date, structured development methods have focussed heavily on process and/or project, and relatively little on product, though the move towards "model-driven development" is redressing this balance.

AN EXAMPLE

We now take an example from high-street banking—to which most people can easily relate—in order to indicate the types of problem that need to be addressed if businesses are to derive value from CASE technology.

Two hundred years ago, customers' bank accounts were maintained in branch ledgers, the structure of which is illustrated in Figure 1, left. The diagram should be read as making the following statements: (1) each branch may have any number of customers, (2) each customer has a unique account number and (3) each customer account belongs to one and only one branch.

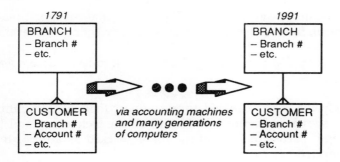

Figure 1   Bank Account Model

At the right is shown the basic structure for 1991's computer files in (so far as we can discover) all long-established UK banks. Such diagrams can be found in many publications on system design, data design, and CASE products, and satisfy the formal requirements of normalisation. Readers may may like to pause at this point and consider their own reactions to this structure.

Now consider some actual examples of problems caused by this structure:

- A customer of 40 years' standing with the same branch of Bank A and with a very healthy balance, wanted to open a second account; he was vetted as if he was a complete stranger. Why? "The computer doesn't let us check for you by name, only by account number."

- The same bank refused to transfer funds because only the payee's name and branch (one of theirs) were known, not the account number. Why? "The computer deals only with account numbers, not people".

- A customer with multiple accounts was irritated by receiving multiple copies of "junk mail". Why? The same reason.

- Bank B told a customer they wanted to give him a new account and account number. Why? "We are closing the branch." So? "The computer allocates account numbers by branch; no one can alter them". In another, similar, case the bank failed to transfer the funds, so that the new account was almost immediately overdrawn!

The diagram indicates that two fundamentally wrong assumptions were made about the business: account is tightly coupled with branch (which is not necessary for the account's existence) instead of account holder (which is). The damage is not, however, limited to customer dissatisfaction. The absence of a total view of the customer undermines debt control, fraud detection, and effective marketing—for example:

- A bank lent £3M to a business that it ought to have known was going bankrupt.

Eventually the banks decided to re-engineer their file structures along the lines shown in Figure 2 and, with all the technology and business modelling expertise they could muster, embarked on a major rework of all the affected systems.

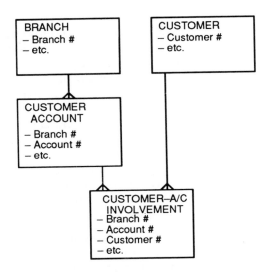

Figure 2   Revised Bank Account Model

Part way through they realised that while their new design would fix the false assumption that customers are accounts, it still left the following problems:

- An account must be connected to a branch and only a branch
- It cannot be moved, nor managed by more than one branch at a time

So the banks re-engineered their re-engineering, threw away some of what they had already done and embarked on a second re-work. *Yet all of the problems identified above were known to be problems long before computers were even considered.* With quills and ledgers as the only tools, these problems were difficult to avoid—and, in the days of stable communities and slow communications, not too damaging.

RMF: A UNIFYING FRAMEWORK

How do we set about dealing with these problems? In order to remove superficial and transient considerations, we have tried to go right back to basics. This has led to the creation of RMF (Reality Modelling Framework) which we have found helpful for seeing both the root of the problems identified in the preceding section and a reasonable approach to dealing with them. RMF itself is completely generic, with multiple levels and dimensions and this allows it to be applied to many disparate domains. In this paper we use a much simplified version.

The influence of RMF in its earlier forms is to be found in Business System Development Method, which was created by the writers of this paper and others.[3] [4] Though the work on the method was done by people who all worked in IBM's marketing function, it was adopted first by IBM UK for internal development, then by IBM Europe, and then became part of an IBM Corporate standard. The framework is also reflected in a number of software products and the structure of IBM UK's "Business System Development" professional services. More recently the authors were instrumental in its adoption by the IBM Corporation for its insurance application architecture (IAA).

Map-Need-Shape-Run

In its simplified version one dimension of RMF contains four elements, normally shown horizontally (Figure 3).

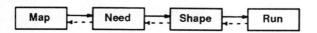

Figure 3 Map–Need–Shape–Run Dimension

- *Map* focuses on understanding those aspects of the field of interest which are universal and stable: its geology. So a manufacturer, for example, ought to have a "map" of the objects, processes, and structural relationships between objects and processes, that are of the very essence of manufacturing—independent of any specific manufacturer, product, place or time. This underpins all work on the other, more changeable elements.

- *Need* focuses on specific behaviour, aspects, and perspectives of the world. These views are often in conflict and many problems in IS result from trying to manage them in isolation. In RMF, these are all reconcilable with the single, shared, Map.

- *Shape* focuses on identifying, defining and building components which can be used ("run") in order to respond to one or more defined views. For IS development, this covers the activities of designing, building and testing new system components—and of making changes to existing ones. It would also cover the specification and manufacture of physical tools, for example, or the formulation and documentation of policies or procedures.

- *Run* focuses on the use or exploitation of what someone has, somehow or other, shaped. In IS, this element applies largely to the area of operations.

The names in both this and the next dimension are all monosyllables, deliberately chosen to minimise clashes with existing terms which mean different things to different people. All can be read as either verbs or nouns, since each element has an intrinsic duality: sometimes there is a need to focus on the activity (e.g. mapping), sometimes on the thing (the map).

Relative Return on Investment

It is only natural that the return on investment from good or bad work in one of the earlier elements will be progressively magnified in the later ones. Figure 4 indicates the relative impact and cost of correctness: the cost of achieving correctness in the Map element is relatively low, but the cost of failing to do so may well be extremely high.

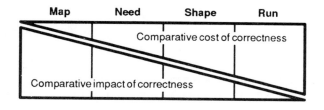

Figure 4   Comparative Cost and Impact of Correctness

Even a day spent in Shape on, say, designing a screen may be grudged, but a far larger consequential loss to the business overlooked; solid work in Need is rare ("come and tell us what you want" seems to be the most that IS asks of the business—and is often more than the business is willing to give); and work in Map is done even less. This pattern will no doubt remain as long as cost of development is measured rather than total business cost.

IS Development and the Elements

The elements should not be confused with phases of a development project, nor with stages in the life of a system component. The relationship between elements is mainly logical, whereas both the latter have a clear time-flow.

Figure 5 relates the elements to a typical development cycle and illustrates the following points:

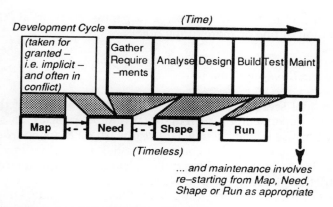

Figure 5 A Common Development Cycle and RMF

- Almost all development cycles that are advocated seem to start from an existing solution (i.e. in Shape), a few from needs (i.e. in Need) and—increasingly popular—a few from current strategies or plans.

- Building a sound map of the business (independent of any particular perspective, strategies, plans, or organization) is, we believe, vital to building simpler, more stable, and yet more flexible business systems in the future.

- At first sight Need might seem to correspond with the "requirements phase" in many approaches. Despite their wording, the statements "I want a house built" or "I need a sales ledger package" are actually statements of solution, for which the real need may or may not have been defined; the mere fact that one particular solution has been expressed as a need may inhibit proper exploration of alternative solutions. In RMF this type of early solution-setting is not treated as part of Need, but of Shape.

Business modelling is sometimes seen as part of Requirements Definition. However, many different kinds of business model are produced. In RMF terms, "as-is" and "to-be" models are variants of Shape models; entity-relationship models, such as the one provided by IBM for its respoistory, are statements of Need; as far as we know, only BSDM and its derivatives contain produce maps. Increasingly we observe that business models contain hybrids between the elements (for example, PERSON from Map, CUSTOMER from Need, and ORDER-LINE from Shape), but without distinguishing them with different constructs.

- Maintenance is not, of course, a separate element at all, but a revisitation of one or more of the others.

Mapping the Banking Example

A Map model seeks to capture only the *essential* aspects of the bank's business, independent of current organization, policies or strategies. Precisely because it focuses on what *must* be true, a Map model opens the way to all the flexibility that could be wanted. It should allow anything which the laws of nature and logic allow, leaving multiple interpretations and restrictions to be applied in Need and Shape.

Figure 6 shows an extract from a (simplified) Map model which avoids the problems identified in section 4 (the diagrams in that section were Need and Shape models). In this model:

- Accounts are between two parties (hence two lines): the account holder and the bank.

- A party can operate singly or as a group (a partnership of three solicitors involves four parties, connected by three party-party relationships).

- Accounts can move branch and can even be managed by more than one branch at a time ...

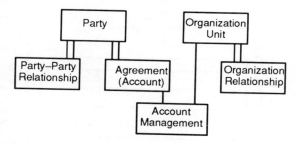

Figure 6 Bank Account Map Model (Reasonable)

- ... and not only by a branch; the unit could be a special account team or head office.

- Customers can be charged and monitored on their *total* position with the bank—and marketing effort can be economical yet relevant.

Entities such as "Customer", "Supplier" and "Employee" do not reflect realities that exist—i.e. people and businesses—but the roles played. To leave it at that is like insisting that J. R. Ewing exists and Larry Hagman does not. In RMF terms they belong in Need and/or Shape.

Complete enterprise modelling actually involves work in all four elements; both constructs and content must, however, reflect this properly.

Aim-Drive-Work-Fuel

Another dimension of RMF contains four elements, normally shown vertically (Figure 7). Solid arrows indicate sequence *only* in the sense of influence. Broken arrows indicate feedback; lack of resources, for example, might cause adjustments to Drive—and even, if appropriate, to Aim.

- *Aim* is concerned with deciding what needs to be achieved and checking whether it has been; it is recursive in the sense that it covers the establishment not only of mission, but of goals in support of the mission, objectives in support of goals—and so on.

- *Drive* is the active component of the management system that institutes and controls Work in support of Aim. It covers the establishment of such mechanisms as policies, strategies, priorities, plans, tasks, and checkpoints and also the verification of conformity with all these.

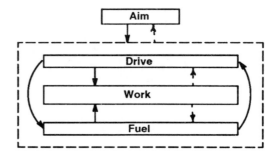

Figure 7   Aim-Drive-Work-Fuel Dimension

- *Work* is concerned with making and managing changes to support Aim, under control of Drive and with resources from Fuel.
- *Fuel* is the supportive component of the management system. It covers the acquisition and maintenance of resources (people, premises, equipment etc.) and their deployment across the work to be done.

The Elements in Combination

Figure 5 shows both RMF dimensions together. The shaded areas indicate interfaces between elements—needed because the elements are quite different in nature. These areas represent definition of one element in terms of another. No element is transformable into another, though transformations are possible *within* the same element, as in the popular "waterfall" analogy, e.g. from pseudo-code to COBOL procedure—all in Shape. No doubt there will be further growth in the industry's ability to automate transformations of this second type.

Constructs and rules are definable for the intersection of each row and column. For example a definition in Map would have clearly defined population subsetting rules in Need, Shape and Run; its status in the business would be reflected in Aim, Drive, Work and Fuel. Observing vertical segregation (of A-D-W-F rows) and horizontal segregation (of M-N-S-R columns) leads to cleaner architectures.

POSITIONING AGAINST RMF

Business System Issues

We can now use the framework to position the issues exemplified in the first section (Figure 8).

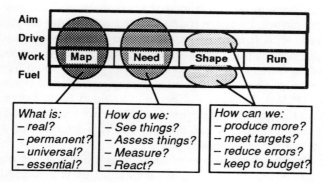

Figure 8 Business System Issues

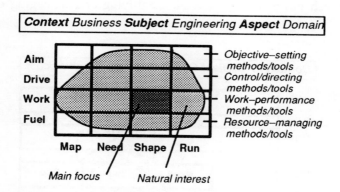

Figure 9 Natural Domain of Engineering

CASE Domain

Similarly we can plot the natural domain of engineering, as shown in Figure 9.

CASE Methods

The first three types of method mentioned earlier (product, process management and resource management) correspond with Work, Drive and Fuel in RMF; project management involves harnessing all three.

Of those development methods that cover more than just notations and/or techniques, most are today focused principally on procedures to be followed, with lists of deliverables and notations to match—that is they are strongly biassed towards Drive, with little guidance on how to do the work. Others combine Drive advice with limited Work advice. In our earlier work on BSDM and our current work on Business Object Modelling (BOM), we have deliberately avoided tying Drive and Work together, on the grounds that, provided there are well-defined constructs and rules, more flexibility can be allowed. This seems to be a feature of other object-oriented approaches.

Figure 10 shows the scope of three major families of method: one strongly procedure-driven (broken rectangle) of which SSADM seems a good example, the second starting from high-level strategic planning (shaded areas), of which members of the IE family seem good examples, and the third based strongly on object oriented approaches (broken oval), which has a strong focus on identifying and managing common objects.

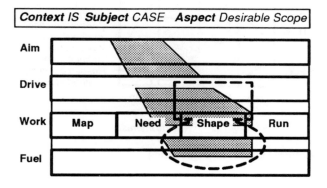

Figure 10   Three Families of Development Method

Desirable Scope of CASE Tools

To the business as a whole, IS plays a supporting role and therefore, in RMF terms, provides part of the Fuel of the business. To IS, CASE should be chiefly concerned with Shape/Work, with appropriate interfaces "vertically" to Aim, Drive and Fuel, and "horizontally" to Map and Need (for input and understanding) and to Run (for prototyping and testing)—Figure 11.

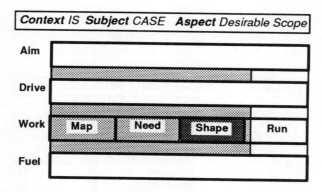

Figure 11   Desirable Scope of a CASE Tool-set

Upper and Lower CASE

A distinction is sometimes drawn between upper and lower CASE (Figure 12). The latter, which covers construction and testing, embraces tools such as assemblers, compilers, and code generators which have been available for many years and is today quite rich. The former, which is generally considered to cover enterprise modelling and, increasingly, business system planning, is less well populated—and much of the support for enterprise and data modelling is for Shape modelling.

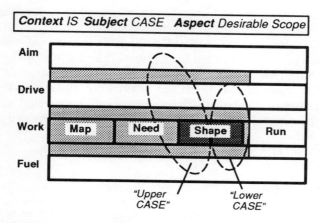

Figure 12   Scopes of Current Upper and Lower CASE

Component and Integrated CASE

A distinction is sometimes drawn between "Component CASE" (C-CASE) and "Integrated CASE" (I-CASE); see Figure 13.

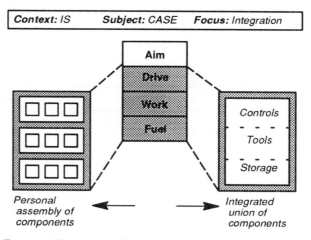

Figure 13   Range of Possible CASE Integration

C-CASE is a vendor marketing strategy which encourages IS staff to choose the components they personally like and create their own mix. The amount of method engineering which this actually requires is often underestimated. In general, the dangers inherent in mixing a new "shade" of method are not appreciated. We are in danger of establishing a plethora of inconsistent and unstable development meta-models to match our inconsistent and unstable business systems.

In contrast, Integrated-CASE (I-CASE) tools rely on pre-selecting the combination of tools permitted for a given job and situation. In principle, I-CASE should ensure that within the set of tools and materials available, decisions on how to use them are reasonably clear cut. To be truly effective, however, this approach requires a well-architected method; the less well the components fit properly together, the closer the result will be to C-CASE.

Once in use, all CASE implementations are I-CASE.

Open and Shut CASE

As with any software, CASE tools should, ideally, be able to both operate on multiple hardware platforms and also from a single specification, be able to produce systems that will operate on multiple hardware environments.

This openness is provided by such tools as TI's IEF, Systematica's Virtual Software Factory (VSF) and Oracle CASE.

In addition, open environments which can support multiple production methods is also a facet of open CASE. While this is the intention of IBM's AD/Cycle and Repository Manager/MVS, care should be taken, as earlier indicated, in mixing and matching within such an environment. Suppose, for example, that a modelling tool produces Map entities separately from Need entities (i.e. it distinguishes the *reality* of "person" from the various *roles* of customer and supplier). A screen design tool which could not discriminate between these types of entity might require users to work with a totally unnatural language, while an undiscriminating data base tool might well produce undesirable designs.

Maintaining layer integrity and separation is essential to the success of such an environment.

In Open CASE, in order to achieve integration for any of these layers, a separate model is necessary. In IBM's AD/Cycle strategy, the information model is intended to integrate Fuel, ADPS has a model to integrate Drive and any production method would require its own model to ensure consistency of the work-in-progress and the finished products. For these reasons we would warn against mixing production methods in any single implementation of a repository manager. If, say, one application system is being developed using SSADM, and another is using BSDM, they would be ill advised to share objects in a common repository.

CONCLUSIONS

We believe it is salutary to dwell on the question: why do UK clearing banks act so cavalierly towards their customers and then fall back on saying: "it's the computer"—as if the machine had ceased to be under human control? Would the bankers of the past have excused their unhelpfulness by pleading "our new quills ran away with us"?

Clearly the computer is not the *cause* of the banks' problems. On the contrary, it offered the first real opportunity to cure them.

The banks pride themselves on their use of advanced IT; an informed estimate suggests an IT budget for UK clearing banks of well over £1,000,000,000 a year and well over a thousand staff engaged in developing and maintaining information systems; many have adopted development methods which claim to place emphasis on "sound analysis of business needs".

Yet their high-technology systems have effectively automated a 200-year-old system which was already creaking before computers were invented—and perpetuated the rules of manual ledger records as if they were immutable laws of banking. By using the power of the computer to build "bigger and faster" solutions on faulty foundations, the banks have increased both the intractability and the scale of their problems.

"Pragmatic" tinkering with symptoms at the technology level, while ignoring root causes, has cost the banks a great deal of money and goodwill. Moreover, they are now having to pay a far higher price to fix problems which it would have been easier to have eliminated long ago. There is also the possibility that the banks' inability to adjust their systems to changing circumstances has made them vulnerable to competition: it is interesting that one clearing bank, which started life as a building society, seems to have been less afflicted by the types of problem identified here.

Though this paper takes banking as an example, similar problems exist in other industries too. Building information systems is difficult. It should be the joint responsibility of IS and the business itself and the true nature of the business should be understood before attempting to define information requirements. *Real* understanding of the business, independently of current business and information systems, requires a huge effort in challenging today's assumptions.

Businesses generally are beginning to realise that what they need for themselves—and from other businesses with which they deal—is fewer, better-quality, and properly unified system components, not a proliferation of quickly written, overlapping, and inconsistent ones. CASE may bring an acceleration of the development process, but if it is used to produce more ill-fitting and inappropriate systems, then this acceleration is counter-productive.

CASE methods and tools are sold largely on the basis of their potential for increasing (a) productivity, and (b) consistency—see the evidence gathered by Spikes Cavell[6]. Too often, however, productivity is seen as a matter of speed—and consistency is seen in terms of the *form* of what is produced. Important though these are, emphasising speed of production often leads to lack of attention to rightness of product—while consistency of form often masks an inconsistency of content and meaning.

Industry is increasingly demanding reusability and open system standards. The response of "component" CASE and shared repositories is good news. However, this will fail if integration is seen only as a matter of providing agreed formats at the interfaces.

Both CASE and the business systems which it is used to produce need not only well-bounded elements with defined interfaces but also a common underlying conceptual framework . Without this we shall continue to add to the existing confusion of business systems and increase the computer-dissatisfaction of business users, business sponsors and the public at large: the promise will go on being broken.

REFERENCES

[1] Milligan, S. (1954). *The Dreaded Batter Pudding Hurler of Bexhill-on-Sea*, British Broadcasting Corporation.
[2] Kent, W. (1978). *Data and Reality*. North-Holland.
[3] Reynolds, W. J. F. et al. (1983, 1985). *Introduction to SDM; SDM Business Model—Data; SDM Business Model—Processes; SDM Systems Architecture; BSDM Requirements Definition* (1989). IBM UK Ltd.
[4] Widger, J. S. (1983). *SDM System Design*. IBM UK Ltd.
[5] Kalra, C. M. and Reynolds, W. J. F. (October 1989). *Integrated Business System Management (IBSM)*. UKCMG.
[6] Spikes Cavell & Co Ltd. (1990, 1991). *Methods and Tools*.

7

Integrated Support for Real-time Control Systems

Martin Beeby, J. S. Parkinson, Vivien Hamilton

ABSTRACT

Rolls-Royce has recognised the need for an integrated project support environment to help the development of real-time control systems, to time and cost, throughout the Rolls-Royce group of companies. The control systems designed within the Rolls-Royce group of companies are used in a wide range of applications with the single common factor being; failure of the control system could lead to risk of life. High Integrity and High Quality are therefore of paramount importance in the system design process so that safe systems can be built that will work and also satisfy independent safety assessment bodies.

Many environments are available which can assist pure Software projects and some exist to support Electronic projects with embedded Software. The Rolls-Royce need is for an environment which can support the development of systems which include Mechanical, Electronic and Software components. Because of the diverse range of applications, any environment must be capable of supporting both large and small project teams with a large degree of project tailoring being possible.

This paper covers the first steps in meeting the Rolls-Royce requirements by describing the work that has taken place, within the Rolls-Royce group, to build a primitive Systems and Software Development Environment (SSDE).

A primitive development environment has been constructed, but is not intended for use on a real project. Our main conclusions from the work were that a process model is of paramount importance to be able to develop an environment and assist users to understand the whole system development process. We also concluded that tool integration technology is not sufficiently mature to allow users to easily create their own environments.

INTRODUCTION

This report describes a project to investigate CASE tool integration with a view to producing, or recommending, an integrated project support environment. The work was undertaken by a specialist High Integrity Systems support centre in the Rolls-Royce group. The intention of the centre is to assist the main production line areas in developing control systems.

At the outset, we recognised that our environment should address the needs of systems development. However, as a major component of these systems is software, and the software process is better understood and supported with tools, we chose to target this process for our primitive environment. To this end we have limited the integration of tools to those which primarily support software development. During the system development process, many computer based tools are already used (e.g. CAD, CIM etc.). Inclusion of such tools into any future environment is expected to be possible.

Primarily we are tool users not tool builders. For this reason we were looking for a tool integration solution that allows us to make most efficient use of "off-the-shelf" software tools while still allowing us to create an environment configurable enough to encapsulate our working procedures.

The project brief was so wide it is no surprise that we were not able to find a total solution, in the form of an off the shelf product, to solve our problem. What we learnt and the conclusions that were drawn have been of great importance to finding the right direction to the future solution . Of these the most important was understanding, rationalising and defining our system development process.

AIMS OF THE PROJECT

As a first step towards implementing an environment, preliminary work was necessary to understand the methods of putting together such an environment and to obtain the prerequisite knowledge to enable implementation. This paper summarises the first steps towards acquiring this knowledge, which covered the following:

- Investigate tool integration technologies.
- Produce a simple environment using an "integration" product.
- Highlight further areas for investigation and learning.

Our initial investigations into tool integration technology showed there to be a small number of tool integration techniques forming the basis of some products. The most common "integration" seemed to be that of other CASE tools allowing menus to be tailored and further tools to be invoked. To us this provides no real benefit over an existing uncoupled set of tools because an effective integration must address data integration, display integration and provide the means for process control.

The most promising approaches seem to be the PCTE and ATIS approaches which aim at data integration and control integration but not display integration. This is acceptable because Data and Control integration is of primary importance while Display integration is in the realm of tool builders. As the basis for our primitive environment we used an ATIS based product, the Atherton Software Backplane. To facilitate tool integration we used the Atherton Integration Softboard in addition to the Software Backplane.

The important features of the software backplane are:

- Central Database (object oriented)
- Version Control (as part of database core)
- Control integration (as part of Integration Softboard)
- Roles and Contexts

The tools integrated were:

- Interleaf (documentation)
- IDE Software through Pictures (analysis and design)
- Cadre Teamwork (analysis and design)
- OS specific tools (editor, compilers, debuggers etc.)

The work was carried out on a Digital VAXstation 3100 and an IBM RISC System 6000 workstation running VMS and UNIX operating systems respectively. The two machines were linked via TCP/IP and NFS, allowing sharing of data between the two machines.

TOOL INTEGRATION

At the start of the project we expected a number of learning problems related to operating systems, integration package problems, etc. It looked like tool integration was the key to being able to build an environment and this would be where the main difficulties would be found. The thoughts were that once tool integration had been achieved, an environment could be built by simply adding and integrating more tools.

The mechanism of tool integration is based around the central object orientated database where each object contains project data and associated control attributes. This data may only be accessed by methods associated with the object type. Tool integration is achieved by using these methods to extract the data and then passing it to the associated tool. The integration softboard allows the definition of object types and their associated methods. The integration of tools involves the building of command lines which include file names and switches to be passed to the tool. Some tools provide direct access to operations on specified objects, others force the user to use the tool's internal operator interface to navigate to the file and operation required. In the former case we can implement total control of the tool, in the latter we have to depend on the tool's internal control procedures. Routines are available to the user, however, which permit the tool's database to be interrogated. Where possible, data is not duplicated between the central object orientated database and the tool specific database, although, where the data is required for control it must be extracted from the tool database and placed in the central database. Methods which integrate tools which support structured analysis and document products can be regarded as sub-processes within the development process.

Having carried out integration of our tools we realised that building a tool integration with some degree of process control "hard-coded" in was not the best approach. For example a tool invocation which forces the user to perform a number of actions from a single invocation prevents other users from being able to access single functions. By addressing the integration of tools in isolation we were not addressing the tool to tool transitions.

Thus the need for a process model was established.

Having understood the mechanism of tool integration and recognised the need for a process model we now believe that the correct approach is to define the process completely prior to integration.

THE PROCESS MODEL

In order to provide a framework for the environment we initially defined an entity relationship diagram for items associated with a project. An attempt was made to cover all activities within a project.

Major sections included requirements capture, design, implementation and test. We used the concept of a role so that certain activities could be assigned to users operating in that role. Accordingly we identified four major roles within the process:

- The Client
- The Implementor
- The Tester
- The Manager

The Implementor designs or manufactures a component. We use the terms "design", "manufacture" and "component" in the broadest sense.

The Tester is someone other than the Implementor of the component under test. Again the word "test" is used in its widest sense. We could be testing compliance with document format requirements or compliance with dynamic response requirements, for example. Note that we test against requirements, if there is no requirement we cannot test.

The Manager monitors work and grants approval to proceed. The Manager also communicates with the Client.

The Client operates outside the environment but an interface must be provided. This is done by accepting statements of requirement, and by requesting amendments to requirements.

We have avoided introducing further roles because the actions permitted to each role can be restricted via associating sets of methods with each role.

In the entity relationship diagram (ERD), the relationship between item entities and role entities define the interactions of roles within the project (Figure 1).

The ERD models the development process in a detailed way. However it omits detail on dataflow, control of dataflow, and specific project processes.

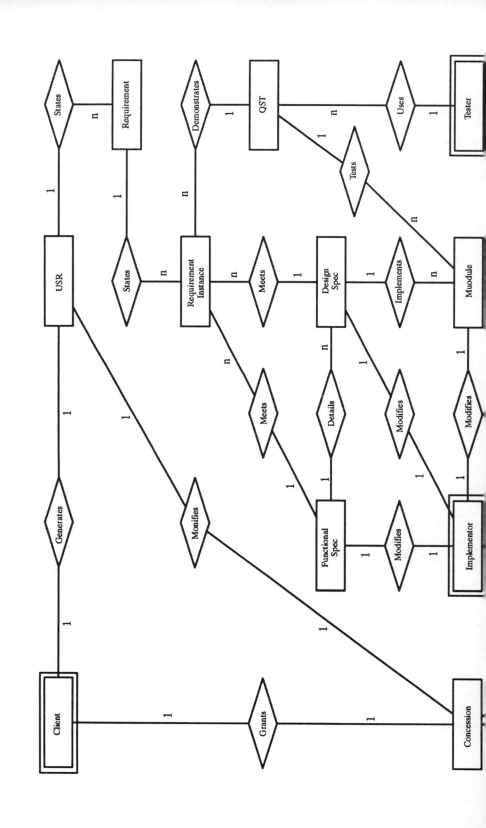

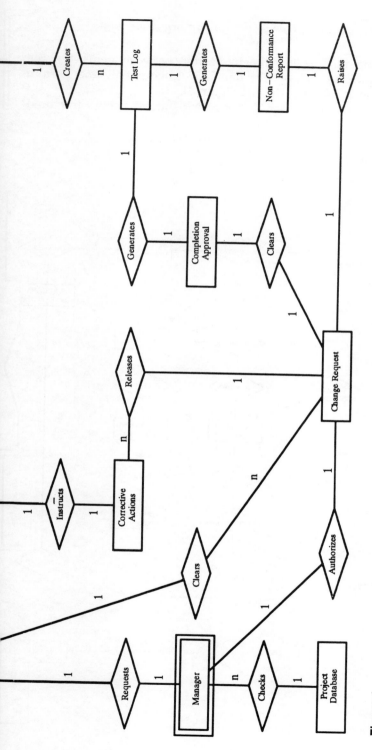

Figure 1

What is being modelled is the interaction between items, not the structure of a project database. The database structure will emerge from further, more detailed, analysis (e.g. Figure 2).

It was decided to model the development process using Structured Analysis with Real Time extensions.

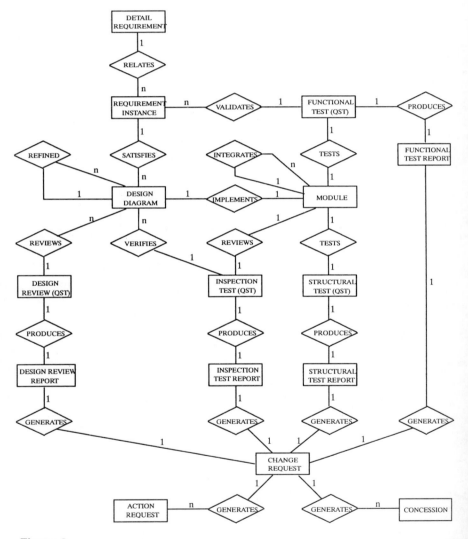

Figure 2

In developing our process model it became apparent that the Change Request Procedure was of critical importance. It is this procedure which controls the flow of work within our development process.

A Change Request (CR) is raised against a failure to comply with a requirement. The failure to comply may have many sources. A CR can have associated with it the following attributes:

- A non-conformance report
- A list of corrective action reports
- A list of affected items
- A list of test reports
- A completion approval report

Each item within the project database must have an associated state transition diagram, for example see Figure 3 (or entity life cycle).

As the CR forms the basis of our model, any item in the model must be controlled by a CR. Failure to allow the CR control implies that that item cannot be changed. It should be noted that project startup is a special case of change request.

Thus a change request must have the potential to control all processes within a project (Figure 4). Access to the tools which support these processes is role dependent. Such processes include:

- Testing
- Impact Analysis
- Approval of Corrective Action
- Release and Implementation of Corrective Actions
- Retesting
- Approval of Retest

Let us now consider some of the requirements of the change request process.

1. The development process must be able to accommodate change requests being assigned to an item while that item is itself subject to ongoing CRs.

2. It should be noted that CRs may be raised against items which may or may not conform to their requirements. If the item currently conforms then it is in a known established state (checked-in). If the item does not currently conform because it has a CR pending because it does not meet its current requirements then it is not in a known state (checked-out).

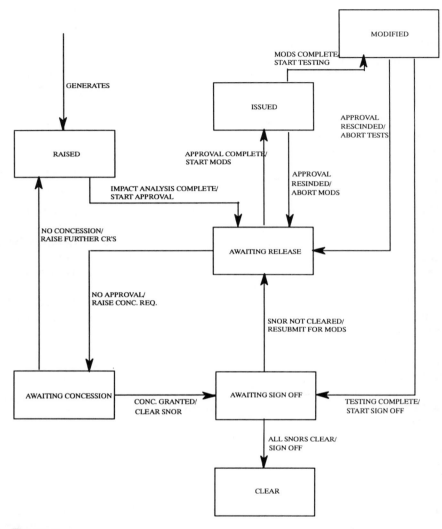

Figure 3

3. If a CR is raised against a checked-out item we have two choices:

a) We reject it until the item is checked-in (i.e. tested and CRs signed off)

b) We go to the previous version of the item and review all CRs raised since the item was checked in.

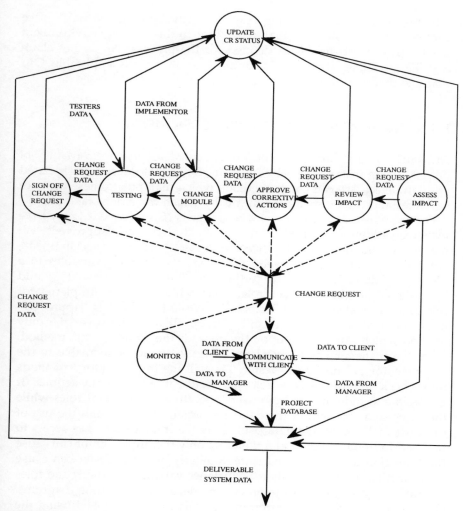

Figure 4

The requirements for a change request show the need for decisions to be made. The exact basis on which the decision is made is not of importance: what is of importance are the possibilities through which the change request is allowed to go.

As the change request sequence operates, it in turn triggers processes which when complete cause transitions for each item associated with the change request.

In the context of developing High Integrity Systems we must place emphasis on control rather than flexibility. To this end any environment would implement the CR as defined for the process. We do not claim that the model, as discussed, is complete or universally applicable. Our example serves to illustrate some of the issues to be addressed.

IMPLEMENTATION OF THE PROCESS MODEL

Attributes of data items can be implemented as instance variables of objects. Using instance variables we can implement the states associated with an object. We can create methods which manipulate these instance variables and thus provide the means by which transitions take place.

For example a database object whose type is "C source code" may have instance variables "released", "modified", "tested" and "approved". We may create methods for the object type "setReleased", "setModified", "setTested", and "setApproved" which set the instance variables to a TRUE condition. The methods "setReleased" and "setApproved" would be assigned to the Manager role, "setModified" to the Implementor role and "setTested" to the Tester role. While the object is "approved" it can be available, as a read only file, to all roles, however the only method which can operate upon the object is the "setReleased" method. Once the manager has released the object it would be available to the Implementor but not to the Tester. Thus all the Implementors' methods must check that the object is "released" before it can effect any actions. (It is possible to hide objects from users operating in particular roles while the object remains within the database organisation through the use of Contexts or Views of the database). Only the implementor has access to the "setModified" method and therefore only the Implementor can cause the transition to the modified state. Similarly only the Tester can cause the transition to the tested state. So instance variables, methods and roles all combine to implement the process model's state transition diagrams. Once in a particular state, appropriate tools may be invoked using the methods we choose to implement for each tool.

GENERAL DISCUSSION

In our opinion the complexity of configuration of the Backplane and the considerable learning curve we have had to ascend has limited the scope of our activities. We, as systems developers, should be concentrating our efforts on activities which contribute directly to contract deliverables. We look to integration product suppliers to provide high level user interfaces which will minimise our overhead activities. The current technology is not sufficiently advanced for users of tools to easily build effective environments. It is our hope that as the open systems philosophy is further adopted by tool vendors and integration tool vendors, this will lead to improvement of existing standards and the creation of new standards to address the user's requirements.

The exercise has been useful in that it has provided exposure to the Software Backplane philosophy which has in turn led to refinement of the process model. Generally the integration of individual tools (i.e. providing a common user interface for invocation of a tool's functions) is relatively easy; determining how tools work together within a project is more difficult.

We have used the Yourdon method to model our development process, our reasoning being that if it is appropriate for our deliverable systems then it is appropriate for modelling our development processes. It has the advantage of being accessible to a wide range of staff, allowing all concerned to contribute to the development and refinement of the model. The method does not lend itself easily to implementation in an object oriented framework. For this reason we believe that appropriate methods should be used for modelling the process and modelling the implementation of the process. These are not necessarily the same. For example we used Yourdon to communicate with users and some high level Booch diagrams to model the implementation on to the object oriented framework.

CONCLUSIONS

Having set out to build an environment through integrating tools, we found that the process model has far greater importance.

The current integration technology is not sufficiently mature for users to be able to create their own environments.

It is essential to have a process model to specify the functionality of any environment. Many people believe that written procedures are sufficient, but they are not.

A process model should:

- Embody the concept of Methods and Roles.
- Accommodate decision making by users. The way in which users make decisions is not the concern of the model, but the result of the decisions is.

- Be based around a critical feature of the development process. In our example the change request procedure was of critical importance and was required to control all processes and items within a process.

A process model provides the best media for evaluating changes to a development process and providing the feedback to allow continuous process improvement. This is necessary to increase process maturity (SEI maturity).

A high level process model can contribute to the understanding of the whole development process by those involved in the execution of parts of the process. By providing a consistent view it can serve as a useful training aid for all involved; Project managers, Engineers, Testers etc.

REFERENCES

Alan Brown, Database Support for Software Engineering (April 1991)
Alan Brown, Integrated Project Support Environments: The Aspect Project (Academic Press 1991)
Grady Booch, Software Engineering with ADA (Benjamin Cummings 1983)
Dewayne Perry and Gail Kaiser, Models of Software Development Environments (IEEE Transactions on Software Engineering 1991)
Watts Humphrey, Characterizing the Software Process: A Maturity Framework (IEEE software 1988)

8

Reverse Engineering Data Using An Integrated Toolset

Nick Sabanis, Anthony Darlison

ABSTRACT

Reverse engineering activities have become increasingly important in bringing old code into maintainable state, understanding its functionality, and linking it with development activities which exploit emerging CASE technology. The REDO project focuses on the analysis and understanding of existing applications, especially ageing data processing applications written in Cobol. This paper discusses the data reverse engineering effort in REDO, particularly with respect to the development of a tool for the reverse engineering of (persistent) data of Cobol applications and its effective use from within the integrated REDO Maintenance and Reverse Engineering Toolset. A brief review of the state of the art is also given, which provides the context for assessing REDO's contribution to advancing the state of the art in (data) reverse engineering.

CASE: Current Practice, Future Prospects. Edited by Kathy Spurr and Paul Layzell
© 1992 John Wiley & Sons Ltd

INTRODUCTION

The focus of the **REDO** project [1] has been the analysis and understanding of existing systems, and the recording in an accessible manner of the results of this analysis. This task, usually associated in software maintenance literature with the term **Reverse Engineering**, has to do with creating models of an existing system, in much the same way as "normal" system specification is related to the creation of models of as-yet non-existent systems.

In many systems, an important subtask of reverse engineering has to do with analysing the data of the application system as they are defined in existing code, and creating (data) models which provide a more abstract, implementation-independent representation of this data.

To address this, **Data Reverse Engineering** in REDO is aimed at producing and evaluating a set of tools which will help analysts produce a logical model of a system from the description of the physical files which implement it.

In particular, the current focus of REDO on ageing data processing application written in Cobol has directed the development of a tool, called the **Data Remodelling (DRE) Tool**, which will assist with the reverse engineering of persistent data definitions of Cobol program into a conceptual-level representation.

This paper discusses the design of the DRE Tool and current progress in its implementation, with emphasis on ways in which it is expected to advance the current state of the art through its effective integration with other reverse engineering tools and other facilities developed in REDO.

REVIEW OF THE STATE OF THE ART

Before embarking on a discussion of the REDO approach to data reverse engineering, let us pause to examine the current state of the art in this field. It can generally be said that the state of the art in methods for data reverse engineering is currently embodied in the tools available or currently under development. There is no flourishing of theoretical work reported in literature. Two early publications ((Davis and Arora, 1986), (Nillson, 1986)) on the translation of Cobol file definitions to an Entity-Relationship conceptual model originated from a slightly different viewpoint and, to the best of our knowledge, were not followed by any major thrust of relevant research.

---

[1]   ESPRIT Project 2487: REengineering, Validation and DOcumentation

A few seminal papers ((Sneed and Jandrasics, 1987), (Sneed and Jandrasics, 1988), (Choobineh *et al.*, 1988), (Bachman, 1988), (McWilliams, 1988)) present the case for Data Reverse Engineering. They also provide a first classification of tasks and levels of abstraction, from the implementation level, up to and including the "conceptual level" representation of information.

More particularly, the following three levels of abstraction are identified, which are very much the same as the levels typically recognised in the forward engineering activities of Data Modelling and Data Base Design:

- **conceptual design level**, where the system and its "real world" is described in an implementation-independent manner (i.e. independently of the data model used in the logical design)

- **logical design level**, where data are organised according to a defined implementation model (e.g. relational, hierarchical or network), but in a DBMS-independent manner

- **physical design level**, where the actual physical structures (files) of the implementation (e.g. DBMS DDL, Cobol files) are created.

By and large, researchers in the field appear to have mostly focused on "first-degree" reverse engineering, i.e. recovering the physical database design from existing schema and subschema code or, accordingly, extracting data dictionary information from Cobol file definitions. Issues addressed also include system-level data reengineering (e.g. data definition and data value reengineering (Ricketts *et al.*, 1989)), and the introduction of abstract data types to improve existing data structures (e.g. (Colbrook and Smythe, 1989)).

In the commercial world, most tools concentrate on the lower levels of the reverse engineering process, capturing physical design information (e.g. DBMS DDL, or Cobol files) and storing it in a repository. This perhaps explains why a large proportion of tool vendors are actually Repository and/or Data Dictionary vendors.

As also found by a recent state-of-the-art study (Rock-Evans and Hales, 1990), very few existing products/tools (actually, only three tools) get above the Logical Design level towards a Conceptual Level representation of the persistent data of a system. And of these tools, only one provides some support for data reverse engineering from Cobol file definitions to an ER kind of representation.

CONSIDERATIONS FOR THE DEVELOPMENT OF THE DATA REMODELLING TOOL

The review of the state of the art in the previous section has indicated a largely unexploited potential for the development of methods and tools for Data Reverse Engineering. In particular, looking at existing tools in the light of the REDO current focus on the reverse engineering of ageing data processing systems written in Cobol, the scenery is rather poor. Even the one tool which supports reverse engineering from Cobol data definitions all the way to an ER model does so in an isolated way, that is without parallel support for **process reverse engineering** to assist with the analysis and improve understanding of the persistent data of Cobol applications.

Reverse engineering is all about creating models of an existing system. In designing a tool for making data models from existing code and manipulating them, we must be clear about what kinds of model are required, and what they may be used for. The study of practices, case studies, and available tools for data reverse engineering has led to a number of considerations for the development of the Data Remodelling (DRE) Tool:

- Derived models must be presentable to staff with a particular culture, training and mentality. This indicates that a credible reverse engineering offering must be to some extent tailorable, and have a graphical interface. This is much the same idea as the CASE meta-tool, and infuses the REDO philosophy.

- Models at various "levels of abstraction" are required, depending upon intended use. For example, change requests are sometimes presented at a functional level, so an up-to-date functional specification, suitably linked to the designs and code which implement it, will be of great benefit for impact analysis and cost estimation. REDO as a whole caters for a range of abstraction levels. As stressed earlier, the data modelling world generally acknowledges three levels: physical; logical; and conceptual. Data remodelling in REDO aims to reconstruct a conceptual model from information contained in the source code and elsewhere, whilst maintaining links from the model to the source. Lower-level models can be reconstructed from this, much as in normal forward engineering, but with additional cues and clues from the implementation.

- Substantial tool assistance is important (Seminar, 1991). We should not expect maintainers to create models of their system by hand any more than we expect programmers to compile their source by hand. Much useful information can be extracted automatically, and the only barrier to doing this presently is the sheer size of the manual task. This suggests a tool which creates a "first cut" view automatically from the information in the Cobol code.

- Not all useful information can be derived automatically. Tools must therefore be interactive, to allow users to modify the first cut view on the basis of information which the tool could not possibly have inferred from the source code alone.

- In REDO, we have a set of powerful reverse engineering tools (at various stages in their development). All information that is used or produced by these tools is stored and managed by the common repository, called the **System Description Data Base (SDDB)** (Ostrolenk, 1990), the schema of which is a direct reflection of a structured (parse-tree) representation of Cobol programs, developed within REDO and called the **Cobol-IF** (Ostrolenk, 1990).

With this set of tools becoming available, we must acknowledge that the "added information" that a user provides to one particular tool may have been derived using another tool. We thus expect a toolkit to be immensely more valuable if different reverse engineering tools are reasonably tightly integrated.So like all the other REDO tools, a DRE Tool must provide "hooks" for invoking other tools.

- The model is not an object in its own right but a model *of* the subject system. We would therefore be able to expect to justify the model in terms of the source from which it was derived, in much the same way as we expect to justify implementations with respect to specifications in forward engineering. This leads us to the idea of connecting derived models to the original source via navigable links, with terminators being nodes in the parse tree of the source ("pieces of code" to the user) and constructs in the derived model (entities, relationships, or whatever). The links may either represent a trace of the automatic tools derivation, or may be subsequently set by users.

TOOL FUNCTIONS

The above considerations have strongly influenced the functionality of the REDO DRE Tool. This section describes in more detail the functionality of the DRE Tool, its source of information and its expected end product(s). The list of functions given below for the DRE Tool is a natural one of the REDO environment, and allows the integration of the DRE Tool with other REDO tools using the (common) repository, thereby exploiting one of the main novelties and advantages of the REDO platform.

Create First Cut Model

Outline

In outline, this function takes as its input a representation of the subject system in the form of Cobol-IF stored in the SDDB, processes it according to some supplied heuristics, and presents a first cut ER model. Like other REDO tools, no direct input from Cobol source is catered for, so only information representable in the SDDB [18] can be processed.

Input

More precisely, the tool will take as input **persistent data information from Cobol** programs. The entire system source will be scanned for information normally residing in the INPUT-OUTPUT SECTION of the ENVIRONMENT DIVISION and the FILE SECTION of the DATA DIVISION of Cobol programs.

Most of the popular file organisations and access methods (e.g. serial, sequential, indexed sequential) are covered, with less emphasis on serial files for which fairly limited information can be derived from Cobol File Definitions.

Auxiliary files, such as sort files, are not considered, as they do not embody any information about the system that the main files do not. Internal data (WORKING STORAGE data in Cobol) may contain useful information, and this issue will be addressed during a later research phase of the tool development.

The DRE Tool does not deal with any other physical file implementations, such as hierarchical, network, or relational Data Definitions due to the overall emphasis of the project. However, these should be in the scope of any mature data reverse engineering product.

Output

The tool will create, store and display a logical/conceptual data model of the persistent data of the system. The target formalism is an **Entity Relationship (ER)** kind of model.

The ER (Chen, 1976) is the most widely accepted technique for logical data modelling. It supports the representation of data at a higher level of abstraction by modelling them in terms of entities, their attributes and (inter)relationships. The ER appears most often as the meeting point for reverse engineering and forward engineering processes and tools, and for conversion procedures for migration towards new database technology (e.g. hierarchical to relational). Variations of the ER are also the underlying data model of popular CASE repositories.

The current version of the DRE Tool uses an extended ER model, which will be referred to as the **Enhanced Entity Relationship (EER) model**, and which supports the following classes of objects:

- **entities**, which are the principal objects about which information has to be collected. Entities are distinguished into:

  - **strong entities**, which have internal identifiers, called **keys**, that uniquely determine the existence of entity occurrences
  - **weak entities**, which do not have keys. Such entities are related to one or more parent entities through an **identifying relationship**.

- **attributes**, which are used to provide descriptive information about entities or relationships. For strong entities, a special set of attributes provides the key of the entity, which is used to uniquely distinguish among the occurrences of the entity. Weak entities and relationships do not have keys.

- **relationships**, which represent real-world associations among one or more entities. The **degree** of a relationship is the number of entities associated through the relationship. Relationships of any degree are supported by the EER model, including so-called **recursive relationships** (those where the domain and the range of the relationship are the same). Also supported are **identifying relationships**, which are used to associate weak entities with their parent entities.

Relationships can have attributes, in the same way as entities. Unlike entities, however, relationships do not have keys. Also, relationships have semantic meaning which is indicated by the following:

- the connectivity, or **cardinality**, of the relationship (e.g. **one-to-one**, **one-to-many**, or **many-to-many** for binary relationships).

- the **participation** in this connectivity by the member entities: **optional** (partial participation), or **mandatory** (total participation).

- special **REDEFINES** associations between a number of entities and/or attributes. This information is used to represent REDEFINES clauses from Cobol : a REDEFINES association involves all entities or attributes that provide a logical-level Cobol definition over the same physical location.

The derived, and evolving EER model of the system is stored in the SDDB, and suitable graphical viewers are provided. Sophisticated CASE users expect an automatic layout facility, and this is being developed within REDO. A textual (predicate calculus-like) view is also provided for users who may find this style more palatable. Finally, interfaces to other data modelling and case environments will have to be implemented eventually for REDO to achieve its goal of an "open toolset".

Processing

Upon invocation the tool will commence a traversal of the Cobol-IF stored in the SDDB, applying the rules and heuristics stored in the knowledge base to build up a first-cut EER model of the system.
    Some of the mappings are rather straightforward. The following are some examples of rules that are applied automatically for mapping Cobol data structures to an EER model:

- Cobol 01 record definitions (i.e. 01 group items and elementary items) naturally correspond to entities

- a clause of the type "field-name OCCURS N TIMES" can be represented as a separate entity "field-name" related to the parent entity via a 1:N relationship.

- 88, 66, and RENAMES clauses in Cobol data definitions are ignored in the first-cut EER diagram, while REDEFINES clauses result in REDEFINES associations among the data items involved.

- PICTURE clause are used to determine data types and values

- naming of components of the derived data model will naturally be based on the names of corresponding Cobol data items.

Other correspondences between Cobol structures and ER primitives are less clear-cut than the above. For example, a group item in Cobol can be represented in the ER either as a separate entity related to the parent entity via a 1:1 relationship, or as an attribute of a parent entity. The tool will provide a choice to the user as to which of the two kinds of representation to adopt. Current prototypes allow this choice to be made globally by configuring the knowledge base *before* the tool is invoked. The DRE Tool will also enable the user to invoke the first cut tool more than once, each time experimenting with different hypotheses and assumptions.

Maintain Links To Cobol-IF

The idea of setting up a web of links between the original source and various kinds of derived information is pervasive within REDO. A data model is just another kind of derived view and so facilities must be provided for navigation from the derived model to the original source. Links will be created by the first cut tool as it traverses the SDDB and creates the model. These links will connect nodes in the parse tree of the source ("pieces of code") to terms in the derived model (entities, relationships, attributes, and so forth) and will be navigable in either direction.

For example it will be possible to point at an EER object and obtain a display of related data definitions within the source, using one of the database editors supplied with REDO. The displayed objects would be elements of source which had somehow contributed to the creation of that EER object, and different link types are provided to express different kinds of relationship. Related source, together with some minimal context, will be displayed.

Once a model has been created it will be possible to create further links between model terms and other database entities. Since we cannot anticipate all of the numerous ways in which such a facility might be used we permit users to create their own link types, with the (non-enforcible) understanding that each type is to be used to express a different kind of relationship.

As an example of the use of such links consider the notion of a *transaction* within the subject system. Some entities in the derived model will have a number of transactions associated with them, and implemented as procedural code updating the data items in the implementation which model the real-world entity. Since we have an association between EER entities and data fields, we can use a REDO tool, such as the Data Flow Analyser, to search for updating code, and once we have found it, link it to the appropriate entity.

Refine and Enhance Model

We recall that the intention behind our effort in Data Remodelling is not to construct a very sophisticated data modelling environment or a CASE tool based on the EER formalism, but primarily to investigate ways in which to derive as much information as possible from the source code about the persistent data of the system, in order to enhance system understanding and maintainability. However, producing a correct and unambiguous representation will require some further manipulation of the first cut model.

Support for this includes:

- an **interactive graphical environment** that will enable the user to visualise and maintain an EER diagram. This will include creating and modifying EER diagrams, and using associated functionality offered by the tool, such as validation and normalisation of the diagram.

- a **knowledge base**, consisting of rules for assisting with aspects of the refinement and enhancement of the EER model. This will include checking for anomalies (e.g. synonymous entities), and discovering potentially useful properties (e.g. hidden relationships, the possibility of ISA hierarchies) in the current model.

Further aspects of knowledge-based support for EER modelling (e.g. automatic merging or splitting of an entity in the EER model, or creation of a subtyping hierarchy among a set of entities) would normally be expected to be addressed by a more sophisticated data (re)modelling environment. These functions will certainly be required if the derived models are to be used for any significant redevelopment, but with the steady move towards open tool interfaces we can foresee that this need may best be addressed by a good connection between REDO and another tool which already offers these features. Relevant research has been identified, for example that referenced in (Benedusi *et al.*, 1990) and (Teorey *et al.*, 1986).

- producing a **normalised data model**. The data model we construct should be as correct, accurate and unambiguous as possible. This is where normalisation of the data model becomes a necessity ((Beeri *et al.*, 1978), (Ling, 1986), (Teorey *et al.*, 1986)).

The information provided by the original Cobol file definitions is sufficient in deriving information about keys in the new data model. However, more information is required in order to produce a logical model from the conceptual representation, such as multivalued functional dependency among data items. It will be imperative for the tool to offer facilities for asserting further semantics and functional dependency between data which are not detected automatically in the original data structures. We are currently working on developing an appropriate environment and a procedure to guide the elicitation of relevant information from the user.

Navigate To And From Other REDO Tools

Typically, in Cobol data processing applications the procedural code is used to formulate transactions and integrity constraints on the data. A significant part of structural information and semantic constraints (e.g. cardinality, inheritance and subtyping information, validation rules), as well as inherent functional dependency information (besides "primary key" information for files) are typically expressed in the code, rather than asserted declaratively or documented in any form directly accessible to the maintainer/reverse engineer.

As stressed earlier, REDO holds a comparative advantage as far as reverse engineering is concerned in that it has developed a set of integrated tools which work on a common repository. The user of the DRE Tool (a Reverse Engineer) can exploit this by having other REDO tools invoked from within the DRE Tool to enhance analysis and understanding of Cobol data, and enrich the information contained in the first-cut model produced by the system.

For instance, for a given subset of the first-cut conceptual model, e.g. an entity, the Data Flow Analyser (OBrien, 1990) can be invoked to provide information on the bits of code that access and/or update it. A closer inspection of this code can reveal interesting information regarding:

- unspecified internal structures of records. In some occasions, the author(s) of a Cobol program are not interested in assigning structure to their persistent data, as long as they can extract this structure in their programs. This is typically achieved through appropriate "READ persistent-record INTO working-storage-record" statements, as shown in the following example of a Cobol program.

```
DATA DIVISION.
FILE SECTION.
FD SALES-PERSON-FILE
    LABEL RECORDS ARE STANDARD
```

```
01 SALES-PERSON-DATA PIC X(80).
WORKING-STORAGE SECTION.
01 SALES-PERSON-RECORD.
    05 SP-REGION          PIC XX.
    05 SP-NUMBER          PIC XXXX.
    05 SP-NAM                PIC X(18).
    05 SP-QUOTA-CLASS     PIC X.
05 SP-COMM-CLASS          PIC X.
05 SP-YTD-SALES              PIC X(8).
05 SP-YTD-RETURNS         PIC X(7).
05 FILLER                    PIC XX.
05 SP-CURRENT             PIC XX.
05 FILLER                    PIC X(35).
PROCEDURE DIVISION.
READ-SALESPERSON-RECORD.
        READ SALES-PERSON-FILE INTO SALES-PERSON-RECORD
            AT END MOVE ''Y'' TO WS-EOF-FLAG.
```

By isolating the fragments of code that read persistent data into working storage structures (i.e. READ statements) throughout the entire system, information can be recovered about the inherent structure of data items that was obscured in the implementation code. The reverse engineer may then decide to include this structuring information as part of a consistent record definition.

Particular attention should be paid to records that are accessed by more than one program with different structures extracted in each occasion—view integration is a possibility.

- any conceptual similarity among data, which will enable the integration/merging of conceptually synonymous concepts. Thus, e.g., two attributes with the same name, or two items which (the Reverse Engineer thinks) embody similar content/role can be checked, using the Data Flow Analyser to slice out relevant code.

- functional dependencies between data items not covered by the key information of file definitions. This will be very useful not only in reaching a richer conceptual model, but also in deriving information that is necessary for the normalisation of the logical data model.

For example, if the value of a data item is always computed by a piece of code based on some other data item, this is a strong indication of an implicit functional dependency between these two data items. The reverse engineer can assess the situation and possibly assert a functional dependency between the two data items.

- the way data structures are updated. This may e.g. provide information as to whether a group item in a Cobol file definition is ever accessed on its own, or only as part of a higher-level group item/entity. This can have a bearing as to whether e.g. this group item should be represented as a separate entity related to the parent one, or as an attribute of the parent entity.

- cardinality constraints not expressed in Cobol OCCURS clauses, as well as optionality information, which are very useful for the semantics of relationships in the EER model

- "mutual exclusion" information not expressed by REDEFINES clauses on a piece of data structure, but defined in the code as a constraint/validation rule.

This is just one example of the benefits of tight tool integration. However it should be clear from the above discussion that to realise the full power of the DRE Tool will require tool navigation. By this we mean that the following facilities will be available:

- other REDO tools may be invoked to access the same SDDB as currently being used by a DRE Tool. Invocation of these additional tools will be possible directly from the DRE Tool interface, or from within a data remodelling function, where appropriate.

- certain REDO tools will need to navigate directly to certain regions of the schema upon invocation, provision being made for this in their parameter lists. "Hooks" (that is, an appropriate generic interface) will be provided for the directed invocation of these tools. For example, pointing to an EER entity would bring down an "auxiliary tools" menu. A selected tool wil be provided with a pointer to the entity from where it was selected.

The whole issue of tool navigation is under active discussion within REDO. Integration through shared data (the SDDB) has largely been achieved. To harness the full power of the variety of tools in tomorrow's reverse engineering toolkit (REDO), we believe that functional integration as described above is required and constitutes a significant advance over the current state of the art.

A FORWARD LOOK

Much fuss is beginning to be made in the trade literature about the new generation of reverse engineering tool which will be used to solve the maintenance crisis. Many pieces of the jigsaw have been developed or are currently being researched. So far they have not been convincingly assembled into an integrated approach although there is almost universal agreement that future developments in Reverse Engineering will concentrate on four areas:

• the active use of an open repository for storing both implementation artifacts and higher-level information recovered via Reverse Engineering

• the use of knowledge-based techniques to assist with labour-intensive aspects of the Reverse Engineering process and increase productivity

• a greater degree of synergy between Data Reverse Engineering and Process/Code Reverse Engineering towards a more coherent, possibly unified, higher-level representation of information concerning both data and processes.

• the integration of Reverse Engineering activities with existing and emerging Forward Engineering tools and methodologies.

The implementation of a basic data reverse engineering tool within the integrated environment of REDO will be a significant step in realising these four goals. In particular, the Ovum report (Rock-Evans and Hales, 1990) for example, makes it clear that whilst a number of commercially available tools are beginning to address the problem of extracting conceptual level data models, there is still a dearth of tools to perform process reverse engineering. Not only does REDO contain both these elements, but also the possibility of sufficiently tight integration to permit both these complementary approaches to reverse engineering to work in tandem.

CONCLUSIONS

Earlier in this paper it was asserted that reverse engineering is not a fully automatable activity: a certain degree of human assistance is required to recover information lost during the development cycle. This was found to be particularly true with respect to the reverse engineering of file and data definitions of ageing data processing systems written in Cobol. Such systems typically lack documentation of the semantic meaning of information and of interrelationships among data (e.g. foreign key information in relational terminology).

It is our belief that automation in the form of a toolset for reverse like the one constructed in REDO can significantly increase human productivity in application understanding and reverse engineering activities. This belief is currently being tested through the use (and evaluation) of the current version of the REDO Toolset by industrial partners in REDO in real world data reverse engineering. Preliminary results have been encouraging, and an enhanced version of the the toolset is currently being produced. This mini-industrialisation phase is expected to provide interesting feedback regarding the usefulness of information obtained through process reverse engineering in the reverse engineering of (Cobol) file and data definitions.

REFERENCES

OBrien, L. (1990). Static analysis and program transformation techniques. 2487-TN-UL-1036.

Davis, K. H. and Arora, A. K. (1986). A methodology for translating a conventional file system into an entity relationship model. *Entity Relationship approach: the use of ER concepts in Knowledge Representation*, P.P. Chen (ed.), IEEE CS Press, North Holland.

Nillson, E. G. (1986). The translation of a Cobol data structure to an entity-relationship type conceptual schema. *Entity Relationship approach: the use of ER concepts in Knowledge Representation*, P.P. Chen (ed.), IEEE CS Press, North Holland.

Seminar 26/3/91. Reverse Engineering, Reality or Hype. *The Belfry, Sutton Coldfield, Salford University Business Services*.

Beeri, C., Bernstein, P. A. and Goodman, N. (1978). A sophisticate's introduction to database normalisation theory. *Proceedings of the 4th International Conference on Very Large Data Bases*, West Berlin.

Benedusi, P., Benvenuto, V. and Caporaso, M. G. (1990). Maintenance and prototyping at the entity relationship level. *Proceedings of IEEE Conference on Software Maintenance*, USA.

Chen, P. P. (1976). The Entity-relationship model: towards a unified view of data. *ACM TODS*, Vol. 1, No. 1.

Sneed, H. M. and Jandrasics, G. (1987). Software Recycling. *Proceedings of IEEE Conference on Software Maintenance*, Austin, Texas.

Ricketts, J. A., Del Monaco, J. C. and Weeks M. W. (1989). Data reengineering for application systems. *Proceedings of IEEE Conference on Software Maintenance*, Miami, Florida.

Sneed, H. M. and Jandrasics, G. (1988). Inverse transformation of software from code to specification. *Proceedings of IEEE Conference on Software Maintenance*, Phoenix, Arizona.

Choobineh, J., Mannino, M. et al. (1988). An expert database design system based on analysis of forms. *IEEE Transaction on Software Engineering*, vol. 14, No. 2.

Stehle, G. J. (1989). The CASE repository: more than another application. *Meta Systems Ltd*.

Bachman, C. (1988). A CASE for reverse engineering. *Datamation*.

McWilliams, G. (1988). Users see a CASE advance in reverse engineering tools. *Datamation*.

Rock-Evans, R. and Hales, K. (1990). Reverse Engineering: Methods and Tools. *Ovum Ltd.*, Vols. 1 and 2.

Ling, T. W. (1986). A normal form for entity-relationship diagrams. *Entity Relationship approach: the use of ER concepts in Knowledge Representation*, P.P. Chen (ed.), IEEE CS Press, North Holland.

IBM Systems Journal 1990. Vol. 29, No. 2.

Ostrolenk, G. (1990). 2487-TN-LR-1057 The ERA model of Cobol-IF

Teorey, T. J. et al. (1986). A logical design methodology for relational databases using the extended entity-relationship model. *ACM Computing Surveys*.

Colbrook, A. and Smythe, C. (1989). The retrospective introduction of abstraction into software. *IEEE International Conference on Software Maintenance*.

9

Second Generation CASE: Can it be Justified?

Peter Haine

ABSTRACT

Experience with first generation CASE tools such as Excelerator, Automate, IEW and the like, has caused users to question whether they provide adequate support for the chosen systems development method, and whether the prescriptive nature of the method is acceptable. The tools support many aspects of their respective methods tolerably will, but most have weaknesses in terms of their breadth of coverage and the usability of the resulting models. In any case, most organisations tend to adopt their own variant of the respective method and often find the tools restrict them or require them to follow a prescribed development path.

Second generation CASE tools—those such as Systematica's Virtual Software Factory and the Ipsys Tool Builder's Kit—purport to remove these restrictions by enabling a bespoke toolset to be produced to fully support local variants of any method (Lewis, 1990). But how realistic is this, and in any case can it be justified?

CASE: Current Practice, Future Prospects. Edited by Kathy Spurr and Paul Layzell
© 1992 John Wiley & Sons Ltd

This paper reviews some experiences with CASE and addresses the question as to whether a bespoke solution can be justified, or whether it is better to adopt the strictures of a toolset designed for a prescribed method. It questions the required scope of any proposed bespoke toolset and considers how it should relate to the corporate repository and any other tools which are relevant to the systems development process. Perhaps most significantly it proposes a strategy for organisations planning to adopt tools as part of their future development strategy: placing in context the role of repository as well as that of current and future CASE tools.

INTRODUCTION

CASE tools have been with us for almost ten years now. By any standards that's a lifetime in our industry! We should expect there to have been a couple of generations by now and that we should be well into advanced technology approaches. In reality there have been quite significant developments over the time period. From the early point toolsets which supported specific analysis or design techniques, we have moved to relatively well integrated toolsets which support many aspects of the development life cycle. Much of the development, though, has been aimed at improving the functionality and the degree of integration of the toolsets rather than extending the life cycle or providing variability in the life cycle or even supporting novel modelling techniques.

Vendors who were early in the market with application generators integrated their products with front end analysis and design tools. Those who specialised in analysis and design workbenches have recognised the need for these to work in the context of an information strategy plan and hence fronted their product with a strategic planning tool.

Many of their toolsets are targeted at very specific development methods such as SSADM or Information Engineering. Some of them enforce the method and this is often seen as an advantage. In as much as it keeps development staff on the straight and narrow, it is indeed an advantage. The problem is that many of today's applications are better developed by an alternative path to the straight and narrow— rapid prototyping for example. Some of the tool vendors have recognised this and are ensuring their toolsets **will** support variants on the standard routes and handle alternative representations of development information. At the end of the day, though, many have earned their reputation from adherence to a rigorous method and cannot easily support any other approach. They perhaps regret that they could not use their own tools to define their tools. If they **had**, they might now be able to take advantage of the CASE approach and regenerate alternative designs of tools with some ease!

What we are now seeing from a few vendors, however, **is** the emergence of a new approach to CASE: so-called second generation CASE. I am referring to such products as the Ipsys Tool Builder's Kit and Systematica's Virtual Software Factory. They are more like meta CASE tools or CASE tool generators. The rules of a systems development method, and the graphical representation of objects and relationships within the method, are described to the generator which then builds a rule-base and a diagram editor specifically for that method. Both the products mentioned are UNIX windows-based and take advantage of many of the workstation facilities. Each has much built-in functionality which can be incorporated into the method specification to handle such matters as consistency and completeness checking in models and object definitions.

Such second generation toolsets therefore enable specific or bespoke method toolsets to be developed. The scope and functionality of these is limited only by the scope and functionality of the chosen method. So, for example, a range of objects and relationships can be defined and a comprehensive set of graphical models described in which these will be represented. Suffice it to say that full function toolsets to support methods such as SSADM and IE have been built using these second generation toolsets.

It is not the purpose of this paper to consider in detail the functionality or feasibility of second generation CASE toolsets. Rather, I want to discuss whether the development of a bespoke CASE tool can be justified—what the benefits are and whether they can be achieved in other ways.

SECOND GENERATION CASE

In this section I want to discuss how second generation CASE tools came to be, and why we should consider them as serious contenders to aid the process of software development.

In the early '80s the Alvey Programme was established, and had as one of its major aims the improvement of the software engineering process. Too many software projects were seen to run into difficultly: greatly exceeding their budgets, taking many times longer to complete than anticipated and, in many cases, being abandoned before completion. A key objective was to provide better control of software engineering projects. The Integrated Project Support Environment, or ISPE, was seen as an important deliverable of the Programme.

In order to control software projects, it was necessary to establish some kind of framework for them, and hence be able to monitor deliverables being produced at each stage. It was recognised by several of the research groups that this gave them a platform in which to construct tools to aid the production of the deliverables. Two of the major contenders in this field were a group working with Plessey in Bournemouth, and a group working with Software Sciences. Out of their project grew two companies. Systematica with their Virtual Software Factory (VSF) and Ipsys with their Tool Builders Kit (TBK). Both products were built on a Unix platform and now benefit from the X-Windows environment and many other Unix facilities. As discussed above, what both of these tools offer is, in effect, a generator for building a bespoke CASE toolset. The rules of a chosen development approach are described to the generator, together with the forms of representation to be used for system objects and their relationships. A diagram editor and rule based system are then generated to support the development approach. Much use is made of macros and templates to build the framework—and this does impose some restrictions on the functionality of the toolset which is generated. But the secret of success lies in defining the rules of the method precisely, and correctly modelling the objects and relationships to be represented. Given that this is achieved, then a toolset can be built in a relatively short time.

Some people feel it is outrageous to even contemplate building a bespoke CASE tool! But we must be careful before we judge—it depends **who** is building it and for what purpose. The average dp shop with ten developers is not going to justify such a project. At the other extreme, IBM's decision to use Systematica's Virtual Software Factory to build their BSDM support tool makes a lot of sense (SDM, 1991). The alternative of building a toolset from scratch would have taken longer, been very much more costly, and not benefited from the available technology. The cost is naturally a factor in any decision to take this path—and here perhaps is the biggest surprise. With a cost of around $\leq$100K for the generator and perhaps the same again for development, the builder ends up with an organisation wide licence for a whole life cycle toolset at a cost less than equipping twenty developers with a proprietary toolset each. Of course there is then the small question of maintenance of the resulting toolset, and the perhaps larger question of enhancing it to integrate with other development tools. To take some kind of view on this we really need to consider the future role of CASE and how it fits into the development, maintenance and re-development life cycle as a whole.

THE ROLE OF CASE IN FUTURE DEVELOPMENT

CASE has already developed from providing diagramming support to specific system analysis and design techniques to cover most elements of the life cycle in a reasonably well integrated way. Integration is achieved by sharing definitions of the objects and relationships described in some form of dictionary or encyclopedia. In the most advanced toolsets this dictionary is shared amongst developers. In others it is, in effect, a single-user dictionary perhaps with some crude form of check out of objects to other tool users and consolidation back into the central dictionary. The inaccessibility of dictionary information to other tools, or other developers, is a major inhibitor to the effectiveness of CASE today. In simple data processing terms, we have been striving for a shared data environment for many years now. Throughout businesses, and for many different purposes, we have a need to take a different view of consistent underlying data. The same is true throughout the systems development and maintenance process. We have a constant need to know how and where particular data is represented in physical files, what its currency is, who is responsible for it, which programs access and maintain it? What purpose does is serve in the business? What activities will be affected if it's not available? These sorts of issues are especially important if we are trying to see through the implementation of an information strategy plan. We constantly need to reflect back on the business objectives which are driving the plan and see whether they are being fulfilled.

We know, too, that a migration from our existing systems resources must play a key part in fulfilling future objectives. Indeed, currently around 80% of systems development resources are involved with the maintenance and enhancement of existing systems. It is therefore important to have a complete and consistent view of those present system resources. These systems were mostly built long before CASE tools were even thought of, and today's CASE tools have a real problem in capturing structured knowledge about such systems and hence supporting their re-development.

A particular aspect of re-development of interest today is migration and distribution of systems to new hardware and software platforms. Communications technology and the availability of high performance PCs and workstations now make distributed applications and distributed data almost essential. Here again, there is little tool support available for the design of distributed database schemas and the transformation of a single (mainframe) application into a multi-platform, co-operative processing application. Indeed, many CASE tools are weak at all aspects

ACTIVITY	OBJECTS OF INTEREST	COMMENT
Business Strategic Planning	Business mission and objectives, strategies, organisation structure, business activities, critical success factors, key performance indicators. Business and IT opportunities.	This is the driving force for system development.
Information Strategy Planning	The above plus information needs, corporate data elements, information architecture, IT infrastructure definition, current systems architecture.	Defining the desired IT and IS infrastructure to meet business needs.
Business Systems Requirements	Information architecture, systems scope, entity-relationships, business processes, systems architecture.	
Business Systems Design	Data flows, logical data structures, process descriptions.	
Prototyping	Screen design, menu design, first cut database design, procedure definition, database navigation.	
Technical Analysis	Current systems architecture, current physical database(s), current code structures.	This is effectively to consider re-engineering or re-use in line with information strategy plan.
Technical Design	Transformation of above logical and physical objects to map onto required architecture. Test harness. Configurations.	
Construction	New data structures, new or transformed system components, application control structures.	
Testing	Test results, performance indicators.	
Implementation	Users, access permission, data conversion plan, implementation plan.	
Post Implementation Review	Fault reports. Task actuals. Performance measures.	
Change Control	Change requests, fault reports, version plan.	

of transformation of a business requirement into any form of technical design.

We see, then, that the scope of the activities coming under the general umbrella of "systems development" is already broad and growing. It would perhaps be helpful if we were just to define the scope of the overall process, and then analyse how it can best be supported by tools. I will do this by defining all the major activities and listing the major object of interest to those activities, together with key relationships (see p. 142).

SYSTEMS DEVELOPMENT ACTIVITIES

There is of course a major snag in presenting activities in this way, namely that it suggests a linear development path, whereas it is in reality iterative. We constantly need to refer back to earlier stages. Furthermore since there is an implied decomposition from an overall strategy to individual systems components—we need to refer between related, parallel developments to maintain the overall integrity of the process.

Overall, we need knowledge of the current business strategy (which is a moving target), knowledge of the implied information needs and how they are being addressed by current developments, also knowledge of present systems, which may or may not address the information needs. The tools we use to progress the above activities need both to manage and use all this knowledge. Little wonder, therefore, that we hear so much talk from the major vendors about **repository** (Xephon, 1989). Without a shared knowledge base, our tools cannot hope to survive the rigours of the dynamic development process!

So, what we come down to then is a requirement for a rich set of tools capable of viewing a whole plethora of knowledge in a variety of ways—each adding their own particular value to the development process (Burdick, 1991).

It is my belief that we should firmly separate considerations about the repository (of knowledge to support systems development) from the tools which support the development process itself.

There are several attempts being made to define some standards for repository (IRDS, PCTE, ATIS, etc) (Jones, 1991). These must quickly converge on something which the major CASE vendors can subscribe to (lest the IBM Repository definition becomes the de facto standard). With this in place we might then be able to interface the portfolio of tools we need to manage and manipulate the array of objects which have a part to play in the systems development process. Undoubtedly, second generation CASE (Meta-CASE) tools will have a part to play in building the specific technique related tools we will need at points in the development life cycle. I believe, though, that their place is as a component of an overall CASE strategy and not as a means for generating an all-embracing CASE platform for any particular development method. Structured development methods are a current "fad" in my estimation. Other branches of engineering don't need "methods" or "methodologies". They just have sound principles applied in a common sense way to each problem. We need the same—namely, a portfolio of techniques (supported by tools) which are rich enough to support us through the very varied cycle of responses to business needs and opportunities. The underlying need is well defined: to capture relevant business data and manage it in a consistent and coherent form; then to be able to view it and to process it so as to deliver a wide variety of information to support business endeavours.

What we need to concentrate on, I believe, is harnessing tools to the knowledge base. Defining the scope of the required knowledge base is a key task within any organisation.

It will not be defined implicitly or explicitly by any repository, since the latter must be open to incorporate the range of objects relevant to a particular organisation at a point in time (Olle & Black, 1989). Once the scope of objects and relationships to be maintained in the repository is defined then populating it and maintaining it is the next big problem. Repository administration is a task likely to be an order of magnitude bigger than the task of the data administrator today!

Software tools will be needed to support repository administration, as well as to enable developers and end users to be able to make use of the repository. An intelligent browser to help find objects of potential use, editors, as well as the full range of diagramming and application generation tools we have in the systems development tool bag today. Also, guidance tools to help run projects and guide developers through the steps necessary to fulfil their customers' requirements.

Speculating about how we might want to do things in the future is perhaps rather dangerous, but the point I really want to make is that future development is likely to be very different to the way we do development today. Hence, we should be addressing the prospects in a very open way—laying ourselves some flexible foundations to support whatever tools we might require. To this end, second generation CASE may have a part to play. My experience with such tools suggests that they are probably trying to generate too tightly integrated a toolset: a closed toolset, rather than the very open tools we seek which can be integrated with others through the repository.

REFERENCES

Lewis, J. (1990). Second Generation CASE. *Ipsys Software plc.*

Software Development Monitor (1991). The UK Approach to AD/Cycle. April 1991, P7.

Xephon (1989). The Repository—centre for all CASE tools. *Xephon Consultancy Report.*

Burdick, P. (1991). CASE Repositories *Ipsys Software plc.*

Jones (1991). Current Progress in Repository Technology *Savant Technical Paper.*

Olle & Black (1988). Data Levels in IRDS. *BCS Database, 1988.*

10

A Comparative Review of the ISO IRDS, the IBM Repository and the ECMA PCTE as a Vehicle for CASE Tools

T. William Olle

1. INTRODUCTION

There are three very distinct approaches being put forward for the handling of the data associated with CASE tools. The aim of this paper is to review how they are different and where the similarities lie. Both CASE tool suppliers and user organizations need to gain an appreciation for the three approaches and a second aim of this paper is to motivate a more in depth comparative analysis.

One of the main similarities is that the three pieces of work recognize (explicitly or implicitly) the concept of systems on different level pairs (pairings of types and instances). The application level pair is the bottom one, and the application types are instances on the next higher level pair which (in ISO IRDS) terms is the dictionary level pair. Since a dictionary has a structure in the same way as any other database, and

CASE: Current Practice, Future Prospects. Edited by Kathy Spurr and Paul Layzell
© 1992 John Wiley & Sons Ltd

most importantly needs to be extensible, the dictionary definition is the very important third level pair.

The ISO IRDS work consists of two international standards with more to come. The two extant standards are the IRDS Framework and the IRDS Services Interface. The former provides an overall architecture for a family of IRDS standards and relates closely to the ISO Reference Model of Data Management. The IRDS Services Interface standard is a standard for the dictionary definition level. It is the intent that it be used to define "content standards". The data associated with CASE tools is a good example of the kind of data which can be handled in a content standard.

A summary of each approach is presented together with an indication of the documentation used. This is followed by the presentation of a number of relevant characteristics and an assessment of how each approach caters for each characteristic. To distinguish the assessment of how each approach caters for a characteristic, this is printed in italics, whereas the presentation of each characteristic is in a normal type font. Each approach is referred to in the summary and in the assessment by an acronym—IRDS, REPOS, PCTE.

Any comment in quotes is a quote from one of the documents reviewed in preparing this paper. The references to the documents on which this comparison is based are included in the summary of each approach and collected at the end of the paper.

2. ISO INFORMATION RESOURCE DICTIONARY SYSTEM

The ISO standards work on Information Resource Dictionary Systems (IRDS) is described in two standards documents as follows:

IRDS FW ISO/IEC IS 10027 IRDS Framework (published 1990)
IRDS SI ISO/IEC DIS 10728 IRDS Services Interface (published 1991)

2.1. Summary of IRDS

The key notions presented in IRDS FW include the idea of specific level pairs (or data levels) for application, dictionary and dictionary definition. The level pairs of concern in the two IRDS standards are the dictionary definition level pair and the dictionary level pair.

IRDS FW contains a processor architecture showing how various processors including a database controller are positioned relative to each other. The aim of this at the time it was written was to establish a basis for harmonising the ISO work with an early ANSI IRDS standard (X3.138) which was for a Command Language and Panel Interface.

The cornerstone of the IRDS SI standard is a definition of a set of 27 SQL tables which collectively comprise the set of IRD Definition tables. These tables are defined using ISO SQL2 and making extensive use of referential constraints and check clauses to capture the rules which the data stored in these tables (which comprise a dictionary definition database) has to satisfy.

The content of 17 of these tables comprises the structure of an IRD (or dictionary database). For example, if the dictionary were to be used as a container for SSADM4 specifications, then the dictionary definition tables would contain the names of the set of tables and columns, which, when created, could in turn be used to record the results of an SSADM4 requirements analysis or requirements specification. This could include the results of preparing a logical data model and/or a data flow analysis.

The 17 tables defined to contain the structure of a dictionary in fact represent (among other things) a definition of the SQL2 "data modelling facility". This means that a dictionary database should conform to the same structuring rules as any SQL2 database and can be accessed by any SQL2 compatible product.

The definition level, in addition to defining 17 tables to contain the structure of a dictionary also contains tables to support what are referred to as "added value functionality". The main example of this is version control. The specifications stored in a dictionary are typically, but not necessarily, the kind of specification which support the iterative process of system development. An important part of IRDS SI is then a generalized approach to version control. Each dictionary object has one or more versions. Data in the dictionary tables then relates to a version of this object.

3. AD/CYCLE AND REPOSITORY

The IBM work on AD/Cycle and Repository (REPOS) is described in several documents. Those used in preparing this review are the following:

[1] Repository Manager/MVS. General Information Version 1 Release 2 GC26-4608-1

[2] Repository Manager/MVS. Repository Modelling Reference Version 1 Release 2 SC26-4620-0

[3] Systems Application Architecture. Common Programming Interface Repository Reference

[4] Repository Manager Overview of Repository Manager-Supplied Entity Relationship Model

3.1. *Summary of REPOS*

AD/Cycle is IBM's Application Development Life Cycle. Repository is the name given to the structured container in which specifications are stored as one goes through the life cycle.

Conceptually, AD/Cycle can be thought of as a framework for, and a set of, application development tools. "The framework is provided ... to support the integration of tools through a consistent user interface, work station services, an AD information model, tool services, repository services, and library services that provide control for defining and sharing application development data."

The Repository Manager uses "three views of information that permit you to specify both data and function from three perspectives: a global repository perspective, a repository application or tool perspective, and a physical storage perspective." These are referred to as the "conceptual view", the "logical view" and the "storage view".

The conceptual view represents data that is common across all tools and functions in the repository. Executable procedures can be defined at the functional level of the conceptual view to ensure the integrity of the information.

The logical view is the repository's "database" of tool functional specifications. It defines the subsets of conceptual view information to which tools have access, and specifies the way tools will process information.

The storage view represents how repository information is physically represented. Repository Manager uses DB2 to store repository information.

4. ECMA'S PORTABLE COMMON TOOL ENVIRONMENT

The ECMA standards work on Portable Common Tool Environment (PCTE) is described in the following document.

Introducing PCTE+ ECMA/TC33/89/48. Copyright April 1989.

This document is not the complete PCTE+ description which is understood to be about 400 pages. This means that some characteristics may be incompletely or incorrectly addressed in this paper.

4.1. Summary of PCTE

"PCTE+ is a tool support interface (or tool interface) that, with the addition of appropriate tools, provides an environment for the development and maintenance of software applications." It is an aim of PCTE to "support inter-operability of tools and data between such PCTE based environments".

One of the goals addressed by PCTE's is the following: "to support an environment that is based on the entity relationship model. That is, it must provide a distributed database management system that manages data as entities".

To meet this and other goals, the PCTE interfaces provide "a distributed database. In a PCTE-based environment, the central database of information is called the object base and is transparently distributed across the network of work stations. It is structured in such a way that it reflects the software development activity it supports."

"The PCTE Object Management System (OMS) is an information management system that accesses and manages the object base in response to requests from users and tools. It defines objects (with or without contents), relationships between objects, and attributes of objects and relationships, as the basic items of the object base."

PCTE is independent of any programming language and currently provides interfaces for tools written in both C and Ada.

5. TECHNICAL CHARACTERISTICS

5.1. Prevailing Paradigm

This characteristic and the name given here to the characteristic may seem obscure. However, it is useful to recognize that the technological driving force underlying one approach may be significantly different from that underlying others. The term "prevailing paradigm" is used to refer to this driving force.

Some examples of typical paradigms are the following. Programming is probably the oldest. Approaches with this driving force tend to place major emphasis on the design of the suite of programs required.

Database management is another paradigm. The emphasis with this paradigm is on a detailed data model although sometimes it is not clear whether the emphasis of the data model is as an analysis of the data associated with the requirements or as a detailed prescription of the database design.

The "object oriented" paradigm is the most recent to emerge. It is closely related to the programming paradigm and is based on the idea of extending object oriented languages to handle the problem of what is perceived as "persistent data" (in other words a database which persists after an executing program has completed its task). The use of the term "object" does not necessarily imply that the object oriented paradigm is used.

IRDS is based on the database paradigm.

Many paradigms have played a role in the design of REPOS. Database, programming and object orientation are all in evidence. No single paradigm prevails.

A significant part of the PCTE+ functionality is the specification of what is a fairly general purpose data base management system. Nevertheless, the underlying paradigm is very much the programming paradigm. The object management system is for use by programmers.

5.2. Focus

This characteristic relates to the three possible focuses for a technique or possibly for an information systems life cycle stage as stored in a dictionary. Alternatively, the focus can be for the use of a technique, implying that a given technique can be used for different purposes.

Sometimes the focus is on the business with temporary disregard for the computerized system aspects. For example, some techniques are meaningful only when applied to business aspects.

There is a considerable body of expertise among computer scientists which focuses sharply on the internals (as opposed to the externals) of computer software. Various programming design techniques have exactly this focus. Algorithms for optimising the indexes in databases to achieve best performance also fall into this category.

Finally, there is the interface between the business and the computerised system. In hardware terms this is typically a screen. The interface to a computerized system can usually be designed prior to the design of the internals such as those mentioned in the preceding paragraph.

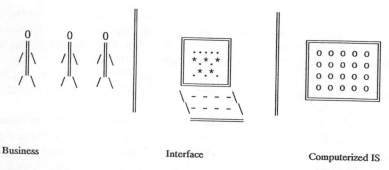

Figure 1

Focus on the interface between human users and a computerized system has two sub-characteristics. One is specific to the information system and covers the specification of the user tasks or user functions which a user is able to initiate from the interface. It also covers assignment of user tasks to menus, and the hierarchical structure of the set of menus.

The other covers the general aspects such as "look and feel", pull down menus, mouse technology and in general what kind of interface technology, including tactile and voice, which the user employs to move through a menu hierarchy and to initiate a user task.

This characteristic applies in this review not only to the content of the dictionary, but also the way in which the dictionary product itself is constructed or intended to be constructed. This also has a focus

In IRDS, a technique supporting any focus can be recorded in a dictionary database. An IRDS conforming to the IRDS SI standard would be built with the focus of a computerized IS. However, a product based on the SI standard would need to provide its own support with an interface focus. (In this way ISO IRDS is different from ANSI IRDS (X3.138) in that the latter defines two human user interfaces.)

In REPOS, enterprise modelling has the business focus. There is a concept of a dialogue which has an interface focus. There are alternative approaches possible to designing the internals of a computerized system. The exact focus of REPOS is not clear from the documents reviewed.

The focus of PCTE+ is the internals of a computerized system.

5.3. Distribution

For each of the three focuses described in the preceding section, distribution techniques may be used. The business may be distributed and appropriate techniques are needed to established how. A centralized or distributed computerized system may be appropriate. The business may be centralized in one geographic location and the interfaces to a centralized computer system scattered around the location.

The centralized computer system may itself be distributed implying possibly a distribution of data and possibly a distribution of data and processing power.

The IRDS FW considers distribution aspects. It is the intention to make use of other ISO standards such as RDA (Remote Database Access) to allow access to a dictionary from a remote system. ISO IRDS SI standard has been encouraged to avoid involvement with the distribution characteristic on the grounds that distribution is being considered on a more general level (for all level pairs) as part of an overall architecture in the ISO Reference Model of Data Management (DIS 10032).

In REPOS, the problems associated with distribution are not mentioned explicitly.

"PCTE+ supports:

> *an architecture based on a network of workstations*
> *the distribution of processes and the communication between processes*
> *management of special data represented as replicated objects*
> *management of workstations and the network"*

"Although a process cannot migrate from the workstation on which it started, there is no limitation on its ability to access remote resources."

PCTE+ manages replicated data. "The choice of which data to replicate is a system installation and administration consideration."

5.4. Information Systems Life Cycle

The term "information systems life cycle" is used in this paper rather than a project life cycle, because the former may subsume the latter. For example, a project life cycle may cover only the analysis and design parts of the life cycle.

Every approach life cycle breakdown. There are different numbers of stages, different names for them, and different boundaries between them. It follows that a life cycle with a large number of stages, each well defined but restricted in scope, has a better chance of mapping to life cycles with a coarser stage breakdown.

In IRDS, the concept of "IRD content status" is intended to allow a dictionary user to define his own life cycle stages. This functionality is likely to be refined and improved in the first extension of IRDS SI.

Closely associated with REPOS, the AD/Cycle is as follows:

planning
analysis/design
produce
build/test
production/maintenance.

However, in theory AD/Cycle is methodology independent which presumably implies that a user of the product could define his own life cycle.

In PCTE, an object base can be "structured to reflect the software development activity it supports". This implies an approach similar to that of IRDS.

5.5. Conceptual Logical and Physical Aspects

This taxonomy is used in some approaches. In some interpretations, it can be seen to compare with the focus characteristic introduced in section 5.2 with the caveat that logical and interface are not necessarily a good match. This means that both logical and physical relate to the internals of the computerized system.

Another way of viewing the conceptual, logical, physical breakdown is in a time continuum and hence related in some way to life cycle stages.

The taxonomy originates in database technology of the mid-seventies and originally related to different ways of looking at data. The logical aspect or model related to a specific way of modelling data in a class of DBMS product (such as network, relational, hierarchical). The physical was the stored representation of the data represented according to a logical data model. The conceptual was some view of the data which transcended the requirements to represent the data according to some logical data model.

The IRDS SI regards data in the same way as ISO SQL2 regards data. This is certainly not in physical terms, but it is a matter of choice whether one refers to it as conceptual or logical.

In REPOS, the first two of these three terms are used to refer to different perspectives of the repository (see 3.1). "Conceptual" implies "global" and "logical" implies "for one tool". These meanings are at variance with those originally intended.

PCTE does not consider this taxonomy.

5.6. Role of Techniques

Examples of techniques are data modelling, data flow analysis, Petri nets and cross reference tables or matrices showing the relationships between pairs of concepts.

Information systems methodologies prescribe a sequenced set of techniques and each technique has a clearly defined place and role.

SSADM4 has the interesting approach that it defines a set of techniques several of which can be used in more than one stage in its life cycle.

The IFIP Working Group 8.1 "Framework for Understanding" [1] concentrates heavily on this characteristic as it relates to methodologies. It identifies and relates the components of several widely used techniques

With IRDS, a representation of the components generated by any technique may be stored in a dictionary database. However, IRDS SI does not define any techniques. This would be the role of ISO IRDS standards still under development. Such standards are referred to as IRDS content standards.

It is the aim of REPOS to support any technique that a user may wish to use.

PCTE+ supports techniques by supporting tools which embody them. "The main design goals of PCTE are to support the construction of integrated tools sets which are widely portable over a range of environments, and to support interoperability of tools and data between such PCTE based environments."

5.7. Data Modelling

This characteristic is related to the role of techniques characteristic described in the preceding section.

Data modelling is widely used and there is growing acceptance of the importance of some kind of data modelling technique. in approaches to computerized systems on any level (see 6.3). Some approaches regard data modelling as the lead technique. This means that a data model is developed prior to an associated process model. This would be the case in approaches with a prevailing database paradigm.

There are also many kinds of data modelling technique. This generalisation applies without taking into account the additional variations in the forms of representation used.

Data modelling plays a major role in IRDS SI. The standard makes extensive use of the data modelling facility provided by ISO SQL2. The associated schema definition statements are used as a definition formalism for defining the dictionary definition level tables. The data modelling facility for use by those defining the structure a dictionary (or some part of it) is that of SQL2. This is a different role from the role of a definition mechanism for definition level tables.

Any data modelling technique which a user wishes to represent in a dictionary as part of his methodology may be defined (using ISO SQL2 as the definition technique).

REPOS uses different data modelling techniques for different purposes. An SQL based technique is used only on the storage level. The technique used for enterprise modelling is a variant of the entity relationship modelling technique. The technique used for modelling tools is a different variant.

PCTE+ introduces its own data modelling technique which is "based on the entity-relationship model". The PCTE+ data modelling technique is not intended for use by methodology users. It is intended as a means of representing tools in what is called an object base.

The relationships appear to be binary (that is associating two objects). Each relationship consists of two links—one in each direction. Hence a relationship is "a mutually dependent pair of links". Links can be created explicitly.

"The user can associate attributes, whose values represent specific properties, to objects and links and as a result also to relationships."

"To support the typed structure of the object base, objects, links, relationships and attributes are typed. That is each instance of an object, link relationship and attribute is created from a pre-existing type definition."

A cardinality (one or many) is associated with a link type "A link type can be declared independently of a relationship type." (The term "relationship" clearly is used to refer to an instance rather than to a type as is the possibly unfortunate widespread practice.)

5.8. Process Modelling

Data flow analysis is an example of one of the most widely used process modelling techniques. As with data modelling it is possible to include a process model for analysing the business, defining the interface between business and computerised system and for defining the internals of a computerised system.

For any approach based on the programming paradigm, some kind of process modelling is always found. It will typically have a focus on system internals but may include one or both of the other focuses.

In IRDS, process modelling techniques may be represented in a dictionary.

It is the aim of REPOS to support any process modelling technique that a user may wish to use.

In PCTE, a set of "OMS operations" is defined. Users can "navigate the object base, by specifying a sequence of "link names from a specified object." User can "modify the object base ... by creating and deleting objects, but always in strict accordance with type definitions...". This kind of process modelling has the focus of the internals of a computerized system (see 2.2).

5.9. Event Modelling

A process (in both business and computerized system) consumes resources and endures for a measurable period of time. An event happens at an instant in time and does not consume resources. There is a school of thought which claims that techniques based on events are more precise and lead to a better information system than techniques based on processes. Others claim that event modelling is mandatory for certain kinds of time critical systems such as process control systems.

One can analyse the events which happen in a business—such as fire employee, send purchase order, and file for bankruptcy. One can also define the events which may happen in a computerized system—such as various kinds of interrupts or events based on the calendar clock.

It is important not to confuse event modelling as described here with the concept of cross referencing data and process (for example preparing a matrix in which it is indicated that one needs to be able to delete a row from a table).

In IRDS, event modelling techniques may be represented in a dictionary.

It is the aim of REPOS to support any event modelling technique that a user may wish to use.

PCTE does not explicitly consider event modelling.

5.10. Access Control

Access control is a requirement for all on-line system and a dictionary system would typically be an on-line system. It is necessary to define who may use which parts of the computerized system and under what circumstances. Typically one has to analyze the requirements for access control using a business focus. Subsequently it is necessary to define the access control system in terms of the interface between the human user and the computerized system.

Access control is part of the overall security problem. Other aspects of security include authentication of user identifications and non-repudiation (in distributed systems using communications protocols).

In IRDS, it is possible to define privileges on working sets (in addition to the access control facilities provided in SQL2). This means a user must have an authorization to use a working set and possible a different authorisation to change its content.

In REPOS, access control restrictions may be defined in the conceptual view and Repository Manager will then map them through to the other levels.

PCTE+ has an extensive discussion of access control facilities. "All OMS objects have an access control list which defines the discretionary rights that designated groups have on the object."

"These access rights are explicitly granted or denied to designated individual users, user groups or program groups."

"Access rights can be left undefined for a group." This means that access to the object by a member of the group is denied.

5.11. Version Control

When a methodology is being used, the specifications which are developed using the various techniques such as data modelling and process modelling are always developed iteratively. If there are many groups working on the inter-related specifications separately, it is necessary to keep track of who is using which version.

The introduction of a version control system is seen as a management function.

In IRDS, the version control mechanism is based on the definition of "working set". A working set comprises a set of objects. A new working set can be based on an existing working set. When a dictionary user wishes to see a working set, then a process of materialisation takes place which effectively produces the most recent version of each object.

With REPOS, this characteristic is not considered in documents reviewed

"PCTE+ provides a mechanism for specifying and implementing versioning policies, in which multiple versions of entities are maintained. PCTE+ version management facilities also support version management of composite entities. If a composite entity represents a configuration, then tools working in that configuration will also work in successive versions of that configuration."

(The document studied does not explain its use of the term "configuration" in this context. It is not in the otherwise comprehensive glossary.)

5.12. Configuration Management

There are two aspects to configuration management. One is during the life cycle and it is concerned with keeping track that the system being designed and constructed in fact relates in a meaningful way to the requirements which were specified at an earlier phase in the life cycle. The concept of **traceability** is used to describe this facility.

The other aspect of configuration is relevant when a system is installed at various locations. These may be different locations in the same distributed system. It is also possible that the computerized system is being sold to customers in different places. The system may be changed for various reasons after it has been installed.

In either case, it is desirable to keep track of who has which configuration of the system installed at any point in time. This is analogous to the problem well known to manufacturers of complex products such as aircraft and cars.

IRDS FW mentions configuration management, but it is not considered further in IRDS SI. However, a computerized configuration management system could be handled in the same way as a computerized project management system.

For REPOS, configuration management is not considered in the documents reviewed.

It is intended that the tools supported by PCTE+ would include a configuration management system. The concept of a complex entity is intended to provide a basis for the management of complex configurations.

6. COMPUTERIZED ASPECTS

6.1. Computerized Help during Life Cycle

It is now widely accepted that the activities of planning for, analysing for and designing large complex computerized systems are almost impossible to progress without some kind of computerized assistance.

CASE tools are now widely accepted. Some are modest £200 packages for preparing and maintaining various kinds of diagrams associated with methodologies (such as data structure diagrams and data flow diagrams). Others cost about £ 200,000 and provide complete life cycle support from planning to automatic system construction. There are many interim points along this very wide spectrum. It is perhaps unfortunate and confusing that the term "CASE tool" should be used all through this wide range of capability. The term "CASE system" could be used for the upper end of the spectrum where the product is based on a DBMS and maintains a dictionary of data about the specifications.

The evaluation and selection of a methodology are for many enterprises inextricably interwoven with the evaluation and selection of a CASE tool. Some choose a CASE tool and let this choice dictate the methodology they use. Depending on the CASE tool, the choice may impact only the choice of a technique.

The work of the ANSI accredited Electronic Industries Association (EIA) Committee on CDIF (CASE Data Interchange Format) should be mentioned. This Committee contains many CASE vendors and have developed a format which can be used for interchanging CASE.

One of the aims of IRDS is to facilitate the task of providing computerized assistance during the life cycle.

This is the main topic for REPOS.

The main aim of PCTE+ is to provide a means of underpinning computerized assistance during certain stages of the systems life cycle. It is not clear how PCTE+ would function in early stages such as planning and analysis. The main thrust is towards construction.

6.2. Construction Platform

The term "platform" is used in the industry by software vendors to refer to the set of hardware and software (typically manufacturers' software such as an operating system) on which a software vendor's product has been constructed and hence is available.

It is also useful to recognize this concept of a platform as a characteristic of the MHF. The concept is closely related to a life cycle stage typically called "system design" and also to the prevailing paradigm (see 2.7).

Some methodologies based on the database paradigm will tend to assume that the construction platform is some kind of DBMS. Others might be rather more specific and assume a relational DBMS. Finally one could go further and assume that the construction platform is a standard SQL compliant DBMS.

Methodologies based on the programming language paradigm will not make assumptions about the construction platform containing a DBMS. Object oriented methodologies may assume an object oriented DBMS.

Whether or not a methodology assumes or prescribes a construction platform is an important categorization of any methodology.

An obvious construction platform for an IRDS product is an SQL2 conforming product. However, IRDS SI states explicitly that this is not a requirement for a conforming implementation of IRDS SI.

REPOS recognizes that different construction platforms could be used. [4] provides a sub-model for IMS/VS and for COBOL.

To some extent, PCTE+ provides a construction platform to the tool builder. Chapters in the complete specification give "the implementor, system administrator and tool writer" some assistance if they wish to use either of the two programming languages C and Ada.

6.3. Data Levels

There may be more than one level of computerized system. On the bottom level is the application system. Data about the structure of its database and about the processes which may be performed on the data are regarded as being stored in a higher level system, typically in a data dictionary system.

For large systems, the amount of data to be stored in a dictionary may be correspondingly large and can differ substantially from one system to another. For example, one may consider access control data and configuration data to be stored in the dictionary system. However, the structure of what is to be stored in the dictionary needs to be defined and this requires a third level of data, here called the definition level.

An aspect of computerized assistance is the use of dictionary systems. The RMDM identifies life cycle support as one of the objectives for a data management system. (The term "data management system" was chosen several years ago to subsume both DBMS and dictionary system.)

While many would regard a data management system as having a role to play only during the operational stage in the life cycle, the RMDM emphasises that a dictionary is a special kind of database and that database is a repository in which data relevant to each stage in the life cycle is gradually built up. Furthermore this would be retained during the operation stage and used to support and facilitate the evolution stage of the information system.

The tie in between CASE tools and dictionary systems is yet to come (at least on the standardisation scene).

IRDS is built on the concept of data levels

A data level concept is part of REPOS although it appears to be different from IRDS.

This concept is implicit. The object base contains instances. The definitions of the types to which these instances conform are called "schema definition sets". These are represented in a so-called "meta-base" as objects. The meta-base is "automatically maintained by the creation and importation of type definitions in SDSs."

Furthermore "the schema of the meta-base is called the meta-schema".

7. ASSESSMENT OF IMPACT OF EACH APPROACH

7.1. IRDS

IRDS provides a container in which various kinds of specifications may be recorded. The data used by CASE tools is an obvious example but there are other examples of data of interest which should be stored in a dictionary. For example, an IRDS could be used as a container for the distribution data needed in a distributed system. The case is even stronger for an IRDS role in an open distributed system (namely one which conformed to a set of standards and was built not knowing at the time of design from which other distributed systems it might need to obtain data.

The impact of IRDS on the data processing community is going to be interesting. It is hard to predict what it will be exactly. In certain ways, there is a clear overlap with REPOS and with PCTE+.

7.2. REPOS

The potential impact of REPOS is extremely hard to assess. While it contains many ideas which support the direction for methodologies which CCTA and others are anxious to follow, it also contains some complications which seem unnecessary. Specifically, three different ways of modelling data are specified. Perhaps the most disturbing aspect is that the repository is an SQL compliant database (being based on DB2) but in order to access it one has to use an DL/I-like interface.

It is clear that IBM is placing considerable emphasis on AD/Cycle and Repository Manager. Many of their customers have been known to accept whatever IBM offers, although this tendency has been less apparent in the last decade as the customer base itself matures. Whether REPOS will a major impact on methodologies is anybody's guess.

7.3. PCTE

ECMA is the driving organization and there is a PCTE Promotion Group which is actively promoting PCTE at software engineering conferences. There is a free PCTE Newsletter which appear periodically with news of PCTE.

ECMA is currently seeking the best way to progress PCTE+ through ISO. The BSI Database Panel has been fully briefed on this effort. It is not clear that PCTE+ would fit well with the existing database standards given the strong SQL emphasis of the ISO database standards work.

When PCTE+ and IRDS are compared, a very clear "paradigm clash" is observable. The PCTE group have invented large parts of early 1970s style database technology in the process of carrying out their work. On the other hand, they have taken into account the problems of distribution and access control to a greater extent than IRDS.

8. CONCLUDING REMARKS

This paper has attempted to identify the similarities and differences which exist among three approaches to a container which can be used for holding the specification data generated by the use of CASE tools.

All three approaches offer a "structured container" in which CASE specifications can be recorded. In the IRDS approach, the container follows the same rules as ISO SQL2 and this must be seen as representing a significant economy for those using the container. A product will be significantly cheaper to build and hopefully the savings can be passed on to the users.

All three approaches make use of one or more data modelling facilities in their own construction. In each case the content of the container may be anything—including a representation of some data modelling facility or other. In all approaches it is important to distinguish among the various roles that data modelling facility can play.

The inconsistencies among the three approaches threaten the ideal of universally inter-operable systems. If an information system constructed using a container based on approach A subsequently wishes to inter-operate in some fairly complete sense with a remote system constructed using approach B then a mapping facility will be needed between the different representations used to define the content of the dictionaries of each.

It more be emphasized that this short paper has done no more than scratch the surface of a comparative analysis and a more in-depth analysis needs to be performed. The results of such an analysis need to be made widely available in order to increase the understanding level which will be the basis for some very important decisions in the standards world, in the world of open and inter-operable systems and in the world of CASE systems.

Most of the following references have been included in the body of this paper in sections 2, 3 and 4. The references are collected here for convenience.

ACKNOWLEDGEMENT

The work in this paper is based on an extract from a report submitted to the Central Computer and Telecommunications Agency (CCTA) in March 1991. The author acknowledges the support received from CCTA in this work.

REFERENCES

[1] ISO/IEC IS 10027 IRDS Framework (published 1990)
[2] ISO/IEC DIS 10728 IRDS Services Interface (published 1991)
[3] Repository Manager/MVS. General Information Version 1 Release 2 GC26-4608-1
[4] Repository Manager/MVS. Repository Modelling Reference Version 1 Release 2 SC26-4620-0
[5] Systems Application Architecture. Common Programming Interface Repository Reference
[6] Repository Manager Overview of Repository Manager-Supplied Entity Relationship Model
[7] Introducing PCTE+ ECMA/TC33/89/48. Copyright April 1989.
[8] ISO/IEC DIS 10032 Reference Model of Data Management (published 1991)

11

DESMET—Determining an Evaluation Methodology for Software Methods and Tools

David Law, Tahir Naeem

ABSTRACT

DESMET—Determining an Evaluation Method for Software MEthods and Tools, is a leading edge collaborative research programme part funded by the DTI IED Advanced Technology Programme. The principal aim of DESMET is to address the problem of objective determination of the effects and effectiveness of methods and tools for the development and maintenance of software-based systems. DESMET is addressing this problem directly by:

- developing an evaluation methodology which will quantify the effects on developers productivity and on product quality;

- validating this methodology by carrying out a number of trial evaluations.

NCC Consultancy are lead partners in the project, and the other partners are **GEC-Marconi Software Systems, Racal Research** and the **Polytechnic of North London**. DESMET began work in November 1990 and is planned to complete by March 1994. This paper reports on the state of the project in mid-November 1991.

INTRODUCTION

The use of methods and software tools to assist the different activities involved in systems development has now become a major focus of attention and development.

Making a choice from the apparently very wide range of methods and tools available can in itself be a complex and costly process because, as well as being numerous, the products themselves are usually large and complex and can have complex inter-relationships with their prospective environment of use. Since the acquisition and installation costs can be very high—in addition to the consequential costs of project disruption and delay—making a wrong choice of methods and tools can be a big risk to an organisation (and to those who made the choice!). Hence their selection and introduction cannot be undertaken lightly.

Current ways and means of evaluating and selecting methods and tools, in isolation or in combination, do not guarantee that a good choice will be made. Furthermore, it is currently very difficult to demonstrate convincingly and objectively that a good choice was made and that the organisation is actually benefiting from this investment. The DESMET Project is addressing this problem directly by developing and validating an evaluation methodology which, amongst other things, will quantify the effects of the use of methods and tools on developers productivity and on product quality.

DESMET is a multi-company project partially funded by the UK Department of Trade and Industry and the Science and Engineering Research Council under the Information Engineering Advanced Technology Programme. The collaborators in DESMET are The National Computing Centre, The Polytechnic of North London, GEC-Marconi Software Systems and Racal Research Ltd. DESMET is extending the substantial work on methods and tools evaluation started during the 1980's, taking note of techniques used to produce the UK STARTS Guide (2nd Edition), recent work on measuring the effects of using methods and tools, and techniques used in disciplines with analogous evaluation problems such as education and medicine. The main advance will be in producing a comprehensive evaluation methodology which will enable independent and consistent evaluations to be made.

The project has recently completed its initial phase, a study of the state of the art in ways of evaluating the methods and software tools used in the development and maintenance of software-based computer application systems. This covered both the work of academic researchers and that of practitioners in industry and commerce, and also covered work in relevant areas of education and medicine (drugs trials in the medical area and curriculum content evaluation in education). It looked at qualitative and quantitative techniques, with the emphasis on quantitative. The 3-volume report of this study will be in the public domain around Spring 1992. References to some of the more important or influential works studied are given at the end of the paper.

At the time of writing the project is in the early stages of designing the methodology and firming up its detailed requirements, and in finding suitable projects in industry on which to do the validation trials. The trials phase of the project is scheduled to start in May 1992 and the project should complete by March 1994. This paper summarises current thinking on the principles to be embodied in the methodology, on its envisaged structure and major components, and on the issues that each will address.

MAIN FEATURES OF THE EVALUATION METHODOLOGY

The goal that the DESMET Project has set for developing an improved evaluation methodology is to provide a set of procedures and guidelines to permit the valid assessment of software methods and tools. The evaluation methodology should provide the following features:

- ensure that evaluations performed in different environments are comparable, and allow evidence for and against various methods/tools to be accumulated systematically;

- support the evaluation of methods and tools for any software production and maintenance activity;

- permit evaluations aimed at method or tool selection as well as those aimed at more general assessment;

- provide the means of assessing the impact of productivity and quality improvement programmes, and risk-reduction strategies;

- highlight potential barriers to take-up and successful use;

- provide firm guidelines to help the user decide which evaluation techniques are appropriate in the user's particular circumstances.

TARGET AUDIENCE

Several types of potential users are targeted:

1. Existing methodology and tool users who are interested in measuring their effect on software quality and productivity.
2. Organizations who are considering adopting a method, methodology or tool:

    (a) as an aid to "process" improvement as a continuing action. Such an organisation will probably have set a comprehensive measurement system to support their process improvement programme;
    (b) as an isolated or infrequent activity.

In both cases they would use DESMET to evaluate one or several methods, methodologies or tools.

3. Purchasers of bespoke systems who wish to evaluate a system suppliers use of good software engineering practices, in particular the methods and tools used.
4. Organizations who are interested in selecting a third party tool in order to sell and support it.
5. Vendors of methodologies and tools who would like to qualify their product. They would use DESMET reports as a promotional aid to market their product.
6. People interested in challenging the many unsubstantiated claims of methodology and tool vendors (for example, academic researchers, market competitors).
7. Indirect users who would use the published results of others applying the DESMET methodology.

PRINCIPLES, STRUCTURE AND ISSUES TO BE ADDRESSED

General Considerations

The experiences of evaluation in the disciplines of education and medicine make it clear that evaluation of methods used by or applied to human beings is extremely difficult; it is not just a peculiarity of the development of software. In software engineering, there has been an intensive search carried out since the late 1970s and through the last decade for a satisfactory evaluation method. Two main approaches, the qualitative and the quantitative, have been pursued in parallel and usually at a distance from each other. The DESMET state of the art study confirmed that there is still no obvious "best" way of performing an evaluation: all the approaches, both quantitative and qualitative, have advantages and disadvantages and are appropriate in some circumstances but not in others.

Furthermore, evaluators must be aware of special situations (in particular the safety-related systems area) where the emphasis in evaluation is very much on quality issues rather than productivity, and may relate to the ability of combinations of methods and tools to achieve a specified level of a quality attribute (e.g. safety integrity level). External requirements of customers and regulatory authorities may severely restrict choice in these areas. Legal requirements may exist to demonstrate that current best practice in development has been followed.

Methodology Design

Initial methodology design is taking place from the point of view of the end-user of the methodology. This has lead to the concept of a "user interface module" (known as EMS) and a number of procedural modules, which contain the technical methods of evaluation which DESMET provides and supporting procedures. EMS will help the user to decide which of the procedural modules should be used for a particular evaluation.

Evaluation Method Selection (EMS)

A number of factors need to be considered when matching the circumstances of a would-be evaluator to a particular evaluation method. EMS will be of the nature of a decision support system and will elicit a number of factors from the user which influence the choice of an appropriate evaluation approach and hence the procedural modules to be "invoked". Factors to be considered include:

- what is the purpose of the evaluation (e.g. selection, has an implementation produced the benefits expected, challenge a "vendor" claims) and what is it that ought to be tested;

- what type of object is to be evaluated (e.g. method, tool, methodology, toolset);
- what information is already available about the object;
- what methods of evaluation are available in these circumstances;
- what influences in the user's environment affect his ability to make evaluations (e.g. previous experience, value of proposed investment, time and resources available).

For example, it is clear that the concerns of evaluation for selection of methods and tools are different from those of evaluation after their implementation but have commonalities. There is a whole raft of concerns which are important influences on the choice of a particular method or tool within a functional category but not so important for post-implementation evaluation of effects on productivity and quality. These concerns include vendor stability and support levels, availability of training and consultancy, enhancement plans, hardware platforms, compatibility with methods and tools already in place, acquisition and support costs, and so on. There may, however, be confounding effects between some of these factors and the "merit" of the method or tool. For example, poor training of staff could mean that it is not being used properly and thus not achieving its full effect on productivity or quality.

The detailed requirements specification for EMS is being built up in terms of a number of usage scenarios. Structurally, it is likely to consist of a key decision module which will recommend what type of evaluation is appropriate and a number of other components (including links to other modules) which will collect the information to enable the right decision to be made.

Investment Analysis and Justification (INVA)

Apart from technical and environmental considerations, the problem still remains of justifying—both as a part of the selection process and after implementation—investment in methods and tools in terms that those who control investment money are familiar with. INVA will provide guidance in this area, in particular on the importance of collecting sound information on delivered productivity, quality and related costs. At the pre-selection stage it is important to set up hypotheses about the benefits (in financial terms) expected to be obtained that can be tested afterwards, expressed in terms of predicted effects and measurements to be made. INVA will also give guidance on the level of investment to be made in the evaluation process itself.

Process Maturity Assessment (PMA)

The previous experience and skills of the people using the new methods and tools is likely to affect the results of evaluation as well as the extent to which the results are likely to generalise to other circumstances. In addition, the attitude of the people to the new method/tool is likely to be critical to the evaluation process. It is therefore important to identify and "measure" state variables such as these in a systematic way and, hence, the process maturity of any software development organisation is likely to affect its ability:

(a) to use methods and tools effectively;
(b) to measure the impact of their use on software quality and productivity;
(c) to do the evaluations it wants to do.

PMA will pay particular attention to this issue. The extensions to the SEI Software Process Maturity Model appear to be a possible basis for the assessment and use of the results of the assessment (process maturity "level") in this context, but this is yet to be established.

Managerial and Sociological Issues (MANSOC)

A particularly important conclusion from the state-of-the-art study was that DESMET cannot concentrate solely on the technical and accountancy issues of evaluation. The distortions that the Hawthorne effect, introduction and learning curve effects, and experimenter influence can impose on the results of a evaluation have to be faced. Medical experience suggests that the effects of introducing a method or tool can be compared with the effects that a placebo and an actual drug have on a patient. The effect the method or tool has may well be determined in part by the extent to which the computer personnel believe that the method or tool will bring benefits (the placebo effect) and on the management style adopted in their organisation (the "doctor" or Hawthorne effect).

Avoiding or minimising these distortions has to be an important influence in selecting evaluation projects and setting up trials, and recognising that they may have occurred is important in analysing the results from previous evaluations, for example as part of a survey. These considerations will be particularly important in selecting and carrying out the DESMET trials projects.

Goal conflicts between staff and line departments can also cause problems with trials by making it difficult to ensure comparable evaluation procedures are followed across different divisions of a single company. This is a particular problem when a staff division is in charge of coordinating an evaluation programme and different line divisions are required to undertake the evaluations.

MANSOC will therefore include advice for organisations on such managerial and sociological issues associated with establishing evaluation programmes.

Experimental Design and Analysis (EXPDA)

Evaluation by the direct use of formal experimentation as such is unlikely to be appropriate in industrial situations, especially if the objective is selection. It, however looks feasible (with restrictions on replication) when diverse systems have to be created to meet high-integrity requirements. Most of the formal experiments reported have been done in academic institutions using students and small projects. Formal experiments appear to be usable and useful in the academic situation because replication and control over extraneous influences is possible. There are inherent limitations on the generalisability of the results from these experiments. It is unlikely that formal experiments could be used to evaluate a CASE "toolset" because the interactions between the different elements of toolset would be difficult to control.

In any case, statistical expertise is required to set up, monitor, analyse and interpret an experiment. It is unlikely that industry will readily accept this burden without support from some body (e.g. a consultancy company or a university, which can be costly) or unless tool support is available. However, the concepts of experimental design and statistical analysis of the results obtained are fundamental to the success of other forms of quantitative evaluation. EXPDA will give an introduction to the subject and point to standard works on the subject for those wishing to know detail.

Case Study Design and Analysis (CSDA)

The industrial experiences reported in the study confirm the need to make evaluation exercises realistic. This emphasises the importance of case studies as a means of quantitative evaluation: case studies are far more practical for industrial evaluations than formal experiments. However, there are good and bad case studies: the good case study being where there is a baseline to draw sound conclusions from the results of the case study. Typically, the baseline provides a means of comparing the effect of the method or tool with the situation before the method or tool was introduced. However, the results from a suitably chosen "control" project in parallel to the case study, ie not using the method or tool under evaluation, may also be used as a baseline.

Since there are few existing guidelines for conducting case studies, this is an area where DESMET will seek—by using the transferable principles and practices of experimental design—to make both a useful theoretical contribution to the State of the Art in evaluation as well as providing a method that would be attractive to industry. CSDA will formalise good practice for the conduct of case studies and, for example, will:

- avoid or minimise Hawthorne, experimenter and initial learning effects;
- use the notions of control groups, blocking and baselines to enable valid comparisons;
- minimise correlations between independent variables in multi-treatment studies;
- systematise the collection of information about state variables;
- provide guidance on appropriate statistical techniques for analysis of the results.

Survey Design and Analysis (SURVDA)

The availability of data from software projects which have used methods or tools, collected and maintained, by independent organisations or research institutions has facilitated the use of surveys by statistical analysis of stored data to evaluate the effects of methods, tools and techniques. The technique allows some of the rules of experimental design to be followed retrospectively so this can be a powerful aid to evaluation.

The correct use of survey data and the value of the results obtained depends very much on how the data was collected and the consistency and validity of the data. Survey data collected in one organisation is usually environment specific, and application of such results to specific method and tool evaluation should be treated with caution.

SURVDA in conjunction with the data collection module described later will give guidance on designing surveys and collecting and analysing data.

Cost Modelling (COSTM)

Mathematical project cost models offer a means of estimating what the effect of the use of a method or tool has been on project effort and timescale. This is done through the retrospective use of a locally-derived model or a locally-calibrated parametric model to estimate what the effort and duration of the project would have been if established practices had been used. COSTM will give advice on the derivation and application of these models.

Feature Analysis (FEA)

The strength of feature analysis is that it is flexible (also a weakness), is conceptually simple to understand and apply, and allows the evaluator to focus on what appears to be important in a particular situation. It does however have intrinsic serious weaknesses. With feature analysis, choosing a set of attributes or features is essentially a subjective activity—there is no scientific truth to be uncovered—and depends on the knowledge, viewpoints, backgrounds and interests of the individuals or groups chosen. It is usually difficult to demonstrate a direct causal link between features and delivered productivity and quality.

There is a further problem of subjectivity in selecting the measurement scales to be used in "scoring" an evaluation, and, even if a common scale is defined and used, in getting consistency in scoring between different judges on the same feature(s). (This was one of the main motivations for DESMET to produce an evaluation methodology which will enable independent and consistent evaluations to be made.)

In practice, feature analysis when applied at the lowest levels of decomposition can generate hundreds of attributes or features to be scored, as a result leaving the methodology or tool evaluator confused about how to make use of all this information. Application of the usual weighted ranking methods has to be done with great care. Further, at this level of use the question of the time and resources required to carry out the exercise is raised.

The methodology of feature analysis does not seem to have advanced beyond the level achieved in the production of the STARTS Guide, second edition; though recent work does show new areas of attention, for example ease of introduction into the organisation, organisational maturity with respect to use of methods and tools.

Despite its limitations, qualitative analysis by feature analysis remains the most often used technique of evaluation as part of selecting methods and tools. In the absence of a comprehensive and well-founded database of quantitative results from actual use of methods and tools, it is difficult to avoid feature analysis for the initial short-listing for selection process. In any case there will always be the problem of new or emerging products for which field-use experience does not exist, and situations in which explicit features are required.

For these reasons feature analysis has to be part of the DESMET methodology. FEA will attempt to define current best practice in feature analysis and give guidance for its effective use.

Qualitative Effects Analysis (QEA)

What is identified by DESMET as "qualitative effects analysis" looks promising as a possible bridge between subjective assessment of features (for selection purposes) and objective assessment by measurement of effects. An example of qualitative effects analysis is the direct estimation of the effects that use of certain techniques and methods will have on the levels of specified quality attributes of the resulting product.

QEA will contain techniques for estimating directly the impact of the use of methods and tools on the levels of those product and process attributes which would be measured post-implementation. Hence quantitative effects can be both estimated and measured. Direct estimation or measurement of qualities of interest can get around the problem of explosion into sub-components (features) that might contribute positively or negatively to quality but it is not known how much and under what conditions they can contribute.

Data Collection and Metrication (DCM)

One common thread underlying all quantitatively-based evaluations is the need for a valid method of interpreting results: i.e. a "baseline" against which productivity and quality changes can be assessed. In the case of formal experiments the baseline is usually built into the experimental design. In the case of industrial case studies and process improvement a baseline should be available prior to the evaluation exercise. In the case of analysing survey data the baseline is constructed from the available data. In all cases, however, measurement values must be valid and comparable. Users who want to introduce method and tools as part of an on-going process improvement programme are likely to need a set of common process measurements that are kept by all projects and monitored over a long time period. DCM will provide guidelines for establishing a measurement baseline.

However, it is clear that obtaining valid and comparable data from which to build a baseline is not as easy as it sounds. It is essential to have commonly agreed definitions of what things/attributes to measure and standard, repeatable and valid ways of measuring them. When selecting attributes and metrics, evaluators must be very aware of the dangers of using proxy or surrogate attributes and metrics instead of direct indicators of the desired end-point or end-effects.

DCM will also cover these issues of establishing and maintaining data collection systems, and will include guidelines for the selection of appropriate attributes and metrics. The GQM paradigm seems a particularly useful starting place for obtaining guidelines for the selection of attributes and metrics for specific evaluation exercises. However, it is clear that the GQM approach is not sufficient to cover all DESMET's requirements. In particular, the need for establishing general baselines as prerequisite for a general process improvement programme is less well supported by GQM: there is a need to look at other "dimensions" to pick up possible side-effects.

Data Collection and Storage System (DCSS)

DCSS is a PC-based software package that will provide valuable practical support to DCM in establishing and running a data collection capability. It gives support in the areas of: data model definition; data collection, validation and storage; metrics calculation and storage and subsequent analysis by external tools.

DCSS was originally developed as part of the ESPRIT MERMAID project, which is concerned with the development and validation of improved models for software cost estimation, and hence the DCSS was originally oriented towards data collection for cost estimation. A number of functional enhancements are in progress, to enable it to meet the more general requirements of DESMET.

Methodology Validation

To ensure the acceptability of the DESMET methodology to the software developing community it is essential to establish that it is both valid and useful. One of the challenges of the project is to develop and apply a set of criteria by which the evaluation methodology itself is to be evaluated. Important considerations are the costs of performing a DESMET-type evaluation against the extra benefits obtained from use of the evaluation information produced, as compared with evaluations done by local present practice.

The detailed criteria are under discussion but it is proposed to carry out a series of trials (beginning around May 1992) on suitable projects at the industrial partners sites, covering a range of methods and tools and the phases and activities of the system development and maintenance lifecycles. The type of trial required will vary according to the nature of the methodology module being assessed, but at each trials site data collection environments will be established or enhanced to provide control measures in order to ascertain the effects of each method or tool evaluated.

Results from the trials will enable the methodology to be refined and enhanced over the final six months of the project.

REFERENCES

Basili, V.R. and Reiter, R.W. (1981). A controlled experiment quantitatively comparing software development approaches, IEEE Transactions on Software Engineering, Volume SE-7, May 1981.

Basili, V.R., and Rombach, H.D. (1988). The TAME Project: Towards Improvement-Oriented Software Environments, IEEE Transactions on Software Engineering, vol 14, No 6, 1988.

Basili, V.R., Selby, R.W., and Hutchens, D.H. (1986). Experimentation in Software Engineering, IEEE Transactions on Software Engineering, vol SE-12,7, 1986.

Basili, V.R. and Selby, (1987). Comparing the effectiveness of software testing strategies, IEEE Transactions on Software Engineering, SE-13, December 1987.

Basili, V.R., and Weiss, D.M. (1982). Evaluating Software Development by Analysis of Changes: The Data from the Software Engineering Laboratory, Technical Report TR-1236, Computer Science Technical Report Series, University of Maryland, December 1982.

Basili, V.R., and Weiss, D.M. (1984). A Methodology for Collecting Valid Software Engineering Data, IEEE Transactions on Software Engineering, vol.SE-10, No. 6, November 1984.

Bishop, ESP, Barnes, Humpherys, Dahll, and Lahti, (1986). PODS- A Project on Diverse Software, IEEE Transactions on Software Engineering, vol SE-12, 9, 1986.

Boehm, B.W. (1981). Software Engineering Economics, Prentice-Hall, 1981.

Browne, J.C., Shaw, M. (1981). Toward a Scientific Basis for Software Evaluation, Software Metrics: An Analysis and Evaluation, (Perlis, Sayward, and Shaw, editors), MIT Press, pp 19–41, 1981.

Card, D.N., McGarry, F.M. and Page, G.T (1987). Evaluating Software Engineering Technologies, IEEE Transactions on Software Engineering, Vol.SE-13, No.7 July 1987.

Cook, V. H., Hartrum, T. H., Howatt, J. W., Woffinden, D. S. (1988). A Framework for Evaluating Software Development Methods, Proceeding of the IEEE 1988 National Aerospace and Electronics Conference (NAECON), 1988.

Curtis, B. (1981). Experimental Evaluation of Software Characteristics, Software Metrics: An Analysis and Evaluation, (Perlis, Sayward, and Shaw, editors), MIT Press, pp 61–75, 1981.

Davis, A.M., Bersoff, E.H., and Comer, E.R. (1988). A Strategy for Comparing Alternative Software Development Life Cycle Models, IEEE Transactions on Software Engineering, vol SE-14, 10, 1988.

DeMarco, T. (1982). Controlling Software Projects, Management Measurement & Estimation, Yourdon Press, 1982.

Disney, J., McCollin, C., and Bendell, A. (1990). Taguchi Methodology within Mechatronics, IMechE 1990, Paper C419/051.

Fenton, N. and Littlewood, B. (1991). Evaluating Software Engineering Standards and Methods Eurometrics 91 Conference Proceedings, Paris, March 1991, EC2.

Gilmore, D.J. (1990). Methodical Issues in the Study of Programming, Psychology of Programming, Editors J-Michael Hoc, T.R.G. Green, Samurcay, D.J. Gilmore, Academic Press, 1990

Kieback, A. and Niemeier, J. (1991). Selecting Methods and Tools for particular Environments: A Toolbased Approach Software Engineering Environments, Aberystwyth 1991.

Kitchenham, B.A. (1990). 'Which Metrics to Measure?', Software Tools 1990 Conference Proceedings, Blenheim Online.

Kitchenham, B.A, and Walker, J.G. (1989). A Quantitative approach to Monitoring Software Development, Software Engineering Journal, January, 1989.

Kitchenham, B.A, Kitchenham A.P., and Fellows J.B. (1986). The Effects of Inspections on Software Quality and Productivity, ICL Technical Journal, May 1986.

Law, D. (1988). Methods for Comparing Methods: Techniques in Software Development, NCC Publications, 1988.

Maddison R.N. (1983). Information System Methodologies, Wiley Heyden, 1983.

Marco, A. (1990). Software Engineering: Concepts and Management, Prentice-Hall, 1990.

Matsumoto, Y. (1989). An Overview of Japanese Software Factories, Japanese perspectives in Software Engineering, (Matsumoto, Y., and Ohno, Y., editors), Addison-Wesley, pp 303–320, 1989.

Merlet, J.M., and Dupont, C. (1991). Measurement of Quality on Clerical Systems: A Case Study, Eurometrics'91 Conference, Paris Mar. 1991.

McCall, J.A., Richards, P.K., Walters, G.F. (1985). Described in Quality Measurement and Modelling — State of the Art Report ESPIRIT REQUEST project ESP/300. July 1985.

Misra, S.K. (1990). Analysis CASE System Characteristics: Evaluative Framework, Information and Software Technology, vol.32, No.6, July/August 1990.

NCC (1987). The STARTS Guide, 2nd Edition A Guide to Methods and Software Tools for the Construction of Large Real-Time Systems.

Necco, C.R., Tsa, R.N.W., and Hoogeston, K.W. (1989). Current Usage of CASE Software, Journal of Systems Management, May 1989.

Olle, T.W. et al (1982). Information Systems Design Methodologies: A Comparitive Review, North-Holland.

Olle, T.W. et al (1983). Information Systems Design Methodologies: A Feature Analysis, North-Holland.

Olle, T.W. et al (1986). Information Systems Design Methodologies: Improving the Practice, North-Holland.

Panzl, D.J. (1981). A Method for Evaluating Software Development Techniques, The Journal of Systems and Software, 2, 1981.

Rombach, H.D. (1987). A controlled experiment on the impact of software structure on maintainability IEEE Transactions on Software Engineering, Vol. 13, No. 3, pps. 344–354, Mar. 1987.

Rombach, H.D., and Ulery, T.B. (1989). Improving Software Maintenance Through Measurements, Proceeding of The IEEE, Vol. 77, No.4, April 1989.

Rousseau, N.P., and Candy, L. (1991). A Pragmatic Approach to Software Development Tool Evaluation within the FOCUS Project, Psychology Programming Interest Group Workshop "The Evaluation of Software Development Tools", University College London, 15th March 1991.

Sayward, F.G. (1981). Design of Software Experiments Software Metrics: An Analysis and Evaluation, (Perlis, Sayward, and Shaw, editors), MIT Press 44–57, 1981

Schas, S. R. (1987). Methodology Characteristic Frameworks and Software Specification and Design: A Critique of "METHODMAN II", IEEE Proceedings of the Fourth Inernational Workshop on Software Specification and Design, vol. 2, pp 667–9, 1987.

Selby, R.W., Basili, V.R., and Baker, F.T. (1987). Cleanroom Software Development: An Empirical Evaluation, IEEE Trans. on Software Engineering, Vol SE-13, 9, 1987.

Skrabanek P, McCormick J. (1989). Follies and Fallacies in Medicine. Tarragon Press, 1989.

STARTS (1987). The STARTS Guide, 2nd Edition, NCC Ltd., 1987

Steadman, S. (1976). Techniques of Evaluation, in Curriculum Evaluation Today: Trends and Implications, Ed Tawney, D., Macmillan Education, 1977.

Troy, D.A., and Zweben S.H. (1981). Measuring the Quality of Structured Designs, The Journal of Systems and Software, 2, 1981.

Vouk, (1990). Back-to-back testing, Information and Software Technology, vol 32, no 1, Jan./Feb. 1990.

Walker, J.G., and Kitchenham, B.A. (1987). Quality Requirements Specification and Evaluation Measurement for Software Control and Assurance (edited by B.A.Kitchenham and B.Littlewood), Elsevier 1987.

Wyatt-Barton, J. (1991). Proceedings of EuroCASE III Conference, Blenheim Online, April 1991.

12

Declarative Analysis in Information Engineering

Paul Sanders, Keith Short

ABSTRACT

This paper outlines the "Declarative Analysis in Information Engineering" project, which is investigating how declarative techniques can be added to Information Engineering in order to allow the explicit representation of business constraints, rules and policies, and the adoption of a more declarative approach to process specification.

INTRODUCTION

The Declarative Analysis project is currently being conducted within Texas Instruments' CASE Research Laboratory. This group conducts medium term research to enhance the Texas Instruments' CASE tool, the Information Engineering Facility™ (IEF™), a full life-cycle I-CASE tool (JMA IEL 1991). Currently, a number of projects within the group are investigating how CASE technology can be applied to problem domains for which systems would be constructed using different mixes

CASE: Current Practice, Future Prospects. Edited by Kathy Spurr and Paul Layzell
© 1992 John Wiley & Sons Ltd

of technologies, such as information systems, knowledge based systems, control systems and real time systems (Short 1991). This requires new techniques to be added in a cohesive and integrated way to the current techniques of Information Engineering (Macdonald 1986, Martin 1990), for example by introducing Object Orientated concepts (Short *et al.* 1992), and by supporting an event driven perspective.

The Declarative Analysis project, which is the subject of this paper, is investigating how the use of declarative techniques can enrich business models by allowing the explicit representation of business constraints, rules and policies, and by adopting a more declarative approach to process specification.

THE CURRENT SITUATION

The IEF supports the Information Engineering (IE) methodology. The stages of IE that are relevant to this paper are:

- **Business Area Analysis**, resulting in a data model, an activity model (functions and processes), and an interaction model (defining the effect of activities on data). The detailed logic of an elementary process is specified using a high level procedural language in a Process Action Diagram (PAD);

- **Business System Design**, resulting in a collection of procedures, each of which may implement one or more elementary processes. During this stage, designers specify the user interfaces and dialogues, and the detailed procedure logic. This logic is specified using the same high level procedural language in a Procedure Step Action Diagram (PSAD), which will directly use the logic defined for the process being implemented (for example, the **procedure** *Customer Maintenance* may collect and validate the necessary information before using the logic defined for the **process** *Register Customer* to actually create the new customer entity);

- **Technical Design and Construction**. These stages are largely automated by the IEF, with the database schema and program code being generated for the chosen target environment.

The current tools of the IEF therefore mean that a full specification can be completed during analysis, from which code will be generated. However, the following criticisms can be made:

- the specification is not normalised, in that it contains different types of knowledge that are not made explicit, and the specification of a single rule gathered during analysis (for example, an integrity rule) may be spread over the specification of a single process, or over many processes;

- the distinction between analysis and design is not complete, as some types of analysis information can only be rigorously specified if design decisions are made (for example, some integrity rules can only be specified by actually defining the necessary logic to check that the rule is not violated by any process);

- specifying a process feels too much like programming. This is unavoidable to some degree if all the details of a process are to be defined, but it is made worse by the fact that the single description language necessitates a complex language, and because it is difficult to represent aspects of the process diagrammatically due to the procedural nature of the specification language.

THE DECLARATIVE ANALYSIS PROJECT

The project is tackling these problems on two largely independent fronts, by:

- making explicit some of the different types of knowledge within the process specification, and separating out that knowledge which has a scope wider than a single process (such that it can be defined as part of the data model);

- allowing processes to **optionally** be specified declaratively, by defining the conditions that must be true upon completion of the process.

The primary benefits of making the different types of knowledge explicit are that the specification is **normalised**, making business models more responsive to changing requirements, and **less design-like decisions** need to be made during analysis. In addition, the use of a declarative process specification means that it is much easier to allow **multiple descriptions** (e.g. via various diagrams), and such specifications are often very **close to the business rules and policies** that they represent.

The **data model** developed during analysis will then include:

- **global derivation rules**: defining how attributes, relationships, subtypes and entity types can be derived based upon other data;
- **global integrity rules**: defining rules concerning data integrity, that must not be broken by any process.

The **interaction model** will include, for each elementary process:

- **control conditions**: defining WHEN, and TO WHAT, a process should execute;
- **preconditions**: defining the conditions that must be true if the process is to be meaningful (the BUT NOT UNLESS);
- **postconditions** (if the process is specified declaratively) **or procedural process logic** (otherwise): defining WHAT the process does;
- **local derivation rules**: defining derived attributes etc that are only relevant within the context of this process;
- **local integrity rules**: similarly defining additional integrity rules that must be obeyed by this process alone.

It is proposed that these objectives can be met by a series of extensions which are compatible with existing IEF supported practices. These extensions are described in more detail below.

EXTENDED DATA MODEL

Global Derivation Rule

Any object in the data model (i.e. attribute, relationship, subtype, or entity type) may be derivable from other basic objects. For example:

> *"sales value equals sales quantity * sales price"*
> *"an order is classified as a due order if it is a back order, or if it is a scheduled order with a scheduled date earlier than today"*

This extends the existing IEF capability of being able to define algorithms for derived attributes. Basic and derived information are therefore both modelled using the Entity Relationship Model.

Some special forms of derivation rules cover the common cases where attributes take their values from related entity types. For example:

"the line scheduled date is equal to the scheduled date of the order containing it"

Global Integrity Rules

Global integrity rules can be defined, that must not be violated by any process. For example:

"orders over 1000 kgs to foreign clients must have export documentation"
"no new order can be created for a customer who is over their credit limit"

The main classifications of integrity rules supported are:

- **general vs special**: A general integrity rule can define any condition that must never be true (or must always be true). A special integrity rule is different only in that it belongs to a commonly occurring class of rules (e.g. permitted values, mandatory relationships), for which we want a simple interface, and for which we can employ particular approaches to ensure violation does not occur (e.g. screen validation). The IEF currently supports a number of such classes of rules;

- **state vs transition**: a state integrity rule refers to allowable states of the pool of knowledge, and a transition integrity rule to allowable changes;

- **error vs warning**: an integrity rule may be classified as an error or warning. The latter may be violated if some confirmation is provided.

EXTENDED INTERACTION MODEL

Control Conditions

The control conditions for a process define a set of conditions under which a process will commence execution, and (for a repeating process) the conditions under which it will cease execution, and the conditions under which executions will be suspended and resumed. They also define how any necessary information should be passed as inputs to the process (including any identifiers necessary) by means of a set of rules that set values of the process imports. For example:

> *"produce a statement upon receipt of a request from a customer, and for each corporate customer every month"*

A control condition can be either activating or passive—a process will execute when its activating condition is met, but only if its passive control conditions are also met at that time. An activating control condition may be:

- the arrival of a **data flow** (from an external entity or another process);
- a **condition** becoming true (often an entity entering a particular state);
- a **real time** event (e.g. end of month);
- a **command** received from a control process (most applicable in modelling Real Time systems).

Preconditions

If the **preconditions are true at the start** of the process, then the postconditions will be true at the end of the process. They define the conditions which must be met in order that no error occurs in meeting the postconditions of the process. For example:

> *"the process Schedule Order is only defined for an order containing normal demand products"*

In the world of transactions and databases, checking such conditions would be called validation. A large subset of preconditions can be derived from the postconditions, by inferring what conditions must be met to ensure that the process will not violate any integrity rule, nor will conduct any invalid action (e.g. divide by zero). Additionally other preconditions may be defined, which will often refer to the entities that must exist.

Postconditions

If the preconditions are true at the start of the process, then the **postconditions will be true at the end** of the process. The postconditions therefore define what conditions will be true upon completion, and are expressed as a set of independent rules of the form **Conclusion IF Premise**. For example:

"the order is scheduled if the customers credit status is ok"

Each rule is a postcondition of the process (i.e. **is a statement that will be true upon completion of the process**), and all the rules are **implicitly** conjoined to form the complete set of postconditions for the process. The rules are independent in the sense that their order is not significant, and each should be meaningful in isolation. The rules may refer to the conditions that are true at the **start** of the process, or at the **end** of the process; it is not possible for them to refer to conditions **during** the process i.e. there is no concept of intermediate values.

When writing the postconditions the analyst will ignore the checks that must be conducted to ensure that no integrity rules are violated, unless the action that must be carried out upon detecting a possible violation involves significant business logic (i.e. goes beyond the simple error processing of "fail and inform the user").

Currently the main types of postcondition rules supported are:

- **entity rule,** defined by a set of predicate rules that apply to every entity meeting the rule condition;

- **predicate rule,** defining the value of an attribute or the existence of a relationship pairing;

- **entity subtype classification rule,** defining the classification of an entity into a subtype (possibly containing one or more predicate rules relating to the predicates specific to the new subtype);

- **entity state change rule,** defining the transition of an entity from one state in its lifecycle to another (possibly containing one or more predicate rules);

- **action block usage rule,** allowing the use of procedural logic if necessary or convenient.

Local Derivation Rules

Data Model objects can be defined that are only relevant within the context of a single process. For example:

"within the context of the process Select Financier, there is an additional classification of financiers into suitable and unsuitable"
"within the context of process Calculate Price, the price increase is an additional attribute of product"

These would be defined in a similar manner to their global counterparts, and they allow the data model to be extended from the viewpoint of a single process. For example, local entity subtypes may be added not because entities of that type have additional predicates, but because they exhibit different behaviour.

Each local derived Data Model object must then have a set of local derivation rules defining it. The form of these is identical to global derivation rules. For example:

"a financier is suitable if they offer a fixed interest loan"
"price increase is equal to final price—initial price"

Local derivation rules provide a method of abstraction, and provide a mechanism to avoid duplicating conditions or expressions between different rules.

Local Integrity Rules

Integrity rules can be defined that are only relevant within the context of a single process. For example:

"the number of sale items imported to process Modify Order is always less than 10"
"the process Modify Order can not change completed order lines (although other processes, such as Archive Order, can)"

These would be defined in a similar manner to their global counterparts, and they extend the current IEF capability of being able to define the common special integrity rules (eg optionality) relating to the process imports.

Local integrity rules overlap with process preconditions in what they can express and the way in which they will be implemented. However, preconditions define the conditions under which a process can successfully execute. If the preconditions were to change, we would need to change the process logic, and hence they are a **property of the process itself**. On the other hand, local integrity rules define additional restrictions that we have chosen to place on the use of the process in this instance, hence they are a **property of the use of the process.**

RULE SYNTAX AND SEMANTICS

The same rule language is used to express all the different types of analysis rule. Whilst the exact syntax has been defined to be consistent with the procedural language used in the IEF, the rule language is based on typed first order logic, with its semantics defined in terms of SLDNF (SLD resolution with negation by failure), as defined by Clark (1978). Hence each rule can be translated into a logical expression.

The basic predicates appearing in rules refer to the attribute value of an object, the relationship between objects, or the type of an object. Each predicate has a form in the initial state (before execution of a process) and a form in the final state (after execution of a process). The premise of each rule may contain predicates of both the initial and final states, and may contain conjunction, disjunction, and negation. The conclusion of each rule is a single predicate, and for a postcondition rule this must be a predicate of the final state (derivation rules are taken to hold in both the initial and final state). Any variable that appears in the rule conclusion is implicitly universally quantified. Any variable that appears only in the rule premise is implicitly existentially quantified.

The semantics of the initial and final predicates can be given using an approach based on the amalgamation of language and meta-language of Bowen and Kowalski (Bowen *et al.* 1982). This allows us to formalise the notion that a predicate holds in the final state if either it was made true by one of the postcondition rules or if it held in the initial state and no postcondition rule falsified it. We can also use this approach to formalise the implicit rules (e.g. the DBMS cascade delete logic).

Another project within the CASE Research Laboratory is investigating how the IEF can support the development of Knowledge Based Systems, allowing knowledge based components to be more easily embedded within other systems, and will be defining the extensions necessary to the rule language to allow its use in this domain.

LINKS TO DIAGRAMS

The entire specification can be viewed and maintained via a textual form. In addition, overlapping subsets of the specification can also be **viewed and maintained** by means of various diagrams. The textual form and the diagrammatic form are merely different views of the same information.

Three of the diagrams are described in more detail below. These make reference to the example presented in Appendix A.

Entity State Transition Diagram

An Entity State Transition Diagram (ESD) defines the possible states in the lives of entities of one type, the transitions made between states, and the processes which make the transitions. This allows events and process to be seen from the point of view of a single entity type. The states and transitions are defined as part of the Data Model.

Figure 2 shows the ESD for the Order entity type. For example, the lines surrounding the state Fully Delivered may be read:

> "An order may enter the state Fully Delivered as a result of process Receive Delivery. It may then move to the paid state as a result of process Pay Invoice. The paid state is a termination state, hence only transitions to the Null state can be made (representing deletion of the entity)."

This information may be related to Figure 9, showing the postconditions of process Pay Invoice, as follows:

> "The transition from paid to fully delivered is the result of rule *Post2*, which also shows that the date paid will be set to the current date."

Activity Dependency Diagram

The Activity Dependency Diagram (ADD) shows the control conditions of processes, and those postconditions of other processes that make those control conditions true (indicating that one process is dependant upon the completion of another). It also shows the source and destination of information produced by the processes. This extends the Process Dependency Diagram as supported by the IEF today, adding greater rigour.

Figure 5 shows the ADD for the Purchasing function. For example, the lines surrounding process Pay Invoice may be read:

> "When an invoice is accepted, execute Pay Invoice, but only if the order is fully delivered. On completion of the process, a

payment is exported and sent to the supplier. Process Pay Invoice is dependant on the completion of process Check Invoice (which results in an invoice being accepted), and process Receive Delivery (which results in the order being fully delivered)."

This information may be related to Figure 6 and Figure 9, showing the control conditions and postconditions of process Pay Invoice, and Figure 2 showing the ESD, as follows:

"We can also see that an invoice is paid when it becomes accepted from rule CC1, which also provides the additional detail that the relevant invoice number is passed to the process. The payment is an export of Pay Invoice (although the rules creating the payment have not been shown). We can also see that Receive Delivery results in fully delivered orders from the transitions shown on the ESD."

Local Entity Relationship Diagram

The Local Entity Relationship Diagram (Local ERD) shows the collections of entities of interest to the process, how they are related, and how such relationships are changed by the process. It also shows the local relationships, subtypes etc defined for the process.

Figure 10 shows the Local ERD for process Pay Invoice. For example:

"Within the context of process Pay Invoice, a supplier may be categorised as an invoicing supplier, and (independently) may be categorised as a payment supplier. The invoicing supplier sends the subject invoice. The payment supplier will, upon completion of the process, receive payment for the subject invoice."

This information may be related to Figure 8 and Figure 9, showing the local derivation rules and postconditions of process Pay Invoice, as follows:

"Rule LD4 also describes the local subtype payment supplier, and fully details the condition under which a supplier is the payment supplier. This condition refers to the invoicing supplier, which is defined by rule LD3. The fact that it is the payment supplier that receives the payment can be seen from rule Post3."

The Local ERD will also provide a method of structuring those post-condition rules that relate to each entity type or subtype. Such rules will then be seen and entered in a very similar manner to the way in which global derivation rules are seen and entered on the normal, Global ERD.

USAGE OF ANALYSIS INFORMATION

The use made of the different types of analysis information will depend upon decisions made during the design phase, which will be greatly influenced by the target environment. To outline the options available, an analysis rule could be implemented:

- **directly in the target environment** e.g. the Data Base Management System (DBMS), KBS environment, or operating system. The implementation would be direct in that we would be using some specific feature of the target environment (e.g. triggers on a DBMS) to implement a particular type of analysis rule (e.g. an integrity rule). However, a transformation of the rules into the target environment would still be required (e.g. a single integrity rule would be transformed into many DBMS triggers, one for each table that effects the rule). Such a transformation would be automatic, based upon designer input. This is an extension of existing IEF capabilities (e.g. currently referential integrity can be maintained by a target DBMS that offers such support, or by the IEF otherwise);

- **by generating the necessary procedural logic**. There are a number of possibilities:

  - generating the necessary logic during the **transformation** of the postconditions of a declarative process specification into its equivalent procedural form as a PAD. During this transformation other information can be incorporated into the generated logic (e.g. to perform integrity checking);

  - generating the necessary logic during the **synthesis** of the Procedure Step Action Diagram (PSAD) that will implement the process. The PSAD defines the design logic (as described earlier), and currently the IEF allows the designer to select one of a number of stereotype designs (e.g. entity maintenance) and tailor it by selecting different design options relevant to that stereotype (e.g. is confirmation on delete required?) and by 'mixing in' other stereotypical components (e.g. providing selection lists). From such explicit design decisions a fully functional PSAD can be synthesised. Extending the stereotypes and design options that are available would allow explicit design decisions to be made regarding the implementation of other analysis rules (e.g. the testing of control conditions);

* generating the necessary logic during **code generation.**

Some of the options available for each type of rule are outlined below. This project is currently investigating how such options can be provided to the designer, and how such design decisions can be made, recorded, and re-used. The number of options available for the implementation demonstrates the benefit of removing such decisions from the analysis phase.

Control Conditions

The control conditions for a process may be implemented in one of a number of ways. For example:

* the control conditions could be implemented as triggers against the relevant DBMS tables, or using a scheduler within the operating system;

* the Procedure Step could determine all the entities that meet the control conditions, and execute the process for each of them;

* the process could be immediately invoked by any other process that makes the control conditions true.

Integrity Rules and Preconditions

Having specified integrity rules during analysis, we implement each rule by ensuring that the rule cannot be violated by any process. We can envisage this being done in a number of ways:

* **take action to regain integrity:** if a process takes some action that would violate an integrity rule, then we could automatically take **further** action to ensure that the rule is not actually violated. An example is the cascade delete logic, where upon deletion of an entity we may automatically delete related entities. The necessary logic may

result from direct implementation or by generating the procedural logic. Such an approach is only relevant for those classes of integrity rules where the corrective action is known;

- **detect violation and rollback:** if a process takes some action that would violate an integrity rule, then we could forbid the process from completing and roll back any changes already made. Such violations can be detected by generated DBMS triggers or by generating the necessary logic during the transformation or code generation. A designer would generally favour the first option (if it is available given the target environment and the type of integrity rule);

- **check for possible violations before initiating a process:** we could ensure that a process is never initiated under a set of conditions that would cause it to violate integrity. This would require us to analyse the postconditions and integrity rules to determine the conditions which must be met for the process to complete successfully (resulting in an additional set of preconditions). During synthesis the designer decides if each condition should be checked, and if so the action to take upon a negative result.

The options and decisions regarding precondition checking are similar to those described above.

Postconditions

The postcondition rules would generally be transformed into a PAD (and then from the PAD into the target programming language, as normal). This transformation would be system led, with designer input. Subsequent changes would be made to the postcondition rules, after which the transformation would be re-made. Alternatively, the postcondition rules could be implemented in a rule-based development environment, after adding the necessary additional details required by that environment.

Derivation Rules

The derivation rules (both local and global) could be incorporated during the transformation to the PAD i.e. the postconditions and the derivation rules relevant to them are transformed as one set. Alternatively, derivation rules may be implemented in a rule-based development environment or as rules in the target DBMS.

RELATED WORK

The benefits of both making explicit the various kinds of knowledge, and of using the rule paradigm, have been expounded in previous work on specification languages. In particular, we have adopted an approach similar to that of the RUBRIC project (Loucopoulos *et al.* 1989) which also argued for the explicit representation of business policy by means of rules, using a similar classification for those rules.

Much previous work has been carried out on both the specification and checking of integrity rules. The most relevant has been that related to deductive databases, using first order logic as the uniform language for data, derivation rules, and integrity rules (Sadri *et al.* 1988, Lloyd *et al.* 1985).

Our approach has also been greatly influenced by the model orientated formal methods VDM (Jones 1986) and Z (Spivey 1989), with a process being specified by means of one or more predicates describing the conditions true for the initial state (and inputs), and the relations between the initial state (and inputs) and the final state (and outputs). The data model can certainly be translated into either a VDM or a Z specification, as can those processes specified purely declaratively (i.e. which invoke no procedural logic). However, the reverse is not true, because (initially at least) our specification language forbids non-determinism (e.g. we could not specify that a process is to export a number which, when squared, is between 1.99 and 2.01 without specifying how it is to find such a number). This restriction is imposed such that we can retain the possibility of automatically transforming the specification into code.

SUMMARY

This research project is seeking ways to improve the results of the analysis phase within the IEF, by making explicit different kinds of knowledge, and by allowing multiple declarative descriptions of processes in rule-based and diagrammatic form. The different knowledge would be implemented according to explicit design decisions.

The benefits of making the different types of knowledge explicit are:

- **normalisation** of the specification, making business models more responsive to changing requirements;
- **less design-like decisions** need to be made during analysis;
- **greater rigour and clarity.**

The benefits of using a declarative specification of postconditions are:

- it is much easier to allow **multiple descriptions** (e.g. via various diagrams) of such a specification, as such descriptions are more easily composed;
- **greater reasoning** about the specification is possible;
- a partial, or **high level, specification** is more meaningful than it would be in a procedural context.

The benefits of using rules in particular include:

- they are a **natural** form of expression and facilitate a top down approach;
- they are often very **close to the business rules** and policies that they represent;
- their **modularity** makes them more easily verified with the users, and promises more **flexible process specialisation** within an Object Orientated context;
- they are a suitable **knowledge representation** tool for Knowledge Based Systems.

ACKNOWLEDGEMENTS

The authors would like to thank colleagues at JMA Information Engineering Ltd. and Texas Instruments for contributions to this paper.

The views expressed in this paper are those of the authors, and should not be construed as a statement of direction for Texas Instruments with regard to the Information Engineering Facility.

Information Engineering Facility and IEF are trademarks of Texas Instruments Inc.

APPENDIX A: EXAMPLE

This appendix contains a simple example of an extended data, process and interaction model, using a simplified model for a Purchasing area.

Figure 1 shows part of the Entity Relationship Diagram for the Purchasing subject area, and Figure 2 shows the Entity State Transition Diagram for one of the entity types (Order). Figures 3 and 4 show some of the global derivation and integrity rules. Whilst these are shown as a simple list in this example, in reality they would be organised according to the entity types to which they relate.

Figure 5 shows the Activity Dependency Diagram for the Purchasing function, including all the processes it contains. Figures 6 through 10 relate to one of these processes, Pay Invoice, and show the control conditions, preconditions, local derivation rules, postconditions, and the Local Entity Relationship Diagram.

The example is discussed in more detail in the body of the paper.

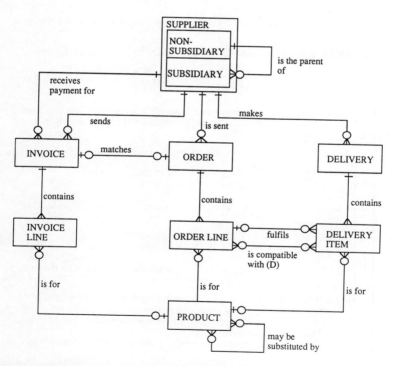

Figure 1   Entity Relationship Diagram (ERD) for the Purchasing subject area

200

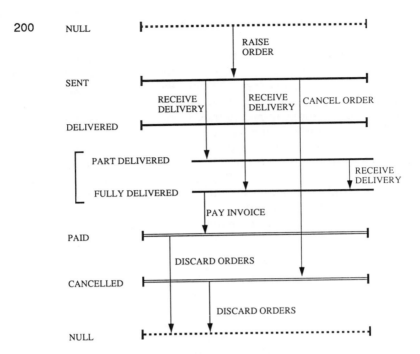

Figure 2 Entity State Transition Diagram (ESD) for entity type Order

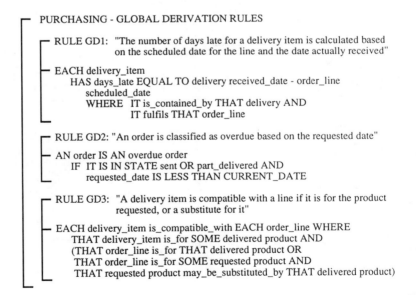

PURCHASING - GLOBAL DERIVATION RULES

RULE GD1: "The number of days late for a delivery item is calculated based on the scheduled date for the line and the date actually received"

EACH delivery_item
HAS days_late EQUAL TO delivery received_date - order_line scheduled_date
WHERE IT is_contained_by THAT delivery AND
IT fulfils THAT order_line

RULE GD2: "An order is classified as overdue based on the requested date"

AN order IS AN overdue order
IF IT IS IN STATE sent OR part_delivered AND
requested_date IS LESS THAN CURRENT_DATE

RULE GD3: "A delivery item is compatible with a line if it is for the product requested, or a substitute for it"

EACH delivery_item is_compatible_with EACH order_line WHERE
THAT delivery_item is_for SOME delivered product AND
(THAT order_line is_for THAT delivered product OR
THAT order_line is_for SOME requested product AND
THAT requested product may_be_substituted_by THAT delivered product)

Figure 3 Global Derivation Rules for the Purchasing subject area

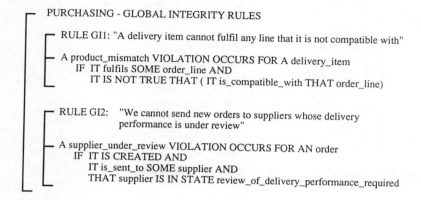

PURCHASING - GLOBAL INTEGRITY RULES

RULE GI1: "A delivery item cannot fulfil any line that it is not compatible with"

A product_mismatch VIOLATION OCCURS FOR A delivery_item
    IF IT fulfils SOME order_line AND
        IT IS NOT TRUE THAT (IT is_compatible_with THAT order_line)

RULE GI2:   "We cannot send new orders to suppliers whose delivery
            performance is under review"

A supplier_under_review VIOLATION OCCURS FOR AN order
    IF IT IS CREATED AND
        IT is_sent_to SOME supplier AND
        THAT supplier IS IN STATE review_of_delivery_performance_required

Figure 4   Global Integrity Rules for the Purchasing subject area

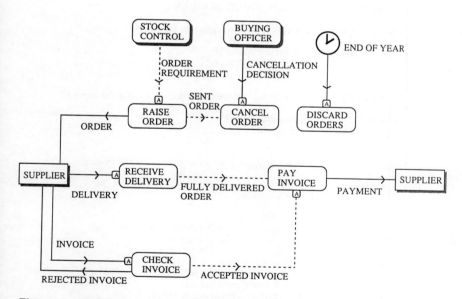

Figure 5   Activity Dependency Diagram (ADD) for the Purchasing function

PAY INVOICE - CONTROL CONDITIONS

    RULE CC1: "Execute when an invoice is accepted, as long
                   as the order has been fully received"

EXECUTE WHEN
    SOME invoice IS IN STATE accepted
    BECOMES TRUE

BUT ONLY IF
    THAT invoice matches SOME order AND
    THAT order IS IN STATE fully_delivered

WITH
    import invoice number EQUAL TO THAT invoice number

Figure 6   Control Conditions for process Pay Invoice

PAY INVOICE - PRECONDITIONS

    RULE Pre1: "The invoice must exist, and only cheque payments can be made"

PRECONDITIONS SATISFIED IF
    THE subject invoice EXISTS AND
    THE payment supplier payment_method IS EQUAL TO "Cheque"

Figure 7   Preconditions for process Pay Invoice

PAY INVOICE - LOCAL DERIVATION RULES

    RULE LD1: "The subject invoice is given by the import"

AN invoice IS THE subject invoice IF
    IT IS IDENTIFIED BY THE import invoice

    RULE LD2: "The order being invoiced is the one matching this invoice"

AN order IS THE invoiced order IF
    IT matches THE subject invoice

    RULE LD3: "The invoicing supplier is the one sending this invoice"

A supplier IS THE invoicing supplier IF
    IT sends THE subject invoice

    RULE LD4: "The supplier paid is either the one sending the
                  invoice, or their parent (for subsidiaries)"

A supplier IS THE payment supplier
    IF   (IT IS THE invoicing supplier AND
          IT IS NOT A subsidiary supplier)
    OR   IT is_the_parent_of THE invoicing supplier

Figure 8   Local Derivation Rules for process Pay Invoice

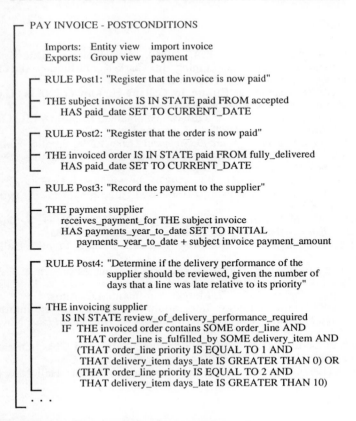

PAY INVOICE - POSTCONDITIONS

Imports: Entity view   import invoice
Exports: Group view   payment

RULE Post1: "Register that the invoice is now paid"

THE subject invoice IS IN STATE paid FROM accepted
    HAS paid_date SET TO CURRENT_DATE

RULE Post2: "Register that the order is now paid"

THE invoiced order IS IN STATE paid FROM fully_delivered
    HAS paid_date SET TO CURRENT_DATE

RULE Post3: "Record the payment to the supplier"

THE payment supplier
    receives_payment_for THE subject invoice
    HAS payments_year_to_date SET TO INITIAL
        payments_year_to_date + subject invoice payment_amount

RULE Post4: "Determine if the delivery performance of the
            supplier should be reviewed, given the number of
            days that a line was late relative to its priority"

THE invoicing supplier
    IS IN STATE review_of_delivery_performance_required
    IF THE invoiced order contains SOME order_line AND
        THAT order_line is_fulfilled_by SOME delivery_item AND
        (THAT order_line priority IS EQUAL TO 1 AND
        THAT delivery_item days_late IS GREATER THAN 0) OR
        (THAT order_line priority IS EQUAL TO 2 AND
        THAT delivery_item days_late IS GREATER THAN 10)

. . .

Figure 9   Postcondition Rules for process Pay Invoice

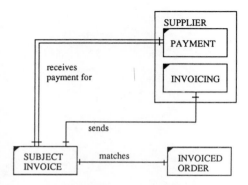

Figure 10   Local Entity Relationship Diagram (Local ERD) for process Pay Invoice

REFERENCES

Bowen, K. A. and Kowalski R.A. (1982). Amalgamating language and MetaLanguage in Logic Programming. In: Clark K., Tarlund S. (Eds.) *Logic Programming*, Academic Press, New York.

Clark, K.L. (1978). Negation as Failure. In: Gallaire H., Minker J. (Eds.) *Logic and Databases*. Plenum, New York pp 293–322.

JMA, IEL (1991). Information on the IEF can be obtained from JMA IEL, Littleton Road, Ashford, Middlesex TW15 1TZ, England.

Jones, C.B. (1986). *Systems Software Development Using VDM*. Prentice-Hall.

Lloyd, J. W. and Topor, R.W. (1985). A Basis for Deductive Database Systems. *Journal of Logic Programming* 2: 93–109

Loucopoulos, P. and Layzell, P.J. (1989). Improving information system development and evolution using a rule-based paradigm. *Software Engineering Journal* September 1989: 259–267

Macdonald, I. (1986). Information Engineering. In: Olle T.W., Sol H., Verijn-Stuart A. (Eds.) *CRIS 86—Improving the Practice*, North Holland, 1986.

Martin, J. (1990). *Information Engineering Volumes 1, 2 and 3*. Prentice-Hall, New Jersey.

Sadri, F. and Kowalski, R. (1988). A Theorem Proving Approach to Database Integrity Checking. In: Minker J. (Ed.) *Foundations of Deductive Databases and Logic Programming*, pp. 313–362. Morgan Kaufmann, Los Altos.

Short, K. (1991). Methodology Integration: the Evolution of Information Engineering. *Information and Software Technology—CASE special issue* November 1991.

Short, K. and Dodd, J. (1992). Information Engineering and Object-Orientation. In: *Proceedings of the CASEWORLD conference 1992*, Santa Clara.

Spivey, J.M. (1989). *The Z Notation: A Reference Manual*. Prentice-Hall, New Jersey.

13

Knowledge Based CASE Tools for Database Design

Michael Lloyd-Williams, Paul Beynon-Davies

ABSTRACT

A large amount of integration has occurred between the disciplines of artificial intelligence and database systems in recent years. This paper examines one such area of convergence—the application of artificial intelligence technology in the form of expert systems to the problem of database design, i.e. 'intelligent' CASE tools for database design. Important criteria in this area are presented, along with a brief comparative overview of several approaches developed to date. The aim is to evaluate progress made, and to identify future research directions.

INTRODUCTION

Database design is concerned with representing a 'real world' situation by means of a database system. This design process can be said to consist of a number of distinguishable steps or stages as illustrated by figure 1. Requirements specification involves eliciting the initial set

CASE: Current Practice, Future Prospects. Edited by Kathy Spurr and Paul Layzell
© 1992 John Wiley & Sons Ltd

of information and processing requirements from the users. Conceptual design can be thought of as comprising two sub stages: view modelling, which transforms the user requirements into a number of individual user views, and view integration which combines these views into a single *global schema* (Vossen 1990). Output from the conceptual design stage is sometimes referred to as the *conceptual model*. Logical design is concerned with determining the contents of a database independently of exigencies that may be imposed by a particular physical implementation. This is achieved by taking the conceptual model as input, and transforming it into the data model supporting the target DBMS. Physical database design involves the transformation of the logical data model into a definition of the physical model suitable for a specific software/hardware configuration. This paper concentrates on systems which attempt to provide 'intelligent' assistance in determining the required content of a database, i.e. within the requirements specification, conceptual design, and logical design stages. Systems for physical design have not been considered within this work as the content of the database has been determined by this stage. Physical design therefore deals with a different type of problem.

Most existing database design techniques have been created for, or adapted to the relational data model, though they may also be used in the design of systems defined by the hierarchical or network models. Examples of such techniques are Normalisation and Entity-Relationship Modelling. Normalisation is a technique based upon the work of Codd (1970) and involves the transformation of data which is subject to a range of problems or anomalies into a form which is free of such problems. Entity-Relationship (E-R) Modelling is based on an approach first described by Chen (1976) and involves the the process of representing the system in terms of entities and relationships. Both of these design techniques have reached a certain degree of formalisation, and therefore would appear to be prime candidates for automation.

Contemporary computer aided software engineering (CASE) tools attempt to increase the productivity of system designers and programmers in a number of ways (Martin 1984). For instance, contemporary database design tools provide graphical interfaces (such as E-R diagrammers), cross checking and validation of systems, and automation of much of the task of system documentation. Although such tools provide assistance in carrying out many design tasks with improved efficiency, they are largely the results of the automation of well established structured design techniques. Existing CASE technology does not address the fundamental characteristic of design. Design is a knowledge-intensive activity that begins with an informal set of

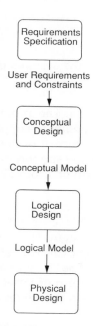

Figure 1   Stages of database design

frequently vague requirements, and ends up in a systematically defined formal object. Database design is therefore currently a labour-intensive process much prone to error. Also, the end result of design is devoid of the design knowledge that led to its construction. It is precisely this design knowledge that is needed to maintain existing systems and develop new systems.

Artificial intelligence technology can be used to develop a new generation of CASE tools capable of overcoming many of these problems. Knowledge-based software engineering is likely to replace contemporary data-based software engineering. The current crop of data-based tools such as data dictionaries will be supplanted by knowledge-based tools. Whereas a data-based tool can merely reason about the structure of a database system, a knowledge-based tool will be able reason about the semantics of a database system (Lowry 1989).

This paper examines several vehicles which apply a knowledge-based approach to the process of database design. This is generally achieved by automating, to a greater or lesser extent, one or more of the recognised database design techniques, and supplementing this automation with a degree of 'intelligence'.

IMPORTANT CRITERIA FOR 'INTELLIGENT' DESIGN TOOLS

The criteria used to evaluate the systems presented in this work are as follows:

Stage of database design covered. The approaches are examined in terms of which of the stages they attempt to support. The stage supported will to a certain extent dictate the format of the final output. For example, if an approach attempts to provide support during the logical design stage, then output will take the form of a logical data model capable of being supported by the target DBMS.

User interface employed. This criterion examines the type of user interface employed by each system. This is generally of one of two types; a menu based dialogue, or some form of natural language interface (NLI). NLI's can be further classified as being a) restricted—the response of the user is restricted to a given form of input or, b) unrestricted—the user has no restrictions placed upon the content or format of response.

Method used to drive design process. Here we concentrate on the method used to provide initial input to the system. That is, how is initial information relating to the application domain gathered? Is it supplied directly by the user or is the input provided by some other means? The driving mechanism is also examined in terms of whether continuous user input is required throughout the design process, or whether the process is largely automatic once initial information has been gathered.

Domain specific knowledge. The use of predefined domain specific knowledge within a system can enhance the appearance of intelligence, and increase the efficiency of a design session. The use of domain knowledge can, for instance, remove the need for certain trivial questions to be asked of the user. We therefore compare each approach in terms of what (if any) domain specific knowledge is used, and if used, how well is such domain knowledge exploited.

Database design technique used. As described in the introduction, several popular database design techniques now exist which are prime candidates for automation. We therefore examine the extent to which the various approaches make use of the opportunity to automate such techniques.

User backtracking. An important feature of a design tool is the ability to 'backtrack' and redesign if dissatisfied with the results. We therefore examine here whether or not a system provides a facility which allows a user to 'undo' chosen design decisions and investigate new possibilities.

Ease of use. A primary function of a CASE tool is to increase productivity. This aim however is unlikely to be achieved if the tool itself is difficult or cumbersome to use. We therefore examine the 'usability' of the systems described.

REPRESENTATIVE APPROACHES

The following approaches were selected either due to their historical significance, or because they illustrate a specific point of interest, the intention being to provide an introduction to work in this area.

SECSI

SECSI™ (Système Expert en Conception de Systèmes d'Informations) (Bouzeghoub *et al.* 1985) was developed as part of the French SABRE project. It is widely seen as the seminal work in the area of knowledge based CASE tools for database design, having influenced a number of researchers.

SECSI provides an 'intelligent' interactive tool for assisting in logical database design. During a design session, the user (i.e. the database designer) is engaged in a dialogue in order to elicit facts relating to the application domain. These facts are then transformed by a series of design algorithms into a logical schema, the schema being stored in an relational database.

The tool consists of a user interface, a knowledge base, and an inference engine. Dialogue with the user takes place via a restricted NLI. User input is required to be in a declarative format such as 'SALESMEN ARE EMPLOYEES' and 'EMPLOYEE-ID IS INTEGER'. The knowledge base deals with two types of knowledge: design facts and design rules. The representation of facts within the knowledge base is handled by a formalised implementation of a semantic network. As information is gathered from the user, a semantic network representing the users application domain is constructed.

Design rules are made up of a series of production rules and cover the areas of *Consistency Enforcement* (verify and maintain the consistency of the conceptual model), *Structural Transformation* (transform the semantic network to a normalised relational schema), *General Knowledge* (relating to semantic network structure and relational theory) and *Design* (controlling the sequence of design steps).

The design process takes place via a series of predefined steps:

1. Verification Step—generation of a conceptual schema in the form described above.

2. Relational Step—interactive generation of first normal form relations, and constraints.

3. Normalisation step—normalisation using attributes of the identified entities.

The completion of these steps results in the production of a set of relations and associated keys, a set of virtual relations specified by view definitions, and a set of constraints. The process can be restarted from any of the steps described if the user is dissatisfied with the results.

SECSI may be summarised in point form as follows:-

- Implementation language: Prolog.
- User Interface: Restricted & declarative NLI.
- Design Technique: E-R Modelling & Normalisation.
- Domain Specific Knowledge: None.
- Backtracking Facilities: Yes.
- Output: Relations plus associated constraints.

SECSI concentrates on the design of a logical schema, starting from a point at which it assumes that a set of user views are already available. Thus, a certain amount of prerequisite work must be carried out before it can be used effectively. However, once this information is available, operation is relatively straightforward. No specific application domain ('real world') knowledge is held by the system, which also has no capability for learning. It is unable to apply knowledge gained during the design of a particular application to a later design of a similar application.

Work Related to SECSI

Two significant pieces of work produced by researchers influenced by SECSI are: UFI (User Friendly Interface) (Moses 1988) and VCS (View Creation System) (Storey & Goldstein 1988).

UFI (User Friendly Interface) was developed by John Moses at Sunderland Polytechnic and attempts to improve on the 'user friendliness' of the original SECSI interface.

VCS (View Creation System) was developed by Veda Storey and Robert Goldstein at the University of British Columbia, Canada. This work can be seen as complimentary to that of Bouzeghoub *et al.*, as SECSI assumes that a set of user views are available before the design session begins. VCS is essentially a tool to create these user views. Views created by VCS need to undergo a process of reconciliation and integration in order to produce a global view of the database. This task must be performed 'externally' as the VCS system constructs individual views, but does not attempt to reconcile or integrate them. Tools such as AVIS (Automatic View Integration System) (Wagner 1989) are able to provide assistance with this task.

I2S

I2S (Intelligent Interview System) (Kawaguchi 1986) was developed at Osaka University, Japan as a direct result of the earlier KDBMS project (Mizoguchi 1985).

I2S provides 'intelligent' assistance in the process of conceptual database design using a query analysis technique. It interviews the user, extracting a series of sample queries to the target database. These queries are then analysed for required data content, and a series of relations produced with sufficient data content to satisfy the queries.

I2S is made up of a user interface, a controller, memory, and a knowledge base. The user interface takes the form of an unrestricted NLI made up of two components; a parser, and a generator. Sample queries supplied by the user are analysed by the parser and used to construct a representation of the user's domain known as a 'plan'. (The plan bears a certain resemblance to Minsky's (1977) 'frame' concept). The generator attempts to verify this process by constructing statements from the plan for the user to confirm as correct. Prior to the commencement of the design session, the user is asked to indicate the application domain of the intended database by selecting from a list of preset options. The domain chosen prompts the system to select an appropriate internal dictionary which is used during the interview process.

I2S memory is divided into three parts. Short term memory holds the model of the current user's domain, the attention list holds items to be discussed with the user, and the working memory holds rules from the knowledge base relating to the current system activity. The knowledge base holds a dictionary for use by the parser/generator, questioning strategy information for use in determining the order/type of question put to the user, planning knowledge for use in constructing the domain representation, and a set of production rules relating to schema design. Overall control of the session is maintained by the controller, which manages the dialogue between the system and the user, and instigates the design of the database schema once it considers the dialogue phase complete.

Once the user has entered all the information requirements, I2S questions the user on any information that has been supplied but which will not be needed by the database to satisfy user requirements. This process reveals redundant data, and also prompts the user into remembering requirements that were omitted during the initial elicitation. This illustrates a critical feature of I2S in that the system asks 'intelligent' questions of the user, directly related to information previously supplied.

The main features of I2S may be illustrated as follows:-

- Implementation language: Prolog.
- User Interface: Unrestricted NLI.
- Design Technique: E-R Modelling & Normalisation.
- Domain Specific Knowledge: Yes, in the form of internal dictionaries.
- Backtracking Facilities: None.
- Output: Relations.

I2S can readily assist a database designer by 'interviewing' end users, provided that the users are wholly familiar with the application domain, and that the information requirements are clear. The use of domain specific dictionaries is unique within this review to I2S. However, they contain only verbs, the advantage being that a much smaller dictionary is required but this may lead to mistakes when parsing user input. These errors should be overcome by the process of confirmation of input. The system does not appear to deal with the integrity constraints in its conceptual schema representation. Future work planned includes an investigation of more efficient use of memory, the aim being to enable knowledge gained to be transferable between design sessions.

EDDS

EDDS (Expert Database Design System) (Choobineh *et al.* 1988) was developed at the University of Arizona USA. This is one of the few approaches that tackles the problem of database design by making direct use of the forms employed in the user's system within the design process.

EDDS provides 'intelligent' assistance in the process of conceptual database design. This is achieved by analysing the forms used within the user's application, subjecting the data content and flow from these forms to a series of design algorithms, and producing a conceptual schema in E-R format.

The EDDS architecture is comprised of a form definition system, a form abstraction base, a design database, a data design knowledge base, a design status base, and an inference engine. The initial phase proper of the EDDS design process is the content analysis of each form, and movement of form fields between forms within the user's application system. The user 'paints' each form on screen using the Form Definition System. The system then originates a dialogue with the user, the aim being to construct a form schema. This process continues until details of all forms have been entered, and the information generated held in the Form Abstraction Base.

The EDDS knowledge base is divided into three parts; The Data Design Knowledge base which holds the design rules used in the design process, the Form Abstraction Base which holds information on forms previously analysed and entered by the user, and the Design Status Base which holds information on design decisions made during the session. The evolving schema is held in the Design Database, which serves as a meta base.

Once collation of the form information is complete, the expert system component applies a series of design rules to the form information in order to construct a conceptual schema. This process is made up of six separate stages, each involving the application of a number of design rules. The application of these stages continues until all forms have been processed. The stages are as follows:-

1. Form Selection—determine the next form to be processed.
2. Entity Identification—determine form fields that identify entities.
3. Attribute Attachment—identify attributes for entities.
4. Relationship Identification—identify and confirm relationships between entities.
5. Cardinality Identification—specify minimum and maximum cardinalities of relationships.
6. Consistency Checking—confirm the integrity of the developing schema.

These stages are carried out at least once for each form held in the form abstraction base. Backtracking is however permitted between the entity identification, attribute attachment, relationship identification, and cardinality identification stages, and is controlled by the database designer. Output from the EDDS system takes the form of an E-R diagram representing the conceptual schema of the user's database.

The main features of EDDS are summarised as follows:-

- Implementation language: Pascal.
- User Interface: Menu driven.
- Design Technique: E-R Modelling.
- Domain Specific Knowledge: None.
- Backtracking Facilities: Yes.
- Output: E-R representation of conceptual schema.

EDDS relies heavily on a number of predefined conditions being satisfied. The system relies heavily on a database designer's involvement in the design process. The design process is also heavily reliant on an analysis of the forms currently used in the system having taken place, and that the expertise to carry out this analysis is available. EDDS does not make direct use of the user's knowledge during the design process.

GESDD

GESDD (Generalised Expert System for Database Design) (Dogac 1989) was developed at the University of Ankara, Turkey. GESDD represents a rare attempt to provide a facility whereby the user has the choice of designing a conceptual schema based on the relational, network, or hierarchical data models.

GESDD provides 'intelligent' assistance during requirements specification, conceptual, and logical database design. GESDD is comprised of two distinct but inter-related expert systems; ESGM (Expert System for Generating Methodologies) for the process of designing and maintaining database design methodologies, and ESDD (Expert System for Database Design) for the process of database design.

ESGM provides a 'shell' facility whereby new methodologies may be developed and stored, or existing methodologies modified. ESDD makes use of this methodology information, along with application centred information provided by the database designer to design a logical schema in the chosen data model format.

The design process of EDDS is highly automated, and requires only certain inputs from the database designer. It does however assume that a detailed analysis of the application domain has been carried out, and the user requirements have been ascertained. The success of the schema generation depends heavily on the quality of this detailed analysis.

The initial stage of the EDDS design process is the selection of a database design methodology from those offered. This is followed by the first stage proper involving the use of ESDD—that of *requirements specification*. This involves the database designer using the information provided by the detailed analysis of the system to build a formalised description of the system.

The *conceptual design* stage is performed in two steps; generating the conceptual schema from the requirements specification, and testing the consistency of this schema. The generation of the conceptual schema involves mapping the requirements specification to a conceptual schema using the rules provided by the design methodology. The testing of the consistency of the conceptual schema is also a two phase procedure involving automatic checking and interactive testing of the schema structure. Interactive testing allows for the possibility of detection and correction of errors before generation of the logical schema.

Logical design involves transforming the conceptual schema into the logical schema and is driven by a series of transformation algorithms provided by the design methodology. Output comprises a logical schema in either hierarchical, relational, or network data model format, and a series of internal constraints derived from the conceptual schema. The database designer may also define external constraints which will be incorporated in the output.

GESDD may be summarised in point form as follows:-

- Implementation language: Prolog.
- User Interface: Menu driven.
- Design Technique: E-R Modelling, but incorporates normalisation if relational model is selected.
- Domain Specific Knowledge: None.
- Backtracking Facilities: Yes.
- Output: Logical schema plus design documentation if requested.

GESDD provides a very flexible facility, being capable of supporting the hierarchical, network and relational data models. It also provides for the specification and use of tailored database design methodologies due to its 'shell' feature. However, this flexibility also necessitates expertise in database design methodologies. No specific application domain ('real world') knowledge is held by the system, and minimum interaction is required with the database designer. This feature leaves the system heavily reliant on the quality of the original analysis of the application domain. GESDD is also dependent on the services of a database design expert to define a design methodology, and a database designer to design the database.

Modeller

Modeller (Tauzovich 1990) is an integral part of a family of 'intelligent' CASE tools being developed by Cognos inc. to assist in the process of application system design. The Modeller system is specifically for use in database design. The final version of Modeller will provide assistance with requirements specification, conceptual design, logical design and physical database design. However, the prototype version provides assistance only during the conceptual design stage.

The prototype version of Modeller is designed to be of use by the database designer, with no direct end-user involvement. Information relating to the application domain is submitted to Modeller via a restricted NLI using LESK statements (an English-like, general purpose knowledge acquisition language). The LESK statements are then translated into a corresponding series of assertions which in turn are used to augment an evolving conceptual representation of the user's domain. Modeller has been designed to provide the designer with passive assistance, that is, only offering advice when it has been asked for. Therefore, at any time during a design session, the database designer can request the system to examine the conceptual representation, to refine it, and to check it for potential problems. Once the session is completed, the system produces output in the form of an extended E-R model. It is intended to use this E-R model as input to later versions of Modeller which assist with logical database design.

The main features of Modeller can be summarised as follows:-

- Implementation language: Prolog.
- User Interface: Restricted NLI (using LESK).
- Design Technique: E-R Modelling.
- Domain Specific Knowledge: None.
- Backtracking Facilities: No.
- Output: Extended E-R representation of conceptual schema.

The prototype version of Modeller concentrates on the design of a conceptual schema, starting from a point at which it assumes that a an analysis of requirements has already taken place. It is therefore totally dependent on this information being available, and the database designer being familiar with the LESK knowledge acquisition language. The quality of the E-R model produced is heavily dependent on the extent to which these prerequisites have been satisfied. No specific application domain ('real world') knowledge is held by the system, which also has no capability for learning. It is unable to apply knowledge gained during the design of a particular application to a later design of a similar application. The system is still at a relatively early stage of development, future work includes the extension of the system to cover all stages of database design, and the development of an interactive graphics interface.

EVALUATION OF PROGRESS TO DATE

Overall, what would appear to be a potentially fruitful area for development has exhibited little commercial progress. Very few commercial examples of 'intelligent' database design tools exist, even though the techniques used are prime candidates for automation. Table 1 illustrates a comparison of the approaches reviewed with respect to the criteria outlined in section 2.

Table 1. Comparison of intelligent CASE tools for database design

	SECSI	I2S	EDDS	GESDD	Modeller
Design Stage	Logical	Conceptual	Conceptual	Req spec, Conceptual & logical	Conceptual
User Interface	Restricted NLI	Unrestricted NLI	Menu	Menu	Restricted NLI
Driven by	Designer	User	Designer	Designer	Designer
Domain Knowledge	No	Yes	No	No	No
Design Technique	Norm & E-R	Norm & E-R	E-R	Norm & E-R	E-R
User Backtracking	Yes	No	Yes	Yes	No
Ouput	Relations & constraints	Relations	E-R model	Logical model & constraints	E-R Model

The approaches provide some support for the majority of criteria described; however, no single approach provides strong support for all requirements. Perhaps the criteria with the greatest potential is also the most neglected—that of domain specific knowledge. Domain specific (i.e. 'real world') knowledge and the ability to reason with this knowledge would be of obvious advantage to an 'intelligent' design tool. Figure 2 illustrates how domain specific knowledge (such as the dictionaries of I2S) can be used to assist in the creation of the initial internal representation of the application domain. This type of use enhances the appearance of 'intelligence' of the tool by removing the need to ask trivial questions of the user.

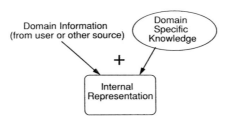

Figure 2   Use of domain specific knowledge

One of the main strengths of CASE tools is their use of graphical interfaces, yet the systems discussed made only limited use of graphical representation. A further area for potential improvement would therefore be the inclusion of improved graphical representation of design input and output.

GESDD provides a limited facility for interactive testing of the conceptual schema during the design session. Interactive schema testing could be expanded to provide a facility whereby the user is allowed to submit test queries to the database undergoing design. This would increase the likelihood of data omissions being discovered at the design stage where they may be corrected prior to the session progressing.

Broadly speaking, all the approaches described follow the same general pattern of operation as illustrated in figure 3.

Information relating to an application domain is gathered and used (in conjunction with domain specific knowledge if it is available) to create an internal representation of the domain. A series of design algorithms are then applied in order to transform the internal representation into a conceptual schema, which in turn may be transformed into a logical schema structure. Although the overall approaches are similar, two

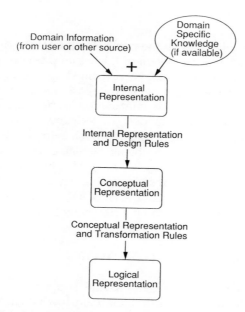

Figure 3   Stages of 'intelligent' database design

distinct methods for driving the design process can be identified. These can be described as:-

1. Those driven by direct contact with users.
2. Those driven by information obtained from an external source.

Direct Contact

These systems use as their driving force, information supplied directly by the user. They assume that an ideal source of information relating to a target database, will be the potential users of that database. This makes the quality of the eventual design heavily reliant on the quality of information supplied by the user. Omitting a simple but semantically important fact may have a significant effect on the final database design. Within this group, the approaches can be further sub grouped into those driven through dialogue with a potential database user (e.g. VCS), and those driven by analysis of sample target database queries (e.g. I2S).

External Source

These systems rely heavily on the presence of database design personnel to drive the design process. Much of the actual processing is automated, but information is required to be presented in the correct format to the system. The primary role of the database designer in this situation therefore is to ensure that the information is presented in the correct format, and to make various design decisions based on his or her knowledge of database design. The approach is totally dependent on the externally supplied information being available, being up to date, and being correctly presented to the CASE tool. This external information may take a number of forms, including an analysis of an existing application system (as utilised by GESDD), or an analysis of forms currently used within a system (as utilised by EDDS).

CONCLUSIONS AND FUTURE WORK

All of the approaches reviewed provide support for the 'traditional' data models (relational, network, hierarchical) which are limited in their expressiveness (i.e. have limited semantic capacity). An 'intelligent' tool using an enhanced model capable of greater semantic capacity would allow construction of a semantically rich representation of the user domain. We are currently involved in such work which combines the knowledge based approach with support structures capable of enhanced semantic content. However, the logical representation of our conceptual schema cannot be fully supported by 'traditional' (i.e. relational, network, hierarchical) database technology. Given this situation, the use of object oriented schema looks like being a fruitful direction in which to progress. Traditional data models are commonly used in standard data processing applications. We are currently examining the suitability of adapting the approach to support non standard applications such as geographical information systems. We also intend to make use of 'real world' knowledge, and the ability to reason with this knowledge within the tool, thus enhancing the appearance of 'intelligence'.

The overall approach of using knowledge based CASE tools for assisting in database design is gradually gaining momentum. The appearance of a limited number of commercial products such as Infosys' version of SECSI, and the forthcoming family of products from Cognos indicates that a pool of interest for this approach does exist. However, the limited number of products emerging does point to an apparent level of commercial inertia in what is potentially a fruitful area. Certainly there is no shortage of activity on the research front, with improved techniques and systems continually being developed. However, relatively little of this research work manages to transfer to the commercial front, even though there appears to be commercial scope for such 'intelligent' CASE tools.

ACKNOWLEDGEMENTS

The authors wish to thank Chris Jones, Roger Stein, Veda Storey, Bob Goldstein, John Moses, Joobin Choobineh and Atsuo Kawaguchi for their helpful comments and advice.
SECSI is a trademark of Infosys

REFERENCES

Bouzeghoub, M., Gardarin, G. and Metais, E. (1985). Database Design Tools: An Expert System Approach. In: *Proceedings of the 11th International Conference on Very Large Data Bases (VLDB)*, pp. 82–95.

Choobineh, J., Mannino, M.V., Nunamaker, J.F. and Konsynski, B.R. (1988). An Expert Database System Based on Analysis of Forms. *IEEE Transactions on Software Engineering.* 14:242–253.

Chen, P.P-S. (1976). The Entity-Relationship Model–Toward a Unified View of Data. *ACM Transactions on Database Systems.* 1: 9–36.

Codd, E.F. (1970). A Relational Model of Data for Shared Databanks. *Communications of the ACM.* 13: 377–387.

Dogac, A., Yuruten, B. and Spaccapietra, S. (1989). A Generalized Expert System for Database Design. *IEEE Transactions on Software Engineering.* 15: 479–491.

Kawaguchi, A., Taoka, N., Mizoguchi, R., Yamaguchi, T. and Kakusho, O. (1986). An Intelligent Interview System for Conceptual Design of Database. In: *Proceedings of the 7th European Conference on Artificial Intelligence*, pp. 39–45.

Lowry, M. and Duran, R.K. (1989). Knowledge-Based Software Engineering. In: Barr, A., Cohen, P. R. and Feigenbaum, E.A (Eds.) *Handbook of Artificial Intelligence, Vol. 4*, pp. 241–322, Addison-wesley, Reading, Mass.

Martin, J. (1984). *An Information Systems Manifesto*. Prentice-Hall, Englewood-Cliffs.

Minsky, M. (1975). A Framework for Representing Knowledge. In: Winston, P.H. (Ed.) *The Psychology of Computer Vision*, pp. 211–277, Mcgraw-Hill, New York.

Mizoguchi, R., Kobayashi, H., Isomoto, Y., Nomura, Y., Toyoda, J. and Kakusho, O. (1985). Interactive Synthesis of Conceptual Schema Based on Queries. *International Journal of Information Processing.* 8: 207–216.

Moses, J. (1988). An Intelligent User Friendly Interface for a Database Design Expert System. *Proceedings of the International Systems Prospects Conference*, pp. 93–96.

Storey, V.C. and Goldstein, R.C. (1988). A Methodology for Creating User Views in Database Design. *ACM Transactions on Database Systems.* 13: 305–338.

Tauzovich, B. (1990). An Expert System for Conceptual Data Modelling. In: *Proceedings of the 8th International Conference on the Entity-Relationship Approach*, pp. 205–220.

Vossen, G. (1990). *Data Models, Database Languages and Database Management Systems*. Addison-Wesley, Wokingham.

Wagner, C. (1989). View Integration in Database Design. PhD Thesis, University of British Columbia.

14

A Knowledge-based Requirement Engineering Assistant

Saimond Ip, Louis C-Y Cheung, Tony Holden

ABSTRACT

This paper outlines the Knowledge-based Requirement Engineering Assistant (KREA) as the support environment for Knowledge Based IS Methodology (KISM). It discusses the architecture of KREA and its three subsystems: elicitation, validation, and support. Then it focuses on the use of abstraction methods as the organizing principle in the design of KREA. Accordingly, three areas supported by KREA are highlighted: rule-based model validation, design history graph, and parameterized design reuse.

INTRODUCTION

We believe that the role of knowledge should be explicitly represented in the development of an information system. Our goal is to develop a

CASE: Current Practice, Future Prospects. Edited by Kathy Spurr and Paul Layzell
© 1992 John Wiley & Sons Ltd

new generation of Knowledge Based Information System Methodology (KISM). The current focus is on the early stages of Information System Engineering, that is, in what is often called conceptual modelling or requirement engineering. A methodology has to be a *coherent* set of techniques, tools, and procedures[1]. Object Relationship Modelling (ORM) and Object Life Cycle (OLC) are the techniques employed in KISM for data and process/behavioural modelling respectively and they are reported elsewhere[9] [10] [11]. The Knowledge Based Requirement Engineering Assistant (KREA) is a knowledge based environment with a set of tools to support these tools. The next section will discuss the system architecture of KREA. The principle of abstraction is an important part of the philosophy underlying the coherence of KISM. The rest of the paper is concerned with three modules of KREA which make extensive use of this principle and the procedures that they support: knowledge based verifier, rapid prototyper, and model re-user.

KREA SYSTEM ARCHITECTURE

IS engineering is considered to involve three parties: the end-user, the analyst, and the programmer. The analyst's job is to build a model to act as a bridge between the end-user and the programmer. A knowledge based environment should support requirement engineering by representing the specification in an explicit knowledge base and by providing a collection of tools to assist in the construction of a "correct" model. This is achieved by the first two subsystems of KREA: elicitation and validation. The third subsystem recognises the interactive and complex nature of the process of requirement engineering and provides some advanced modules to cope with it. Figure 1 shows these three subsystems with their modules.

The Elicitation Subsystem

The elicitation subsystem has three components:

- *Diagram Editor*: this module allows the analyst to construct ORMs and OLCs graphically. It includes all the usual facilities in a powerful interactive environment: menus, icons, and windows. The modelling techniques are designed to facilitate the elicitation of requirement specifications entirely by building these graphs and filling in appropriate predefined forms and tables.

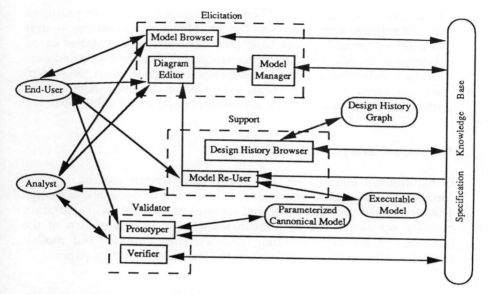

Figure 1 Architecture of KREA

- *Model Manager*: the model manager is concerned with the translation of the diagrammatic representation of ORMs and OLCs to the frame-based specification knowledge base. It is also responsible with the maintenance of the knowledge base, for example, by eliminating duplicate objects. It contains a set of utilities (that is used by other modules) for the manipulation of the knowledge base.

- *Model Browser*: this module allows the end-user/analyst to inspect and to make enquiries about the specification knowledge base.

The Validation Subsystem

Once a conceptual model is built, it has to be validated to see whether it represents a correct specification of the end-user's requirement. This subsystem consists of two parts:

- *Verifier*: a rule-based system is used to check the completeness and consistency of the models. Errors can be classified into two types. Some have to be pointed out once they occur since they will have substantial effect on further development of the conceptual model. Others will be included in a completeness and consistency report which can be requested at different stages of design.

- *Prototyper*: OLCs have a Petri-Net based formalisms and the processes have a rule-like characteristics. The prototyper will assist the analyst to build an executable model and provide an active presentation of the conceptual model. A number of scenarios with sample objects and data can be constructed to allow the end-user to check whether the system actually meets his requirement. Examples of the implementation of such executable data and process models can be found in Ip (1991)[11].

The Support Subsystem

IS requirement engineering, like many other design process, is often complex and interactive and makes intensive use of domain knowledge. This subsystem provides advanced features to support this exploratory building up and re-use of domain knowledge. Details of two of the modules we are experimenting (design history browser and model-reuser) will be discussed in detail in the last sections of this paper.

KREA AND ABSTRACTION

An abstraction is the "model of a system in which certain details are deliberately omitted"[18] in order to present the "relevant" parts of the system. It is an important principle in knowledge representation and forms the cornerstone of KISM. It is possible to consider the significance of any abstraction method in many different perspectives[11] [19] but, for the purpose of this paper, its main function is to provide meaningful organizing principles in the design of KREA. The construction of a conceptual model can be considered along several different dimensions. The most fundamental is the *enrichment* dimension with ordinary addition, deletion and modification of the model. Then there is one dimension for every abstraction method employed. The importance of functional decomposition as an abstraction method is seen in its extensive use in popular modelling techniques such as data flow analysis. However, KISM focuses on two other abstraction methods which is usually associated with object-orientation. The *aggregation* dimension concerns with how a complex object is refined into its components or how several objects are aggregated to form a complex one while the *generalization* dimension deals with the relationship between subclasses and superclasses. These dimensions of modelling turns out to be especially useful in three areas of KREA: rule-based model verification, design history browsing, and parameterized model re-use.

RULE-BASED MODEL VERIFICATION

This is a relatively well-understood area with notably successful applications (e.g. [2]). A heuristic, instead of formal, approach is adopted and forward chaining rules are found to be suitable for the task. Some rules are used to highlight incompleteness in the model, for example, totally isolated objects or relationships, complex objects without components defined, or undefined value object classes (as domains for attributes). Consistency checking rules can be classified and reported according to the modelling dimensions. A number of examples of such rules are given as follows: 1) along the aggregation dimension: the cardinality of an inherited relationship of a component object cannot be more relaxed than its "parent" relationship; 2) along the generalization dimension: any objects related to a superclass of A must either be related to A or be superclasses of objects related to A; and 3) along the enrichment dimension: two objects and/or relationships cannot have the same name. Finally, special classes of aggregations and specializations are governed by more vigorous rules of inconsistency. For example, the relationship between a strictly hierarchical object (which basically models a physical object) and its direct components must be specifically-dependent and exclusive[9].

DESIGN HISTORY GRAPH

Requirement analysis is a highly iterative process with a lot of trial-and-error. It is simply not enough to record a linear sequence of different versions of design. What designer wants is a simple and clear way to visualise all the meaningful changes in the history of the design and to be able to try different designs before committing to a "correct" one. We are currently experimenting with the technique of *design history graph*.[1] The nodes of a design history graph are versions of part of the conceptual model. A version has the following attributes: 1) a unique identifier (shown as a version number in figure 2); 2) the name of its author; 3) the most currently updated time and 4) a comment.

A directional link in the graph indicates a new version is created. There are three groups of links reflecting the three dimensions of changes. Along the aggregation dimension, a link can be either a refinement (ref) or an aggregation (agg); along the generalization dimension, it can be

---

[1] The design history graph extends the idea of "design schedule" in Reisig (1986) with more dimensions and the temporal element.

a specialization (spe) or generalization (gen); and along the enrichment dimension, it can be an enrichment (enrich), a simplification (sim), or a modification (mod). All the links, except modification, are transitive, e.g. if A enrich B and B enrich C, A also enrich C. For simplicity, all such transitively formed links are not shown on a graph. Figure 2 shows a typical design history graph, in this case, only with changes in the enrichment and aggregation dimension. Dummy versions (shown as dots in figure 2) are sometimes necessary to show how new versions are created from old ones but they are not stored and have no attributes of their own. For example, a version (ver 1 in figure 2) may be simplified, refined, and then enriched to form another (ver 4 in figure 2), thus requiring two dummy versions in the design history graph.

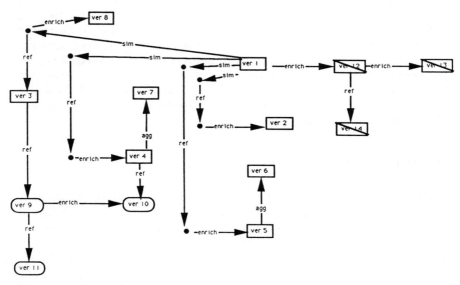

Figure 2   Design History Graph

A large number of versions created at different times usually co-exist to form the current "correct" design.[2] Outdated "incorrect" versions are shown as crossed out boxes on the graph. When a version is designated as outdated, all its refinements, specializations, and enrichments must

---

[2] Conceptually, the current design is a version formed by taking the most refined, most specialized, and most enriched versions and joining them by further refinement, specialization, and enrichment. But it need not be drawn explicitly in practice. The proof of the existence of such a "final" version is a matter for future research.

also be crossed out (e.g. ver 12, 13, and 14). But when the version is revived back to the current design, a designer has the choice of whether to revive its refinements and enrichments. Some versions are designated as hypothetical and do not form part of the current design. All the refinements and enrichments of a hypothetical version must also be hypothetical (e.g. ver 9, 10, and 11). Such a version will either be dumped as outdated or be promoted to the current design in which case the designer will have to decide whether to promote its refinements and enrichments.

Not all typologies are possible in a design history graph. Since a link has temporal significance, any loops are forbidden. There are also rules expressing a number of other inconsistent typologies. For instance, if A enrich B, and C specialize B, A cannot enrich, simplify, or specialize C. Another rule states that, if both A and B refine C, A cannot enrich or simplify B.

KNOWLEDGE-BASED DESIGN REUSE

A highly structured conceptual model with objects at different levels of abstraction (in this case, aggregation and specialization) facilitates reuse of design. We are investigating into further enhancing this process of reuse by the construction of a *parameterized canonical model* for each domain. A parameterized model is a conceptual model (in our case, ORM and OLC) with a *s-value* (value of significance) assigned to each object and relationship. A s-value indicates, in the designers' opinion, how significant the item is to the domain and how likely it would be useful for future designs. A s-value can take any of the following three descending values: essential, useful, and optional. If uncertain, designers are always recommended to give an object a lower s-value. Relationships can also be assigned s-values but it must not exceed the s-value of any of the objects it relates (unless the role relating that object is optional).

The use of aggregation and generalizaton imposes some more constraints on feasible s-values. For example, a strictly hierarchical complex object must not have a lower s-value than any of its direct components and the s-value of an inherited relationship of a component object must not exceed that of its parent relationship.

Each object and relationship in a canonical model also has a *name-set* which contains all the names considered to be equivalent to each other. Given such a model, an analyst can generate the first draft of a new design by using all the essential objects and relationships and selecting from the useful and then the optional ones. Each name-set should of course be eventually narrowed down to one most appropriate name for that application.

When the new model is completed, it can be parameterized and fed back to modify the canonical model. The designer has to decide whether an object or a relationship in the new model has an equivalent in the canonical one. The name of this object/relationship should then be added to the original name-set if it is not already included. The s-value of the object/relationship in the canonical model should also be modified according to the following table:

can.....new	Essential	Useful	Optional
Essential	Essential	Essential	Essential
Useful	Essential	Essential	Useful
Optional	Essential	Optional	Optional

For example, if the s-value of the object is optional in the canonical model and useful in the new one, it is optional in the new canonical model. For an object/relationship with no equivalents, the original canonical model can be regarded as having a virtual equivalent with an empty name-set and a s-value equals to optional.

CONCLUSION

KREA is being developed on a Symbolics Lisp Machine. The diagram editor is developed on top of MAXIM (Holden, 1989) which is a graphical interface builder. A typical input session using the diagram editor is shown in figure 3. Most of the other subsystems are built with ART[4]. The specification knowledge base, the design history graph, and the parameterised models all employ their tailored representation of the ART schemata system. The verifier makes use of forward chaining production rules in ART. The prototyper constructs the executable OLCs by a rather detailed schemata representation of objects and events with special forms of forward chaining rules. The interactive environment of ART is also used extensively as part of KREA, for example, for browsing and manipulating various representations. A number of modules and facilities (e.g. most of the model manager) are implemented in Common Lisp for efficiency reasons. It is our belief that the use of well-proven knowledge representation techniques and the assistance of knowledge based tools in the design process will greatly enhance the job of a requirement engineer.

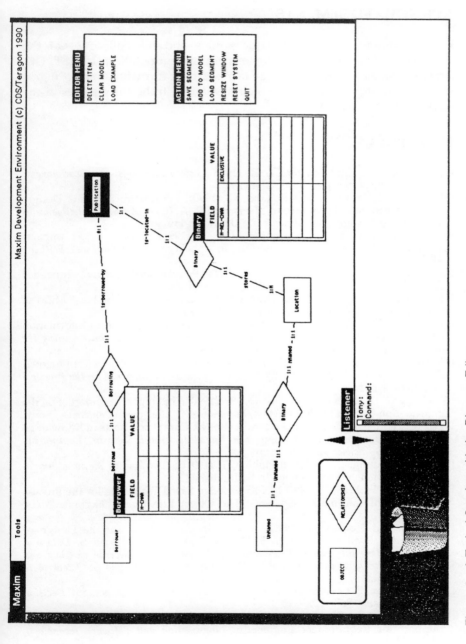

Figure 3 A Typical Session with the Diagram Editor

ACKNOWLEDGEMENTS

We are grateful to Prof P. Loucopoulos and his colleagues at the Information Systems Group, Department of Computation, UMIST, UK, for discussions and the exchange of research information and to Ingrid Hopley and Stephen Wang for their assistance in the early stages of the development of KREA.

REFERENCES

[1] Avison, D. E. and Fitzgerald, G. (1988). *Information Systems Development: Methodologies, Techniques, Tools.* Blackwell.
[2] Cauvet, C., Proix, C. and Rolland, C. (1990). Information Systems Design: An Expert System Approach. In Meersman, R. A. (eds), *Artificial Intelligence in Databases and Information Systems (DS-3).* North-Holland.
[3] Cheung, L. C.-Y., Ip, S. and Holden, T. (1991). Survey of AI Impacts on Information Systems Engineering. To appear in *Information and Software Technology.*
[4] Clayton, B. D. (1987). *Inference ART: Programmers' Tutorial,* Inference Corporation.
[5] Dittrich, K. R. (1990). Object-Oriented Database Systems: The Next Miles of the Marathon. *Information Systems,* 15(1):161–167.
[6] Falquet, G. et al. (1988). Concept Integration as an Approach to Information Systems Design. In Olle T. W. et al., (eds), *Computerized Assistance During the Information Systems Life Cycle,* North-Holland.
[7] Holden, T., Wilhelmij, P. W. and Appleby, K. A. (1989). Object-Oriented Design of Visual Software Using MAXIM. *European Conference on the Practical Applications of Lisp.*
[8] Holden, T., Cheung, L. and Ip, S. (1990). Intelligent Support for the Information System Design Process. *European ART User-group Conference, Rome.*
[9] Ip, S., Cheung, L. C.-Y. and Holden, T. (1991a). Complex Objects in Knowledge Based Requirement Engineering. *6th Knowledge-Based Software Engineering Conference, Syracuse, New York,* Sep.
[10] Ip, S., Cheung, L. C.-Y. and Holden, T. (1991b). The Use of Aggregation in Object Relationship Modelling. To be Published.
[11] Ip, S. and Holden, T. (1991c). A Knowledge Based Technique for the Process Modelling of Information Systems: The Object Life Cycle Diagram. To be Published.
[12] Ip, S. and Holden, T. (1990). A Knowledge Assistant for the Design of Information Systems. In Deen, S. M. and Thomas, G. P., editors, *Data and Knowledge Base Integration, Proceedings of the Working Conference on Data and Knowledge Base Integration held at the University of Keele, England on October 4–5, 1989.* Pitman.
[13] Lockemann, P. C. (1989). Object-Oriented Information Management. *Decision Support Systems,* 5:79–102.
[14] Loucopoulos, P. and Champion, R. E. M. (1989a). Knowledge-Based Support for Requirement Engineering. *Information and Software Technology,* 31(3):123–136.

[15] Loucopoulos, P. and Layzell, P. J. (1989b). Improving Information System Development and Evolution Using a Rule-Based Paradigm. *Software Engineering Journal*, Sep.

[16] Rehm, S. et al. (1988). Support for Design Process in a Structurally Object-Oriented Database System. *Lecture Notes in Computer Science*, 334:80–97, Springer-Verlag.

[17] Reisig, W. (1986). Petri Nets in Software Engineering. *Lecture Notes in Computer Science*, 255:63–96, Springer-Verlag.

[18] Smith, J. M. and Smith, D. C. P. (1977). Database Abstractions: Aggregation and Generalization. *ACM Transactions on Database Systems*, 2(2):105–133, Jun.

[19] Theodoulidis, C., Wangler, B. and Loucopoulos, P. (1990). Requirements Specification in TEMPORA. *Conference CAiSE'90, Stockholm*, May.

15

ISTEL Applications Architecture

John Alexander, Kenyon Hicks

ABSTRACT

The ISTEL Applications Architecture has been evolved over the past 6 years. The objective of the programme has been to simultaneously improve the quality of the company's software products and greatly increase the productivity of the development staff. The paper gives an overview of IAA and briefly reviews the major changes that the introduction of the programme has made to the management, staff and customers. The final section covers the role of CASE and its importance in achieving productivity gains.

BACKGROUND

In 1985 a small development team was set up to investigate and introduce a more structured approach to systems development in AT&T ISTEL. The vision of the team was to eliminate application programming by establishing rigorous, logical definitions of business solutions which could be automatically translated into a form which

CASE: Current Practice, Future Prospects. Edited by Kathy Spurr and Paul Layzell
© 1992 John Wiley & Sons Ltd

a computer could understand. This approach is known as the ISTEL Applications Architecture (IAA). Although AT&T ISTEL was the systems development and computer operations organisation of the Rover Group at that time the company had a mission to expand into other areas. The company focussed on value added and data services (VADS) in selected vertical markets and the development of IAA has mirrored the development of this market thrust. The approach has evolved over the past 6 years and in order to make the necessary productivity gains and quality improvements both first and second generation CASE toolsets have been considered and subsequently rejected for IAA. The current approach has no dependency on third party CASE suppliers and gives the company the ability to further develop its use of method and tools without key dependencies on other parties. The AT&T buy-out coincided with the development of the functional specification for the first IAA tool and the development team was further strengthened by the inclusion of Ken Hicks from Bell Labs to assist in user interface technology and subsequently enable technology transfer of the IAA tools back to the US.

The objective of IAA was agreed as the provision of quality, high specification, portable software (bespoke, product, VADS) using less resource and in a shorter timeframe than our competitors. The first half of the objective needed to address the problems of traditional application development, the latter part ensured that in so doing the company remained competitive in the marketplace. The components, tools and underlying software used to achieve the goal are described briefly below.

IAA COMPONENTS

The three major components of IAA map onto the first half of the objective.

First, **Jackson Systems Development** (JSD) was chosen as the most rigorous of the structured systems analysis techniques.

This equates to the high specification element of the objective in that the other popular techniques and methods in use are less thorough in their analysis, particularly with regard to the timing of events and inter-relationship of entities. It is not possible to record the complex procedural requirements of a commercial application without strong emphasis on the valid ordering of events in the systems analysis phase. See note 1 for more detail.

Second, the **ISTEL Software Architecture** (ISA) is used to build on the strengths of JSD by allowing the modularisation of application software based on the logical requirement (JSD specification) being separate from its physical implementation. This separation of concerns led to more portable solutions as the same business rules could be implemented on different hardware/software platforms by changing only the relevant physical interfaces. See note 2 for more detail.

Third, the ISTEL Quality Programme led to the adoption of Phil Crosby's Quality Philosophy and the implementation of his ideas was a key element in the establishment of the **Standards and Working Practices** now in place in AT&T ISTEL. The implementation of consistent processes has not only led to a more consistent product but also highlighted the most appropriate areas for automation and hence been fundamental in the move to application generation.

IAA TOOLSET

The starting point of IAA was the introduction of JSD and a key component in the success of that introduction was the use of the supporting CASE tools from Michael Jackson Systems Limited. Initially the tools were beneficial in increasing productivity but as the competence level grew in the method the tools became a constraint on further productivity gains. This was because working practice changes could not be accommodated by the tools. This led to an evaluation being undertaken on possible software platforms for a bespoke toolset and the company decided to use an internally supported object store as the underlying software, hence by-passing second generation CASE tool vendors.

The IAA Toolset comprises four separate but closely related products.

First, the **Analyst Workbench** enables the JSD specification details to be captured by the systems analyst. This replaces the existing third party and in-house tools currently used by capturing all the relevant information to enable code generation from specification. It supports an extended JSD developed by AT&T ISTEL which combines the strengths of JSD and object oriented analysis.

Second, the **User Interaction Specification Tool** allows the user interface to be specified. This tool captures the logical requirement of the user interface and allows the analyst to manipulate its physical presentation. It also describes the user interaction in terms of navigation and security. This tool gives AT&T ISTEL a major competitive advantage through the use of the Regions logical windowing system allowing the analyst to deliver the contents of the screen painter to three different physical windowing systems (Windows 3™ for PC/PS2, X-Windows™, Toolbox™ for Mac).

Third, the **System Generation Facility** will enable the generation of applications directly from the IAA Analyst Workbench. The generators transform the logical specification into industrial strength software on a selected set of commercial environments. The software created by the generators is not available to developers and the only route available for the correction or enhancement of software is through amending the specification.

Fourth, the **Specification Re-use Tool** enables systems analysts in AT&T ISTEL to take advantage of other analysts' previous experience. The benefits are derived by holding all completed IAA specifications centrally and classifying the specifications into generic categories. A systems analyst would then use the central repository to ascertain whether another member of staff had already developed a similar application. This will in the future save considerable time in the development of new applications.

UNDERLYING SOFTWARE FOR IAA TOOLSET

There are two pieces of software on which the IAA toolset has been built.

First, **UADS** is a strongly typed object store developed in academia. The company acquired the exclusive rights to UADS in 1989. There are approximately 200 object types in the Analyst Workbench and there is a need for flexible navigation within the tool. We do not believe it would be possible to implement a tool with the power of the Analyst Workbench on any other type of file/database mechanism.

Second, **Regions** is a logical windowing system based on representing windows and their contents through high-level primitives. These primitives express relative positioning of objects which are then mapped to different physical environments. Presently Windows 3, X-Windows and Mac Toolbox interfaces are supported by this generic software.

CURRENT STATUS/FUTURE DIRECTION

The delivery of the toolset is the immediate priority. A single user Analyst Workbench is currently available and the rest of the toolset is scheduled for completion in 1991. The complete toolset is the result of constant refining of the JSD method in commercial projects over 6 years and is driven by experienced practitioners with the desire to produce better products for customers. It has involved major changes in the approach to application development and we believe the tool to be in advance of any commercial offering. Once available the toolset is applicable to the development of solutions in most commercial domains, it is neither constrained by geography nor technology for the class of problem for which it has been built. The ability to penetrate new markets quickly through code generation and reusable specifications represents an enormous opportunity. The next stage involves expanding the scope of application domain tackled, based on the effectiveness of the above tool in production.

LESSONS LEARNT

The past 6 years have been very interesting. There were many challenges to face and obstacles to overcome in bringing the IAA programme to fruition. Some of the major changes/obstacles are listed below. These are not in any order and would obviously be weighted differently depending on individual circumstances.

Organisation—It is important to ensure that any new skills are developed as cost effectively as possible. This may involve reorganising staff to separate the enhancement/maintenance tasks from new developments. This separation should also ensure that a constant flow of new projects is channelled through the new group. This is not an easy policy to introduce but the alternative leads to extended learning curves, lack of focus and loss of impetus.

Staff Resistance—The major change in the introduction of IAA, and this is likely to be even more true of object-oriented analysis, is viewing the customer's problem at the abstract level rather than in concrete terms. The traditional career path in the industry adds to this problem with analysts normally beginning their careers in software development. Many staff find this transition very difficult and it may well be easier to bring in graduates and train them in the new disciplines rather than retrain some existing staff.

Customer Awareness—The use of IAA requires more dialogue with the customer at an early stage and the customer needs to be made aware of his extended role and also has to be familiarised with the new notations and documentation. It is very important to inform the customer of the rationale for the new approach highlighting any additional effort required by him and the benefits to the customer of adopting the approach.

CASE Tools—Having chosen an approach it is important to select a CASE tool which will facilitate the introduction and adoption of the new process. It is highly unlikely that a tool will fit the process exactly but this should not be used as a reason to delay committing to CASE. CASE tools have become a convenient scapegoat for the failure of the management of change in applications development.

Consultancy—I.T. consultancy is expensive but the extended learning curves caused by scrimping on consultancy are likely to be considerably more expensive. The key issue is to agree quantifiable measures with the consultant and ensure that he is used correctly. It must be accepted that there is an on-cost in the short-term whilst adapting to the new approach.

Focus—The goals of the programme must remain uppermost in the minds of the management.

Quality—There is much talk in the computer press about software quality. There is very little documented evidence of the application of quality processes in software development. The introduction of Phil Crosby's ideas into the development process made a major contribution to the system generation process within IAA.

Commitment—The senior executives of ISTEL have been very supportive of the IAA programme from the early days. This support has now been extended to AT&T. This high-level support helps to persuade the middle managers of the need for change.

Extended JSD—Use of the method in various application domains has led to the extension of the method. This was particularly true in the development of the functional specification of the IAA Toolset. Most of the extensions involve combining the strengths of JSD with those of object orientation.

Object Store—It is the view of the development team that a tool with the power of the IAA Analyst Workbench could not be built using more traditional datastores.

CASE ON TRIAL—GUILTY OR NOT GUILTY?

The above list shows CASE to be only one of a series of factors to be considered when looking to implement a software engineering strategy. The most important factor is changing the mindsets of developers, managers and customers to the new disciplines and establishing consistent development processes.

From the work done in evolving IAA the use of first generation CASE tools helped significantly in the process of change in the early stages. It was only after a couple of years that the new processes had evolved to the point where the toolset became a constraint. The verdict is therefore not guilty in that the use of CASE tools allowed the development teams to focus on specifying solutions and enabled the capture of specification details.

Looking at the market generally it would be easy to conclude that CASE has not lived up to the great expectations of it through the 1980's. This is a marketing issue rather than a technical issue as CASE, like most other new technologies, has been greatly oversold. The real problem, as stated above, lies not with the vendors' ability to develop tools but changing the whole approach in application development from a cottage industry to a more rigorous process as used in other more established engineering domains. It will undoubtedly take some time to establish these processes and build the toolset to support them.

NOTE 1

Yourdon uses a very simple diagram to illustrate the 'three dimensions of data processing'.

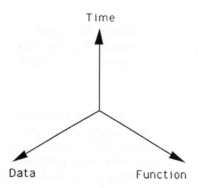

The above diagram says that there are essentially three elements which must be taken into account in systems analysis.

1. Data—The analyst must capture the data requirements of the application. This data needs to be captured by the application and is then subsequently used therein. This leads to the second dimension.

2. Function—The customer does not solely wish to capture data but needs to do this in order to later manipulate the data to produce functional output on which he then bases future business decisions. As the above events do not occur simultaneously and there are dependencies between data capture and functional output then the third dimension which is important is

3. Time—Systems are based on mirroring/modelling the real world. In the real world the state of objects changes through the application or sufferance of events. e.g. a person buys a car, this event changes the state of the car from the dealers viewpoint from stock to sold and alters the state of the purchasers bank account.

In structured systems analysis although there are dozens of 'methods' they are nearly all based on three diagramming techniques. The descriptions and diagrams below show how the notations relate to Yourdon's framework.

1. Data Flow Diagram (DFD)—A DFD does not separate data capture from functionality and although it provides the analyst/customer with some vague notion of how the events occur there is no precise definition of how events alter the state of objects through time.

2. Logical Data Model (LDM)—An LDM shows the relationship between objects and their attributes. This is a static representation which says nothing at all about events nor does it cover functional requirements of an application.

3. Entity Life History (ELH)—An ELH shows the relationship between logical atomic actions and the object which performs or suffers those actions. It is solely focussed on data capture and each atomic action contains attributes associated with that particular event. This gives a very precise, concise picture of the states and events of all objects in an application.

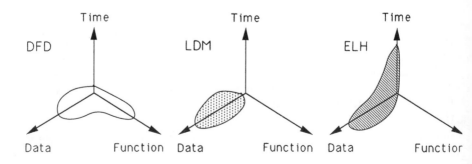

JSD modelling is based on the ELH notation and in IAA the JSD experience since 1985 has been used to supplement the basic technique to capture other requirements to enable all contextual checking to be stored in the elaborated models. The validity of the elaboration has already been proven by the existing code generators in use within MIG.

This leaves the capture of the functional requirements. The path taken here was to use the same notation as with data capture to describe the internals of function processes. This led to the creation of a logical function language which is used within the function process description. In effect the internals of the function processes are similar to JSP programs, the major difference being the use of the business entities and not physical files/tables.

IAA therefore captures all three dimensions of the logical requirements in a concise, precise notation.

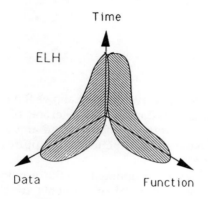

We have therefore gathered all the information that we require about the logical system. What is now required is a toolset to enable us to capture and store this information efficiently and effectively in order to exploit our rigorous analysis.

NOTE 2

As discussed in Note 1 the data capture processes and the functional processes are both described in detail using JSD/JSP notation. These processes are linked by the passing of data between them in the form of either data streams or inspections (one process looking at the data in another process).

At the highest level therefore the business logic contained in a JSD specification can be viewed as a network of communicating processes as shown below.

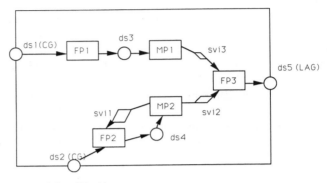

Logical Specification

MP = Model Process   FP = Function Process
ds = data stream   svi = inspection
(CG) = command group   (LAG) = logical appearance group

The JSD specification as viewed above shows the relationship between the processes in an application and the internals of the processes above shows how the data is captured, manipulated and logically grouped.

The scope of the **Analyst Workbench** is to capture all the requirements of the logical system.

The JSD is the logical component of the application and the link between the logical and physical components are the interfaces in the ISTEL Software Architecture (ISA). This is best illustrated by James Martin's pyramid.

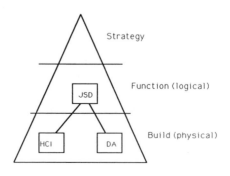

The network diagram does not extend to either the human computer interface (HCI) nor the physical data access (DA). In fact in the logical network the exits from and entry points back into the logical specification from the HCI are the logical appearance groups (LAG) and command groups (CG) shown at the boundary of the system. The mapping between the logical specification and the physical data stores (DA) is not shown at all. Automating the two physical interfaces required two different approaches to be adopted.

The first interface to be considered is the HCI. As can be seen from the network above there are datastreams going outside the system boundaries (LAG) and also entering (CG). In IAA the toolset allows the analyst to specify the structure of datastreams. This is similar to a JSP data structure and shows the grouping of attributes on structure leaves. Due to the power of the UADS object store the view of the objects in the datastream can be changed to a default window view based on the data structure.

The **user interaction definition tool** is then used to amend the window view to the customer's satisfaction. In addition to this the associated command groups are linked to the appearance group. The final function of the screen painter is then to link the appropriate performer type to the appearance group/command group pair.

This is all the static definition required to enable the specification of the user interface to be completed. The definitions captured are then passed to a generic user interface management system which ensures that the correct definitions are used when the application is executed.

The second interface is the data access (DA). This is the mapping of the logical entities onto files/tables. There are three components required to achieve the automatic translation of specification and subsequent execution and these have been grouped into the term **system generation facility**.

The first is the translation of the specification details into software modules. This comprises the model process internals and function process internals as specified using JSD and several other modules derived from that data. The most important of the derived modules being the action processor which enables the logical specification to be implemented directly by standard JSP inversion with the model processes being inverted with respect to the logical actions.

The second component is the mapping of the logical entity roles to physical files/tables. A simple set of guidelines has been in operation within ISTEL with the existing in-house generators and in the first instance these rules will be copied for the new generators. This mapping requires the analyst to specify the relationship explicitly by building a cross-reference table between the entity roles and files/tables.

The third component is the JSD process machine. This is a high level operating system which controls the scheduling of the application processes. It contains all the necessary operating system features to ensure that all error conditions are handled correctly. This JSD process machine is generic and will handle all applications specified using the IAA toolset for a particular operating system.

The final element in the toolset is the **Specification re-use tool**. In the first instance this will simply be a common repository for all completed specifications. Once in the common repository the specifications will be classified into a generic category. A systems analyst will then have the opportunity to browse through the classifications and specifications therein when a new customer requirement is identified and may thus save considerable effort if a similar application has been previously specified using the IAA Analyst Workbench.

REFERENCES

M. Jackson, Jackson System Development
P. Crosby, Quality is Free
E. Yourdon, The Yourdon Structured Method—An Introduction
J. Martin, Structured Techniques—An Introduction to CASE

TRADEMARKS

Windows 3 is a trademark of Microsoft, Mac Toolbox is a trademark of Apple and X-Windows is a trademark of M.I.T.